JOHN TRUMBULL

The University of North Carolina Press, Chapel Hill, N. C.; The Baker and Taylor Company, New York; Oxford University Press, London; Maruzen-Kabushiki-Kaisha, Tokyo; Edward Evans & Sons, Ltd., Shanghai; D. B. Centen's Wetenschappelijke Boekhandel, Amsterdam.

John Trumbull. From a miniature painted by his second cousin, John Trumbull, in 1793. Courtesy of the Gallery of Fine Arts, Yale University.

JOHN TRUMBULL
CONNECTICUT WIT

By
ALEXANDER COWIE

CHAPEL HILL
THE UNIVERSITY OF NORTH CAROLINA PRESS
1936

COPYRIGHT, 1936, BY
THE UNIVERSITY OF NORTH CAROLINA PRESS

PRINTED IN THE UNITED STATES OF AMERICA BY EDWARDS & BROUGHTON
COMPANY, RALEIGH, N. C.   BOUND BY L. H. JENKINS, INC., RICHMOND, VIRGINIA
THIS BOOK WAS DIGITALLY PRINTED.

To
E. C.

PREFACE

THIS BOOK is devoted to the life and writings of the most celebrated American poet of the eighteenth century, John Trumbull. Although it must be granted at once that Trumbull was a minor writer, it is not hard to understand the enormous popularity once accorded his works. He lived in a day when it was difficult to estimate the true proportions of a new American writer. On the bleak prairies of our early national literature every shrub appeared a tree, and every tree a giant of its species. Trumbull was hailed as a writer great enough to be compared favorably with Butler, Swift, and Pope. The encomia he received were extreme but natural. Was he not by common consent the most brilliant writer in the most distinguished coterie of eighteenth-century American poets, the Hartford Wits? Did not his *M'Fingal* go into more than thirty editions during his lifetime? Did not English critics admit it to a parity with *Hudibras?* Was it not the most popular American poem of its length before Longfellow's *Evangeline?* These things may be granted. Yet the benefits conferred by priority are short-lived, and Trumbull's fame has suffered adjustment at the hands of posterity. Now he seems further from Dryden or Pope in ability and, to choose a man of temperament akin to his own, closer to Churchill. If he had only one rival (Freneau) for supremacy in American poetry before Bryant, it now appears that he achieved that distinction partly because of the dearth of good native poets. The leveling process of time has long since crumbled the peak of his fame. His general public has greatly dwindled. Yet it is a mistake to estimate an early writer's intrinsic merit by the number of general readers he draws in later generations. Who except the scholar now reads Butler's *Hudibras*, admittedly a greater poem than *M'Fingal?* Obviously other tests than popular interest must be relied upon in any attempt to appraise a writer of an earlier generation. Trumbull's fame has now reached something like equilibrium. No general revival of interest in him can be expected, but neither is it likely that he will ever be divested of the modest honors now attached to his name. He is a substantial minor writer. Few of the productions of the Hartford Wits have been proof against the decay of time, but *M'Fingal* was so thoroughly steeped in the best of all literary preservatives, humor, that it retains freshness and vitality even today. It has become a minor classic. Hence this critical biography of Trumbull. A poet of the first order Trumbull was not, but assuredly he may be reckoned one of the little masters of our literary art.

The present work is intended not merely for the scholar but for the general reader of more than average curiosity regarding the literary history of our country. It will be useful, it is hoped, to those who wish to become acquainted with American poetry of the Revolutionary era and the transition from the neoclassical period to the romantic period. The study first took form as a doctoral dissertation, at Yale University, but for the present purpose it has been greatly condensed and almost entirely rewritten. Controversial matter has been cut to a minimum, and only the major errors of other commentators have been noted. Nor has it seemed necessary to burden the work with the detailed evidence of all the conclusions and hypotheses here set down. The biographical chronology has been carried in detail only through the first twenty-five years of the poet's life, for after writing *M'Fingal* Trumbull virtually deserted letters for the law. The criticism and interpretation of the poet's work, however, have been made reasonably full. This, the first extended study of Trumbull, contains considerable new material, but discoveries have not been emphasized. The constant aim of the writer has been to present a balanced study of the creative life of one of the most popular of our early poets.

A brief bibliography at the end of the volume indicates some of the sources generally available for a study of Trumbull. It has not seemed wise to list all the material used in the preparation of this study, for the work is of necessity based largely upon primary sources (referred to in the footnotes) difficult of access. There are two principal collections of manuscript material relating to Trumbull. The larger of these consists of the Trumbull Papers bequeathed by Moses Coit Tyler to the Cornell University Library. A considerable body of Trumbull manuscripts may also be found among the Woodbridge Papers in the possession of the Burton Historical Collection, Detroit, Michigan. I have been generously granted permission to use material in both these collections. These two groups of papers comprise most of Trumbull's unpublished poems, a considerable number of unpublished philosophical and critical essays, and a smaller number of unpublished letters, as well as various items that have already been printed. A great deal of material relating to Trumbull may be found at Yale University, which possesses not only a number of Trumbull manuscripts but also many official manuscript records and printed documents that are essential to an understanding of Trumbull's academic life. The Yale University Library also contains a nearly complete file of *The Connecticut Journal*, in which Trumbull printed some forty essays. Many of Trumbull's letters have been destroyed or lost, and those that remain are for the most part scattered. Acknowledgment is made in the footnotes of the kindness of those persons who have enabled me to use little-known letters in their possession.

I am deeply indebted to those librarians who have courteously facilitated my research, especially at the following institutions: the Cornell University Library, the Burton

Historical Collection, the Yale University Library, the Connecticut State Library, the Connecticut Historical Society, the Watkinson Library, the Boston Public Library, the Massachusetts Historical Society, the manuscript division of the New York Public Library, the New York Historical Society, the Library of Congress, the Widener Library, the Brown University Library, the Newberry Library, the William L. Clements Library, the Philadelphia Library Company, the Historical Society of Pennsylvania, and the American Antiquarian Society. The Huntington Library has graciously forwarded a full description of its editions of *M'Fingal*.

The publication of this book has been made possible largely through the generous financial aid granted me by the Research Committee of Wesleyan University. A number of persons have kindly assisted me in the progress of the work. It is a pleasure to record my special gratitude to Professor Stanley Williams of Yale University, who first suggested that I undertake a critical biography of Trumbull. His direction of my doctoral studies increased the great admiration I had long felt for his scholarship, and his friendship has been the cherished experience of years. Dr. Arthur H. Nason of New York University has read the entire manuscript of this book and has made a number of valuable suggestions, which I have gratefully adopted. Many other persons have rendered assistance in ways too various to specify in detail: Dr. Nelson Frederick Adkins, Dr. Theodore A. Zunder, Mr. E. R. B. Willis, Miss G. B. Krum, Miss Anne Pratt, Dr. George Seymour Godard, Mr. Albert C. Bates, Mr. Walter R. Benjamin, Mr. Thomas Madigan, Mrs. Charles Horton Metcalf (a great-great-granddaughter of Trumbull), Dean F. W. Nicolson, Mr. Victor H. Paltsits, Colonel Francis Parsons, Professor Ralph Rusk, the Reverend Anson Phelps Stokes. In addition I am happy to acknowledge, however inadequately, the assistance of Elspeth

Cowie, my wife, who has been the cheerful victim of many demands on her time and skill.

A. C.

Middletown, Connecticut
August, 1935

CONTENTS

Chapter		Page
	Preface	vii
I	The Times and the Man	2
II	Early Days	8
III	Student at Yale	25
IV	Teacher and Essayist	65
V	*The Progress of Dulness*	94
VI	The Eve of the Revolution	125
VII	*M'Fingal*, Comic Libretto of the Revolution	145
VIII	Apostate Poet	207
	Bibliography	215
	Index	225

JOHN TRUMBULL

CHAPTER I

THE TIMES AND THE MAN

As a critical biography, the present study treats of the poet's life and works in relation to each other. Commentary on the times is included in so far as it appears necessary for a full understanding of Trumbull's poetry. Although research has yielded many new facts about Trumbull's life, yet the strictly biographical material is limited by the inevitable difficulty of assembling trustworthy data regarding an American born as early as 1750. The biographical element, however, is naturally subordinate to the critical: the important fact is not that a poet lived but that a poet wrote. The chief aim of the book, therefore, is to lay the basis for an interpretation of Trumbull's poetry. For this purpose the body of his poetry as it exists in the familiar 1820 collected edition of his poetical works has been used in conjunction with many less accessible editions of single works and a considerable number of poems now first printed from manuscript.

Although this study will deal more with effects than with causes, some of the factors which partly accounted for the nature of Trumbull's poetry need brief exposition. Principally these are three: Puritanism, neoclassicism, and the Revolution. The Puritan belief concerning literary art was essentially that literature justified itself only when it served the ends of religion or morality. This purpose might be achieved directly in lyric poems which sang the praises of the Deity and in miscellaneous didactic writing. It might also be achieved indirectly by praising the deeds of virtuous individuals, recounting the history of a chosen people (the Puritans), and by writing controversial pamphlets designed to confound the enemies of the chosen people. The Puritans did not wish to banish art but to direct it and to render it subservient to special purposes. The results on the whole were baneful to belles-lettres. Art flies out of the window when the air becomes too heavy with doctrine. It shrinks from authority. Manifestly it is unfair to imply that Puritanism was the sole reason why New England produced so little real literature in its early days, for the middle and southern colonies did no better. Nor must it be assumed that religion is inimical to art. Yet our literary heritage from the early Puritans bears but a poor proportion to the number of able writers among them. Now and again the Puritans gave a "timid greeting" to art and frequently a certain spiritual fervor lent eloquence to their pens; but for the most part they "left humor and the external beauty of this world out of account as too trivial to waste precious paper and ink upon."[1] Sermon, chronicle, and elegy, as Mr. Lewisohn points out,[2] were the natural vehicles of early Puritan literature.

In Trumbull's time the demand for piety in verse was enormous. Trumbull himself was never a creed-bound Calvinist; yet he was the son of a Congregational minister who was at least orthodox. He could not escape the atmosphere he was bred in. Even when he violated the code of the Puritan by writing for mere amusement, he did so in a manner indicating that he realized his transgression. This matter must not be pressed too much, for Trumbull had a catholic training in books long antedating the Puritan period; but as an ambitious poet he could not avoid consulting the tastes of the people who patronized American poetry in his time. The newspapers of the day, reeking with piety and patriotism, showed the character of that taste. The first American

---

[1] Kenneth Murdock, "The Puritan Tradition," in *The Reinterpretation of American Literature* (ed. by Norman Foerster, New York, 1928), pp. 103, 104.

[2] *Expression in America* (New York, 1932), Introduction, p. xxx.

anthology of verse, Elihu Smith's *Columbian Muse* (1794), was a clear sign that the poet who wished recognition must write elegant, elevated verse—verse that was, as the phrase ran, "just in its sentiments and elegant in its numbers." Satire, humor, and mere entertainment were proscribed. There was a peculiar prejudice against satire, for it was felt to be "in some sense a prostitution of poetry, to busy it with the faults and follies of men."[3] Humorous productions of all sorts were looked upon askance as being mere entertainment and so—like novels, dice, and rum—virtual invitations to the devil. The one alternative to writing moral verse was writing heroic verse on a national theme: next in importance to being right with one's God was being right with one's country. There were doubtless many readers who would have welcomed a more profane poetry—witness the secular jokes and poems which sometimes slipped into the almanacs of the time—but it so happened that literary reputations were largely in the hands of persons who set great store by decorum and morality (as well as pecuniary profit). The Puritans did not constitute the entire population of early New England, but they had something like a monopoly on publicity.

Puritanism, then, was one of the factors that molded John Trumbull the poet. An associated factor was the vogue of neoclassicism. It is a commonplace that in nineteenth-century America poets too often adhered to the outmoded neoclassical tradition of eighteenth-century England. It appears not to be so well understood that eighteenth-century American poets were in pretty close touch with contemporary British poets.[4] True, the influence of a few seventeenth-century Eng-

---

[3] Samuel Kettell, *Specimens of American Poetry* (3 vols., Boston, 1829), I, 182. This dictum, set down in 1829, typifies one of the common critical attitudes of Trumbull's day.

[4] S. Foster Damon, the author of a recent book on Thomas Holley Chivers, unaccountably writes, for example, that "the whole tendency of neoclassical

lish writers lingered here, notably that of Milton and Cowley; but the principal models for our writers of the eighteenth century must be sought among British authors of the same period: Prior, Swift, Addison, Pope, Young, Thomson, Gray, Goldsmith, Johnson, Churchill. The backbone of neoclassicism was conformity to certain laws (codified by Pope) which governed "correctness" in writing. Much may be said for the theory of poetry endorsed by Pope; yet, in effect, neoclassicism paid premiums to many dull, didactic poems. The limitation it set upon subject-matter, metrical forms, and diction in the long run produced undesirable characteristics. Neoclassicism, however, was congenial to Puritan America, partly no doubt because it emphasized rule and propriety. But whereas for a time, at least, the English poets proved that much may be accomplished even in the scanty plot of neoclassicism, the inspiration of Pope yielded little American poetry that was more than mediocre. Trumbull naturally followed in the main the poetical practices that were current in England. To be sure he occasionally disparaged those writers who prized form too highly, but he himself was partial to "elegance"; and had he not possessed the compensating quality of humor, he might soon have been completely lost in the legion of neoclassical poetasters.

A third (and more beneficent) factor was the American Revolution. By temperament Trumbull was a poet of the library. He had a certain critical turn, but his forte seemed to be light comic verse. Excepting *The Progress of Dulness*, his poetry before the Revolution marked him as little more than a dilettante. He seemed destined to remain an obscure versifier, a purveyor of poetical delicacies for a small public of connoisseurs, and a persistent experimenter in ode and elegy. He had mastered the technique of poetry, but he lacked a suitable subject. He was trained but not commis-

---

form meant nothing in the new land."—*Thomas Holley Chivers* (New York, 1930), p. 4.

sioned. The Revolution was his opportunity. He did not recognize it immediately, however, for he was constitutionally a moderate conservative. Like many another colonial gentleman, he regarded himself as fundamentally English. His blood was English; his culture had come mainly from English institutions and traditions. By profession a lawyer, he deplored violent interruptions of the established order of things. He preferred evolution to revolution. He of course did not approve of British acts of tyranny, but, like Franklin, Hancock, and Dickinson, he hoped for a peaceful solution of the difficulties between the Crown and the Colonies. He was a patriot but not a radical. A democrat in the Jeffersonian sense he never became, for he distrusted popular movements in governmental affairs. After the war he shared the Federalist belief that the hope of a nation lay in strongly centralized government. At the beginning of the Revolution, therefore, Trumbull was not among the first to urge a violent separation from Great Britain. Nor did he immediately put his pen to service in the revolutionary cause. At the instigation of friends, however, he finally exerted his brilliant comic powers in a long poem satirizing the Tories and burlesquing the British arms. This satire, *M'Fingal*,[5] proved to be one of the most popular American poems ever written.

It was with some difficulty that Trumbull adapted his poetical abilities to times that were Puritan, neoclassical, and Revolutionary. Although he was not a radical in religion, he did not share the Puritan tendency to identify religious zeal with poetical inspiration. He respected morality and his private life was apparently exemplary, but he could not accept pious platitudes in lieu of poetry. Nevertheless, covetous of the fame of a poet, Trumbull naturally attempted

---

[5] Although eighteenth-century usage called for a turned comma instead of an apostrophe in the name *M'Fingal*, the more modern form is observed throughout this study except where the wording of a title-page has been reproduced.

to write verse for which there was a market in Puritan times. Strictly religious verse it did not lie in him to write. Nor were the comic and burlesque verses, some of them mildly vulgar, which as a youth he threw off from time to time, adapted to please Puritans. Accordingly he kept them under his hat, despite the fact that they exhibited his principal talent—a talent for burlesque. Apparently he did not at first pride himself on this gift. Rather he seems to have cherished the delusion that he might become a master of the elegy and the ode, forms which were quite acceptable not only to the Puritan moralists but also to the less biased monitors of eighteenth-century neoclassicism. He indulged in all the minor vices of neoclassical poets: elegant circumlocutions, clumsy inversions for the sake of rhyme, frequent elisions, stock metaphors and allusions, polished but stereotyped phraseology, and an excess of balance and antithesis. Yet although he achieved a degree of success, he was attempting a genre which he was destined never to master. He was not formed to write odes and elegies. His lyric gift was slight; his imagery was arid; his ideas (in the elegies) were commonplace. In short, despite his belief to the contrary,[6] his gifts were far more intellectual than imaginative. His saving resource was humor.

The Progress of Dulness (1772-73), Trumbull's satire on collegiate education, gave some token of his brilliant critical and comic faculties. The Revolution opened up even larger possibilities. Yet Trumbull, although only twenty-five years old at the outbreak of the war, was already beginning to show signs of conservatism. He deprecated the premature resort to violence. He was thrown among patriots, but he was no roaring democrat. Moreover, he was probably not anxious to draw upon himself the wrath of the Crown: after all, the war might go against the Whigs. Not only political

---

[6] See below, p. 18.

expediency but literary discretion bade him hesitate. His friends who urged him to wage poetical warfare against the Tories suggested that he write a comic poem. Now Trumbull was loath to stake his reputation as a poet on humor, which was ephemeral, or on satire, which was of the devil. Nevertheless he ultimately complied with the request of his friends and wrote the first half of *M'Fingal*, which he published anonymously early in 1776. Completed in 1782, *M'Fingal* did incur censure at the hands of those moralists who did not distinguish between humor and irreverence; but its vast popularity, first as a political manifesto and later as a work of art, proved that a gifted writer may safely ignore the critical mandates of his day.

Thus Trumbull somewhat fortuitously rose to fame in a perplexing environment. Although for a time Puritanism stifled his wit and neoclassicism dulled his pen, the Revolution freed him from their bondage and evoked his best talents. The scholar, the critic, the humorist in Trumbull combined to produce his masterpiece. A true humorist, he never quite lost faith in his serious writing; but his public knew better: it remembered him as the author of *M'Fingal*.

CHAPTER II

EARLY DAYS

MASSACHUSETTS has had her Mathers and her Adamses; Connecticut, her Trumbulls. Perhaps deficient in those temperamental or emotional qualities which capture the public imagination, the Trumbulls have never been so conspicuous in history as the Mather dynasty or the Adams succession. They were not a family of aberrant geniuses but rather of men of very great abilities, primarily intellectual, which they devoted to the service of their state. The name of "Trumbull" is interwoven with Connecticut history to an astonishing degree. A general, three governors, an historian, a philologist, an artist, and a poet—these are the principal members of the Trumbull family whose achievements have reflected glory on their state, and most of them have had some right to national attention as well. Jonathan Trumbull, the first member of the family to become governor, was not only an able chief executive of his state, but was also, it is said, so renowned for his services against John Bull during the Revolution that he earned the sobriquet "Brother Jonathan," a name which was soon transferred to the American people as a whole. John Trumbull the artist made a reputation for himself which transcended state boundaries during the early years of our history, and even now he is almost universally known (if not always applauded) as the painter of the signing of the Declaration of Independence and the Battle of Bunker Hill. John Trumbull the poet (second cousin of the artist) was a son of Connecticut, but the nation claimed him when he wrote *M'Fingal*, a political satire which not only won immediate praise as a patriotic document but remained for many decades the most distinguished poem of its type written on our continent. Today the name of Trumbull is as dear as ever to genuine Connecticut Yankees. Moreover, although details have become a bit clouded in the public mind, even the most casual students of history are at least aware that a powerful clan called the Trumbulls once adorned the political, military, social, and cultural life not only of Connecticut but of the American nation.

The Trumbull family is an old one. Genealogical record alone carries it back to the year 1635; and if an alloy of legend be admitted to history, the record may be stretched back considerably further. There are two versions of a tradition which purports to explain the origin of the name Trumbull. According to the first of these, in the year 1315 a peasant named Rule rescued King Robert Bruce from an infuriated bison in a forest near Stirling. In return for this service Bruce granted him certain lands and changed his name to "Turnebull." There is some foundation for credence in this tale, for it is a matter of record that there did occur "a grant from King Robert Bruce in 1315 of lands in Fulhophalch (*i.e.*, Philiphaugh, a short distance west of the Rule), to *Willielmo dicto Turnebull*."[1] The name "Trumbull," of course, can easily be derived from "Turnebull" by natural linguistic processes. On the other hand it is impossible to prove that the earliest representative of the family from whom the poet's line can be definitely derived was a descendant of "*Willielmo dicto Turnebull*." Furthermore it is a bit disturbing (though not necessarily disastrous to the legend) to discover that the name of the earliest known representative of the poet's family was spelled "Trumble."

There exists, however, a variation of this legend which the poet apparently preferred. The heroism it reports is

---

[1] *New England Historical and Genealogical Register* (Boston, 1895), XLIX, 150.

similar to that ascribed to the Scottish peasant. The setting this time is near London, but the date of the action is left somewhat vague, being referred merely to the reign of "King Henry." John Trumbull the poet wrote down this version in a note appended to his "Sketch of the Genealogy of the Family of Trumbull in New England Drawn May 1809":

> The ancestor of this family was one of the Yeomen of the guard to King Henry. — As that king was walking in the park a mad bull, escaped from Smithfield, made at him—& his life was saved by the courage of this Yeoman. For that service the King gave him a pension of 100 marks per Ann, the name of Turnbull & a coat of Arms, *three bull's heads* with their fronts displayed and a *Bull's Head* for the crest. Afterwards a younger Son of that family married an heiress in the West of England & procured his name to be changed to *Trumbull*, with a grant of the same coat of arms, with small variations distinguishing it in heraldry. Sir William Trumbull, secretary of State in the reign of King William, was the most distinguished of the family in England. The last male heir of the family, who inherited an Estate in the West of England of £700 a year, died just before the American war, having no legitimate issue. I believe the name is extinct in England, unless assumed by some of his connections.[2]

The ultimate truth in regard to these attractive legends can never be definitely established, and essentially legends they must remain, for further back than 1635 no genealogist has been able to carry the Trumbull line with certainty. In that year John Trumble of Newcastle-on-Tyne was married to Elinor Chandler at All Saints Chapelry, Newcastle.[3] Four years later he transplanted the Trumble stock to Massachusetts, whence it soon spread to Connecticut. John Trumble of Newcastle, a cooper by trade, became a person of some

---

[2] This manuscript, which hitherto has remained unpublished, is in the Cornell University Library among a considerable number of Trumbull papers, which will be referred to hereafter in this study as Cornell MSS.

[3] *New England Historical and Genealogical Register*, XLIX, 325.

EARLY DAYS

local eminence in Rowley, Massachusetts, where he acted as selectman,[4] town clerk,[5] and schoolmaster.[6] He died at Rowley in 1657.[7]

John Trumble of Newcastle had several children, among them Joseph, who was the progenitor of the most distinguished members of the Trumbull family. Joseph removed from Rowley to Suffield[8] between 1675 and 1679.[9] Of the four sons of Joseph Trumble, three had issue. The first of these, John of Suffield,[10] had a son, John of Watertown, who was the father of the poet. A second son of Joseph Trumble, also named Joseph Trumble,[11] was the father of the first Governor Jonathan Trumbull. A third son, Benoni,[12] was the grandfather of the historian, Benjamin Trumbull.[13]

John Trumbull the poet was thus the great-great-grandson of John Trumble of Newcastle.[14] His father, respected clergyman and trustee of Yale College, was born in 1714 and he died in 1787. His character and achievements were by no means a prophecy of his son's literary abilities, for although a minister he was essentially a practical person. He was

---

[4] *The Early Records of the Town of Rowley, Massachusetts* (Rowley, 1894), pp. 70, 80, 95.

[5] *Essex Institute Historical Collections* (Salem, 1888), XXIV, 55.

[6] *The Early Records of the Town of Rowley, Massachusetts*, pp. 90, 122.

[7] *Essex Institute Historical Collections* (Salem, 1863), V, 162.

[8] Suffield, Connecticut, remained under Massachusetts jurisdiction until 1749.—*Documentary History of Suffield* (Springfield, 1879), p. 11.

[9] *Essex Institute Historical Collections*, XXIV, 56, 57. See also *Documentary History of Suffield*, p. 42.

[10] *Ibid.*, pp. 42, 150, *et passim.*

[11] *Ibid.*, p. 42. See also Jonathan Trumbull, *Jonathan Trumbull, Governor of Connecticut, 1769-1784* (Boston, 1919), pp. 5, 7, 8, 22, 59.

[12] *Documentary History of Suffield*, p. 42.

[13] A useful, though not infallible, guide to Trumbull genealogy is a chart prepared by Mrs. Louis Richmond Cheney and Miss Eliza Trumbull Stickney, entitled *A Genealogical Chart of Some of the Descendants of John Trumbull of New-castle-on-Tyne.* It bears no date but was printed about 1915.

[14] The spelling "Trumble" obtained generally until the poet's generation, and the poet's name was so spelled when he entered Yale College in 1763; but the older form was dropped soon thereafter.

graduated from Yale College, where, if one may judge from an anecdote, he exhibited a strain of mischievousness which his son seems to have inherited but soon lost. It is said that he stole a sign from a shopkeeper, hurried to his room with it, and, when pursued there, tossed it on the fire, taking advantage of the college rule that a student should not be disturbed at his devotions by remaining on his knees in the attitude of prayer until the sign was completely burned. Meanwhile he prayed: "A wicked and adulterous generation seeketh after a sign; and there shall no sign be given."[15] This legend has been found among the remains of so many distinguished men that it is quite possibly apocryphal, but the elder Trumble seems to have as much right to it as any one else, for it fits his character. His interests were varied. By profession a clergyman, he also practised farming, dealt in real estate, and traded horses.[16] Sports attracted him greatly, especially wrestling, in which, although an ordained minister, he engaged with such vigor on one occasion that he threw his opponent into the fire.[17] He was apparently a good pastor but an indifferent preacher. Frank, generous, jovial, and witty, he was very popular with his parishioners including the poorer members of his flock, whose welfare he did not neglect. His method of raising money for one in trouble was to place a dollar in his cocked hat, remarking that he was "sorry a dollar" and then to pass the hat around with the query, "How much are you sorry?"[18] If one of his congregation turned Episcopalian, the Reverend Mr. Trum-

---

[15] *History of Ancient Westbury and Present Watertown From Its Settlement to 1907* (n.p., n.d.), pp. 16, 17.

[16] So great was his interest in horses that he was known as "jockey Trumbull." —Henry Bronson, *The History of Waterbury, Connecticut* (Waterbury, 1858), p. 259.

[17] *Ibid.*, pp. 259, 260.

[18] Robert Pegrum, *A Memorial and Historical Sermon, Woodbury (Conn.)*, (Woodbury, 1890), p. 7.

ble would buy his farm, so it was said.[19] Possessed of a talent for organization, he soon became known outside of his own parish (Westbury, Connecticut), and he was sought for committee work throughout the state. Additional recognition of his ability was shown by his election as a fellow of Yale College in 1772[20]—a position to which he was apparently called not more for his godliness than for his knowledge of real estate. By this time his land holdings were considerable, and he was accounted wealthy.[21]

This, then, was the poet's father, a vigorous, jovial, and (the episode of the sign notwithstanding) honorable man, a fair scholar, an adequate preacher, a faithful pastor, an efficient business man, and a valued servant of Yale College. His reputation, at first merely local, grew until at the time of his death, which occurred in 1787, he was moderately well known throughout the state of Connecticut. Doubtless John Trumbull the poet profited by the prestige and the material resources of his father, but it seems clear that the wrestler-preacher, although not hostile toward his son's early literary attempts, was by no means an ideal tutor for an incipient poet. Indeed, it may be that the extremely practical strain which characterized him reappeared in the boy to some extent and set up a struggle with the more sensitive elements which he seems to have inherited from his mother. Certainly the rational element was strong in the son, and even in his maturity Trumbull manifested little sympathy with those tendencies in English poetry which prophesied the romantic

---

[19] *Proceedings of the North and South Consociations of Litchfield County* (Hartford, 1852), p. 77.

[20] "Acts of the Corporation" (manuscript in the possession of Yale University), September 9, 1772.

[21] Ezra Stiles noted in 1762 that Trumble had "£1000 L. M. at Interest" and owned "1000 or 1200 acres in Westbury besides Lands in other Towns." —"Itinerary" (6 vols. Manuscript in the possession of Yale University), I, [643].

movement. His temperament was rather that of a critical observer with a penchant for witty analysis and trenchant comment. He did not excel in colorful imagery or in lyric expression, and his best poems demonstrate not so much strength of feeling as of thought, not so much the powerful overflow of emotion as the facile operation of a lively intellect. Perhaps the cool blood which he inherited from his father inhibited the flow of more imaginative poetry in John Trumbull. At all events, it is less to the paternal than to the maternal side that one looks for signs of poetic "temperament."

Probably quite as able a person as her spouse, Sarah Whitman Trumble was accorded as little space in the annals of her time as most eighteenth-century women. One genealogist, however, has vouched for the fact that she was "in every respect a superior woman."[22] This may mean much. Distinguished blood ran in her veins, for she was a granddaughter of Solomon Stoddard of Northampton and a cousin of Jonathan Edwards. The clerical heritage of Trumbull was rich, for it was present on his mother's side, too: Sarah Whitman's father was a clergyman of high reputation in Farmington, Connecticut.[23] Like the poet's father, he was long a fellow of Yale College, an institution with which, first and last, John Trumbull had many contacts. As far as his mother was concerned, she apparently imparted to him a love of letters. It is certainly true that her encouragement was responsible in large part for the astonishingly rapid progress that Trumbull made, even as a boy.

John and Sarah Trumble had eight children, of whom John, the author of *M'Fingal*, was the fourth.[24] His birth oc-

---

[22] Charles H. Farnam, *History of the Descendants of John Whitman of Weymouth, Mass.* (New Haven, 1889), p. 65.

[23] *Ibid.*, p. 43.

[24] The births of only three of these children are recorded in Waterbury, where are located the only official birth records of early Westbury: "John

EARLY DAYS 15

curred at Westbury, Connecticut, a small community north and west of Waterbury on the site of what is now Watertown, on April 13 (old style), 1750.[25] Here the Reverend Mr. Trumble was settled as a Congregational minister in a parish of about fifty families. Here John Trumbull the poet spent his childhood.

Trumbull's childhood was remarkable chiefly for the extremely early manifestation of his poetical talents. All allowances made for parental pride and for the natural tendency of the public to exploit precocity, it may confidently be declared that Trumbull was one of the most precocious persons who ever put pen to paper. True, he did not fulfill every promise of his childhood and youth; perhaps he exemplified Bacon's dictum concerning those persons who have "an over-early ripeness, which fadeth betimes." Certainly Trumbull survived himself as a poet. Although he lived to be eighty-one years of age, he produced nothing after the age of thirty-three which added substantially to his fame. Perhaps the early fruition of his powers was responsible for this falling

---

Trumble the son of Jon Trumble the first of Suffeild [sic] was married to Sarah Whitman the daughter of Samuel Whitman of Farmington July 3 Anno Dom. 1744. Their first child a Daughter name Sarah Born June 20th A.D. 1745. Their second child a son born 27th February 1746/7. Their third a daughter name Elizabeth born March 17th A.D. 1747/8."—*Family Records, Town of Waterbury*, p. 355. Four other children were born of this marriage: Samuel, Elizabeth, and Lucy, born respectively in 1753, 1755, and 1758, and a daughter stillborn in 1761.—Farnam, *op. cit.*, p. 65.

[25] Ezra Stiles, *op. cit.*, IV [204]. An examination of the Waterbury birth records discloses no entry for John Trumbull. The parish records of the Congregational Church at Watertown, Connecticut, do not go back as far as 1750. The date given by Stiles in his "Itinerary" may be regarded as authentic, however, for he received it orally from Trumbull himself. As far as can be ascertained, there has never been difference of opinion in regard to the date of Trumbull's birth. In the scores of biographical notices of Trumbull which I have consulted, the birth-date has always been given as April 13, 1750, or, according to the new style, April 24, 1750. This date also appears in a "Memoir of the Author" prefixed to the collected edition of Trumbull's poems which appeared in 1820. The "Memoir" is almost certainly from Trumbull's pen. —See below, p. 16, footnote 27.

off. In any case, at an age when most boys are busy spinning tops and accomplishing as much general destruction as possible, Trumbull was engaged in intellectual pursuits which astonished the Colonies. Nor can the authenticity of the reports of his precocity be questioned seriously. President Stiles of Yale College vouched for the truth of many of the statements, and the most remarkable of all the boy's feats—passing the entrance examinations for Yale College at the age of seven—has been established beyond all doubt.[26]

Unlike his father, young Trumbull had a delicate physique, and from his earliest years his mental activity far surpassed his physical. He was particularly favored by his mother, who, having had "an education superior to most of her sex,"[27] was able to give him good instruction. The boy's active mind and prodigious memory showed themselves very early. Before he was two, his mother taught him "all the primer Verses, and Watts Childrens Hymns."[28] At the age of two he "began Primer & learned to read in half-year without School."[29] The first poet he read was Isaac Watts,

---

[26] Although boys commonly passed the (then easier) examinations for college entrance at an earlier age than they do now, Trumbull's achievement, if not unique in the history of American colleges, was extremely unusual. At Yale, at least, no comparable feat has been recorded.

[27] "Memoir of the Author," in *The Poetical Works of John Trumbull, LL.D.* (2 vols., Hartford, 1820), I, 9. This sketch of Trumbull, which will be referred to hereafter in these pages as "Memoir," is an important source of material concerning the poet's life, especially the years of his childhood. It is almost indubitably autobiographical in spite of the fact that Trumbull's direct testimony on the point is not available. It is certain, however, from a letter (now in the possession of Thomas Madigan, of New York) which Trumbull wrote to James Hillhouse, that Trumbull personally supervised the publication of his *Poetical Works*. Moreover, the absence of critical comment in the "Memoir" points to Trumbull's authorship. Even stronger evidence is the fact that most of the first paragraph of the *Sketch of the Life of Governor Jonathan Trumbull* ([Hartford], 1809), which is known to be the work of Trumbull, is identical in wording with the third paragraph of the "Memoir." On the basis of this and other concurring evidence, I have concluded the "Memoir" to be autobiographical.

[28] Stiles, *op. cit.*, IV, [204].   [29] *Ibid.*

EARLY DAYS

a prolific British versifier whose combination of piety and elegance recommended him to serious American readers in the latter half of the eighteenth century. Trumbull memorized Watts's "Lyrics."[30] Another work he read at an early age was the *Spectator* which, with the poems of Watts, appears to have comprised the belles-lettres section of his father's library.[31] Before he was four, he had read the entire Bible.

When he was about four, Trumbull began to compose verses, but he unaccountably waited until he was five before "he attempted to write & print these."[32] The earliest poem of Trumbull consisted of four stanzas, of which only one has been preserved. The manuscript of this stanza, dated in his own hand "1755," is accompanied by a note on the history of the composition. Trumbull writes:

Shall I add the earliest recollected specimen of my attempts at Verse; composed before I had learned to write or knew any other poetry, than the Psalms & Hymns taught me by my Mother. I was not then Five years of Age. My first endeavour to write was an Attempt to copy it, in an awkward imitation of printed characters . . . I remember only the first [stanza]—and the reason of my retaining it in memory is that it was the only stanza which I disliked, & laboured at the time to alter and correct—

. . . .
      Come, Blessed Saviour, quickly come,
    And call a sinner to thine home,
      Where in thy bosom I may dwell,
    And in the ways of grace excell.
. . . .

The last line stood thus at first.
    In knowledge of thy grace excell.
. . . .

---

[30] *Ibid.*—The "Lyrics" referred to are probably the *Horae Lyricae*.
[31] "Memoir," p. 10.
[32] Stiles, *op. cit.*, IV, [204].

I felt, even then, the want of connection between this & the foregoing line—and after lying awake some nights, corrected it as above, by inserting the conjunction, *And*, &c.[33]

This manuscript, written in Trumbull's mature hand, also contains a note on the poet's opinion of the nature of his own poetical endowment:

An account of the studies and reveries of my Boyhood might contain some curious traits in the history of the human mind. That one must be born a Poet is an old adage, but that any one, tho' formed with the keenest sensibility, & the most extravagantly romantic feelings, should have an innate attention to the minutiae of Criticism, is perhaps uncommon. I was born the dupe of imagination. My satirical turn was not native. It was produced by the keen spirit of critical observation, operating on disappointed expectation and avenging itself on real or fancied wrongs.[34]

Trumbull's character and writings are a tacit demonstration, as will be seen, of the essential falseness of this self-estimate. Although it is quite probable that he was "formed with the keenest sensibility," he gave no sign even in his earliest literary attempts of possessing "extravagantly romantic feelings." If he was "born the dupe of imagination," harsh contact with a world of circumstance clarified his vision before he had given literary proof of his bondage. Yet this misconception Trumbull seems to have held for many years. It was doubtless on this account that he so frequently essayed odes and elegies and even contemplated a serious epic. The truth, however, seems to have been that his "satirical turn" *was* native and that it was his propensity for satire, together with another native endowment, humor, which enabled him to attain even a modest ranking in American letters.

---

[33] Cornell MSS, p. 6.
[34] *Ibid.*

EARLY DAYS

Not only did Trumbull begin his creative work in a marvelous fashion at a tender age, but he also seriously undertook to learn Latin at an age when the average boy has much ado to learn his mother tongue. Like most clergymen of his time, Trumbull's father prepared young men for college. When in 1756 Mr. Trumble began to prepare a Waterbury youth, William Southmayd, for college, John also, with the approval of his mother but without his father's knowledge, began to study Latin.[35] He "learnd half Lillys Gramar before his Father knew it," and it took him only a day to memorize *quae genus*.[36]

There would seem to be no other conclusion to draw from this record of intellectual devotion than that the boy was an impossible bookworm and prig. Yet although it is true that the mature Trumbull, a bookish person, seems to have valued decorum in conduct unduly, two boyhood escapades indicate that he had a normal love of mischief which it was probably his misfortune to have lost too early. One anecdote bearing the marks of genuineness shows that he was more precocious in letters than he was in developing a sense of chivalry:

Mr. Trumbull raised his own tobacco. John, when a small boy, was put to the task of succoring the tobacco. Having filled his hat with the unsightly worms which infest that plant, he told a little sister that he had found a hen's nest on the scaffold in the barn, but could not get down with the eggs. Parading her below with her apron spread, he let fall the contents of his hat. She fainted; and the father, soon on the ground, exclaimed, "Now, John, you shall be whipped." "Father, father," said the excited

---

[35] Stiles, *op. cit.*, IV, [204]. The "Memoir" refers this undertaking to Trumbull's fifth year. Since Stiles derived his information on the point from Trumbull in 1788, it is perhaps wise to prefer his testimony to that of Trumbull's "Memoir," which was not written until 1820.

[36] Stiles, *op. cit.*, IV, [204]. There is a slight discrepancy between Stiles's evidence on this point and that of the "Memoir."

urchin, "I deserve it, but I beg you won't whip me until Madam Prichett is gone."[37]

Another incident illustrative of the want of reverence proverbially ascribed to the sons of ministers shows the poet's fondness for ludicrous situation and burlesque:

Tradition says that the parson's [the Reverend Mr. Trumble's] grave old dog, who was usually as regular an attendant upon the services as any member of the family, scandalized the good people of the congregation one Sunday, by marching in after the sermon had begun, with the minister's second best wig tied on his head, and took his seat on the pulpit stairs. The parson looked at him, struggled to maintain his gravity and remarked, "That is some of John's work."[38]

The surreptitious Latin studies continued until, after a few weeks, the father discovered his son's waywardness. Finding that John's astonishing memory enabled him to excel the seventeen-year-old Southmayd, Mr. Trumble, instead of becoming angry, "encouraged him to proceed."[39] Ultimately, Southmayd and Trumbull were presented for examination and passed at the same commencement, September, 1757. Legend has it that the Reverend Mr. Trumble and his son went to New Haven a-horseback, "the boy, of course, behind."[40] *The Connecticut Gazette*, very meagre at this time in all but political news, thought fit to notice the feat of young Trumbull:

At the Commencement in this Town the 14th Instant . . . Among Those that appear'd to be examined for Admission was the Son of the Rev'd Mr. *Trumble* of *Waterbury*, who passed a good Examination, altho' but little more than seven Years of

---

[37] *Proceedings of the North and South Consociations of Litchfield County*, p. 77.
[38] *History of Ancient Westbury and Present Watertown*, p. 17.
[39] "Memoir," p. 10.
[40] Bronson, *op. cit.*, p. 441.

Age but on Account of his Youth his Father does not intend he shall at present continue at College.[41]

Returning to Westbury to commence a six-year "miscellaneous course of study,"[42] young Trumbull, the future poet of the Revolution, may have been stirred by the martial spirit of the neighboring town of Waterbury. The French and Indian War was in progress, and during 1757 "the militia marched away in headlong haste; some on horseback . . . the residue on foot," for Fort William Henry.[43] Yet Trumbull was always more fond of books than of bullets, and the probability is that he spent a very quiet half dozen years engaged in sundry household tasks, playing games, and above all, reading.

As far as the classics were concerned, his reading consisted of the Greek and Latin authors generally taught at Yale College.[44] These were not many, for although there is no reason to doubt that in the eighteenth century schoolboys and college students were harassed by drill in declension, conjugation, and parsing to the point of desperation or dullness, it is easy to exaggerate the breadth of their knowledge of the classics. They took their classics in small quantities, which they sipped. The required classical reading cited by President Stiles as operative for a period not long after Trumbull's graduation from college, called for the study of Vergil, Cicero (the orations and *De Oratore*), Horace, and the Greek Testament—not a very formidable list.[45] Probably Trumbull read these, and in addition he himself reported having read Homer.[46]

---

[41] *The Connecticut Gazette*, September 24, 1757, p. [3].

[42] "Memoir," p. 11.

[43] Joseph Anderson (ed.), *The Town and City of Waterbury, Connecticut* (3 vols., New Haven, 1896), I, 393.

[44] "Memoir," p. 11.

[45] *The Literary Diary of Ezra Stiles, D.D., LL.D.* (ed. by F. B. Dexter, 3 vols., New York, 1901), II, 387, 388.

[46] Stiles, "Itinerary," IV, [205].

The opportunities for reading good books in English, not theological in character, were very limited in the village of Westbury. The principal English works Trumbull was able to secure were *Paradise Lost, The Seasons, Telemachus,* the *Spectator,* and "some of the poems of Dryden and Pope." These, Trumbull told Stiles, were "all the poetical & belles Books [he read] till aet 13."[47]

Trumbull's father, given to such secular pursuits as horse-trading, wrestling, and real estate, evidently made no attempt to develop a general library. It is to be presumed, however, that he required his children to read works calculated to improve their souls, for although he himself had apparently small genius for the life of the spirit, he was not the man to neglect the moral development of his charges. His library contained, of course, many theological books; for example, among the new accessions to it when Trumbull was ten years old were such works as Shepard's *The Parable of the Ten Virgins,* Hucheson's *Exposition of the Book of Job,* and Marshall's *The Gospel-Mystery of Sanctification.*[48] Whether at the age of ten even the precocious and nimble-witted Trumbull could find his way through these labyrinths is a question, but it is certain that by the age of nineteen he had examined many such treatises, for he discusses them in some detail. Moreover, *The Progress of Dulness,* which he wrote at twenty-three, shows an acquaintance with a variety of philosophic and religious works, some of which he may have read as a boy. At any rate the books were there as a grim element in his early environment. He could not have become the sort of man and poet he was, if it had not been for the severe Puritan background he acquired in his father's house. The man Trumbull never embraced the extremes of Calvinistic belief, but his later diatribes against Bolingbroke,

---

[47] *Ibid.*
[48] Ezra Stiles, "Folios, Collected and Sewed Together July 19, 1762" (manuscript in the possession of Yale University), p. [91].

EARLY DAYS

Hume, Shaftesbury, and other deists clearly were motivated in part by the simple orthodoxy he learned at home.

In addition to reading such classical and English books as he was able to secure, Trumbull worked on a versification of the Psalms, half of which he finished before he was nine.[49] He also attempted to imitate a number of English writers whose work he was studying,[50] but none of these earlier attempts has been preserved. The boy's memory apparently continued to provoke astonishment, for at the age of nine, on a "wager laid—to commit to memo. one of Salmons Pater Nosters in a quarter of an Hour—he effected it—recits by memo the Pater Noster in Hungarian and Malabar in Salmon." Furthermore, Trumbull retained the matter in memory so well that he was able to repeat the Hungarian to Ezra Stiles in the year 1788.[51]

The record of Trumbull's boyhood indicates that it was largely devoid of excitement except that which was attendant upon his extraordinary mental accomplishments. After he had passed his examinations for Yale at the age of seven, six years elapsed before he began his formal studies in New Haven. Meanwhile, like a younger and lesser Milton, he lived in leisured rustic seclusion, devoting himself largely to the reading of the classics and exercises in versification. His home was one of comfort and refinement: not all early Americans led rough pioneer lives. No direct comment on the appearance and personality of the boy has come down to us; but in the light of his activities one can picture a slight youth with a somewhat shrewd countenance, well-mannered, fond of play, but fonder of study. One suspects that he was not a good fellow: geniality was never a distinguishing trait of the mature man. He seems to have been inclined by nature to be rather reserved, almost secretive.

---

[49] Stiles, "Itinerary," IV, [205].
[50] "Memoir," p. 11.
[51] Stiles, "Itinerary," IV, [204], [205].

Perhaps his bodily frailty tended to make him so. The few pranks recorded of his boyhood seem incongruous in the light of his later love of decorum. Whether the brilliant intellectual exploits of his infancy and childhood and the publicity in which they resulted, developed in him an undue sense of his own importance, one does not know. No doubt he valued himself a little upon his accomplishments, but he probably had less pride than ambition. Certainly his achievements were amazing for a boy of his age. It can hardly be said that he ultimately fulfilled every promise and hope of future greatness, but his accomplishments for the next twenty years at least were all that could be expected of him.

CHAPTER III

STUDENT AT YALE

YALE COLLEGE played a large part in molding the career of Trumbull during his youth and his most productive period as a poet. Between the ages of thirteen and twenty-three, he spent nine years there, four as an undergraduate, three as a bachelor, and two as a tutor. In addition, he later acted as treasurer of Yale for six years. When it is recalled that his father, a Yale graduate, was a fellow of the College for fifteen years and that his maternal grandfather was a trustee for an even longer period, it becomes apparent that without straining terms unduly Trumbull may fairly be called "a Yale man." Yale was both an effect and a cause in Trumbull's life. It was the natural Mecca of a studiously inclined lad living in Connecticut; and his relatively sequestered life there confirmed in him those habits of scholarly retirement for which he had very early shown a proclivity. Whether the total result of his residence at Yale was fortunate or not is a matter of speculation. True, in an academic environment Trumbull produced poetry of a bookish sort; but judging from what is known of his life before he entered Yale (as well as after he left), it is difficult to suppose that a different environment would have made a very different poet. Trumbull was probably intended by the gods to be not a singing poet or a rhapsodic bard, but a witty rhymester with a faculty for making agreeable use of the by-products of his literary and scholarly studies. His wit came straight from nature, but his literary store he accumulated largely while in retirement at Yale College. Essentially in retirement he lived, for although there were stormy episodes during the régime of President Clap and sounds of the approaching conflict with Great Britain occasionally penetrated the seclusion of the College, all such interruptions were more than counterbalanced by the days of lettered ease which Trumbull enjoyed. This at least is clear from his high scholarship and his frequent poetical practice.

The College was small—about one hundred and eighty students were cared for in three buildings: Old College, Connecticut Hall (then new), and New College or Chapel. Besides the President, who bore a considerable part of the instruction, there were three tutors. The curriculum for the years of Trumbull's undergraduate career has not been preserved, but a schedule drawn up by President Stiles for the year 1779 probably gives a fair idea of what the poet was obliged to study:

Freshman Class.

Vergilius, Ciceronis Orationes, Greek Test[a], Wards Arithmetic.

Sophimore [sic] Class.

Græcum Test., Horatius, Lowths Eng. Grammar, Watts' Logic, Guthrie's Geography, Hammonds Algebra, Holmes Rhetorick, Wards Geometry, Vincent's Catechism Saturdays, Wards Math.

Junior Class.

Wards Trigonometry, Atkinson & Wilson D°, Græc. Test[a], Cic. de Oratore, Martin's Phil. Grammar & Philosophy 3 vol. Vincent Saturdays.

Senior Class.

Locke Human Understand[g], Wollaston's Rel. Nat. delineated, & for Saturdays Wollebius, Amesij Medulla, Graec. Test. (or Edwds on the Will sometime discontinued). Presid[t] Claps Ethics. . . .[1]

It is obvious that undergraduate study at Yale at the time centered around theology, the learned languages, and

---

[1] *The Literary Diary of Ezra Stiles*, II, 387-88.

mathematics. Hebrew was also in the curriculum during Trumbull's undergraduate residence.[2] These studies comprised the chief elements of "solid learning," a term much in vogue in that period. The chief defect in the curriculum from the point of view of Trumbull was that he found "little regard paid to English composition, or the acquirement of a correct style."[3] As a graduate student and tutor he later made several attempts to reform the program of study, among them the composition of his celebrated humorous poem, *The Progress of Dulness*, the first part of which constitutes a severe indictment of educational methods employed in American colleges. Though the criticism embodied in the poem purported to be general, it was of course understood to apply particularly to Yale College.[4]

Even before he entered college Trumbull was well prepared in one of the three principal focuses of study, the learned languages. Theology was presumably required of all students without regard to previous condition of enlightenment. In the third major branch of learning, mathematics, Trumbull was probably less proficient. Therefore upon the advice of his tutor he "turned his thoughts to Algebra, Geometry, and astronomical calculations."[5] For the first three years he devoted considerable attention to science,[6] in which he probably received good instruction, for the teaching staff, particularly President Clap and Tutor Woodhull, were especially interested in it.[7] Although Trumbull had

---

[2] Thomas Clap, *The Annals or History of Yale-College* (New Haven, 1766), Appendix, p. 81.
[3] "Memoir," p. 11.
[4] *The Progress of Dulness* is discussed below in Chapter V.
[5] "Memoir," p. 11.
[6] *Ibid.*
[7] Ezra Stiles said of President Clap: "In Mathematics & natural Philosophy, I have not reason to think that he was equalled by any man in America, except by the only man by whom he was surpassed, the most learned Professor Winthrop. . . ."—"The Letters of Ezra Stiles" (12 vols. Manuscript in the possession of Yale University), IV, [292].

probably little taste for the sciences, his knowledge of them stood him in good stead in the composition of *The Progress of Dulness*. Moreover, figures from astronomy and other sciences abound in his poetical work. His senior year, however, he appears to have devoted more fully to literature.[8] Unquestionably he also made excursions into belles-lettres on his own account throughout his four undergraduate years, for the Yale Library was surprisingly well stocked with good poetry.[9]

Probably Trumbull met all the scholastic requirements of the College with ease, but the routine he was obliged to follow was rather arduous. On a typical day, as the Laws of the College inform us, Trumbull was awakened "intra Horam Sextam et Solis Ortum" by the ringing of the bell by the butler. After prayers conducted by the President, he went to breakfast in the commons, where, as at all meals, he was expected to exhibit the utmost decorum. Breakfast over, he had liberty for a half-hour, after which the ringing of the bell warned him to his studies in his chamber. Here he was to remain unless called out by the President or the tutor for a College exercise, until dinner. Dinner was followed by a free period of one hour and a half. Then study was once more the order of the day, until supper. After evening prayers, there was another recess until nine o'clock, when study began again. How late the students were expected to study is not indicated, but the tutors were required to visit the chambers of all students "ante et post Meridiem, et post nonam Horam" in order to see whether they were present. A variation from the routine of study and recitation occurred on Tuesdays and Fridays when every undergraduate declaimed in English, Latin, Greek, or Hebrew, "circiter sex una Vice," and later delivered to his tutor a

---

[8] "Memoir," p. 11.
[9] See *A Catalogue of the Library of Yale-College in New Haven* (N[ew] London, 1743), pp. 6, 7, 44.

written copy of his oration. Saturdays were devoted chiefly to the study of theology. Throughout the week and throughout the four undergraduate years, from time to time, the students recited the Westminster confession of faith, Wollebius' *Christian Divinity*, and Amesius' *Medulla*—"aut aliud quodvis Theologiae Systema, a Praeside et Sociis approbatum." On Sundays, of course, no recitations were heard, but on that day, as on days of fasting and thanksgiving, divine worship was held morning and afternoon in the chapel.[10] It can be seen from these allusions to the College Laws, of which each student was required to own a copy, that the regimen of Yale at the time was a strict one; but, despite the fact that the Laws bristled with references to fines ranging from one half-penny to ten shillings, it is not to be believed (or hoped) that there were no infractions of the rules.

In addition to the *Statuta*, there was operative in Trumbull's time a harsh code of "Freshman Laws," the outgrowth of established customs, which provided rules (apparently approved by the administration) governing fagging for seniors, the proper manner of entering a room, the regulation of dress, and general conduct.[11] The enforcement of this code was probably efficient, for violators of it faced not only official penalties but also the informal punishment meted out by their superiors in class.[12] Thus the undergraduates, par-

---

[10] *Collegii Yalensis, Quod Est Novo-Portu Connecticutensium, Statuta, a Praeside et Sociis Sancita* (New Haven, 1764), *passim*. This edition of the Laws, issued during Trumbull's sophomore year, was apparently used until 1774, when the first edition in English was published. The work here cited is referred to hereafter as *Statuta*.

[11] Broadside in the possession of Yale University. The broadside is not dated, but it was in existence in 1764.

[12] The futility of resisting the hazing methods of the upper-classmen is illustrated by the case of John Treadwell, a classmate and friend of Trumbull. Arguing that the authority assumed by the seniors was "illegally exercised," Treadwell refused to fag. As a result of his independent stand, he "afterwards

ticularly the freshmen, were hedged about by such an elaborate system of major and petty regulations that their condition has been described as no less than "servitude."[13] Yet President Clap, who appears not to have realized that his charges were little more than boys, was not satisfied with this degree of legal protection, for in Trumbull's second year he drew up a supplementary list of "crimes" with provision for their punishment:

> There are many other Crimes and those of a heinious [sic] Nature which are not particularly mentioned or referred to in the Laws such as Sacriliege malicious setting the College on Fire Burglary Defiling the Chappel taking away the great Bible out of the Desk destroying the Monitors Bills &c All these Crimes whenever they Happen are to be punished by such kind and degree of Academical Punishments as shall be adequate to the Crimes and necessary to suppress them.[14]

The college body, as will be seen, was capable on occasion of breaking down the entire disciplinary structure of the institution; but it is unlikely that Trumbull, despite the pranks of his boyhood, was guilty of any but the most venial "crimes." Indeed he became shortly an active ally of the law; and in his senior year, partly no doubt because of his good conduct, he was elected "Scholar of the House," a post not only of academic honor and monetary value but also of proctorial responsibility.

It is not likely that Trumbull was a popular fellow, but there is little reason to suppose that he was peculiarly unhappy at college. His high social standing is to be inferred from the fact that, when he entered, his name appeared

---

suffered much persecution."—Denison Olmsted, *Memoir of John Treadwell, LL.D., Late Governor of Connecticut* (Boston, 1843), p. 6.

[13] Theodore Dwight Woolsey, *An Historical Discourse . . . August 14, 1850* (New Haven, 1850), p. 54.

[14] "Some Observations Relating to the Goverment [sic] of the College 1764" (manuscript in the possession of Yale University), p. [19].

STUDENT AT YALE

second on the list of matriculants.[15] The adequate allowance which his well-to-do father doubtless granted him must have been a comfort, but it could hardly have been a temptation to one of his cool blood. Curiously enough, he appears not to have been a member of the principal literary society of the College,[16] but his friends included interesting men, among them Nathanael Emmons, the eminent theologian, Samuel Wales, who subsequently became Livingston Professor of Divinity at Yale College, and John Treadwell, later governor of the state. In later years Emmons testified to one benefit derived from his intimacy with Trumbull when he said, "I have learned more about English style from Jack Trumbull, than from any other man."[17] Whatever his extra-curricular activities may have been, Trumbull's study and reading probably engrossed him very largely, for upon graduation he was to be regarded as one of the four most distinguished scholars of his class.[18] In addition, of course, he devoted a great deal of time to the development of his poetical gift.

---

[15] Thomas Clap, "Admissions of Students Cellars Occupied Rents of College farms Sundry Accounts 1757-1766" (manuscript in the possession of Yale University), p. [6].

[16] The only statement which he made in regard to this subject is slightly ambiguous:

"During their residence at the university, several young gentlemen were associated in their literary and poetical society, particularly Messrs. David Humphreys and Joel Barlow."—"Memoir," p. 15. The membership lists of the Linonian Society do not contain Trumbull's name. He was not a member of Brothers in Unity, for that organization was not established until 1768, the year after Trumbull was graduated. There is a possibility that he belonged to a society older than either of these, the Critonian Society, but no membership roll of this older society exists. Certainly Trumbull's literary gifts and his social standing qualified him for membership in one of the undergraduate literary societies. Whether he refused membership or failed to be elected cannot be determined. By nature an introspective, somewhat secretive person, Trumbull may not have been regarded as a "good fellow."

[17] *The Works of Nathanael Emmons, D.D.* (6 vols., Boston, 1861-63), I, 27.

[18] William B. Sprague, *Annals of the American Pulpit* (9 vols., New York, 1857-69), I, 710, 711.

JOHN TRUMBULL

Although Trumbull's academic career was probably quiet on the whole, there were a few events which disturbed the even tenor of his cloistered studies. Among the more interesting of these was the "poison plot." In his freshman year, most of the college body were seized one morning with a violent and extremely painful stomach disorder, resulting in many cases in "convulsion fits."[19] It is probable that Trumbull was among the victims of the illness, for only ten of the College boarders escaped it.[20] On account of the delicate international situation attendant upon the conclusion of the French and Indian War, it was believed by many people that a French neutral, offended by some of the students, "conveyed . . . poison privately into the dough that was mixing for the biscuit for breakfast."[21] President Clap, however, preferred to interpret the episode as a malicious prank on the part of certain students who, disgruntled at being obliged to take their meals in College, attempted to bring discredit upon commons. In a letter intended to reassure parents of the students, he expressed the opinion that the trouble was caused by "some strong Physic and not any mortal Poyson."[22] Most of the cases yielded to emetics and "Oleaginous and mucelaginous Draughts."[23] No one seems to have died; the President was probably right in his diagnosis. Yet he ordered that in the future the kitchen personnel should include no French cooks or servants.[24]

---

[19] *Memoirs of Doctor Seth Coleman, A. M. of Amherst, (Mass.)* (New Haven, 1817), pp. 96, 97.

[20] *Ibid.*, p. 96.

[21] *The British Magazine or Monthly Repository for Gentlemen & Ladies*, V (July, 1764), [381].

[22] "The Disasters which befell the Commons" (manuscript in the possession of Yale University, 1764), p. [1].

[23] "Correspondence of Ezra Stiles" (manuscript in the possession of Yale University), V, [14].

[24] "The Disasters which befell the Commons," p. [2]. By an odd coincidence, within two weeks after this poisoning or purging of the college body, the evangelist, George Whitefield, made a visit to the campus. The efficacy of his

STUDENT AT YALE

Another incident which occurred during Trumbull's freshman year suggests that the boy's earlier love of mischief was being replaced by that regard for law and justice which characterized the future judge. In August, 1764,[25] the case of one Griswold, a dissolute student, came up for final disposition. During the preceding April, Griswold had been found guilty of leading a group of students who had broken into the hen-house of a widow living near the campus and stolen therefrom eight fowls, which they had taken to the rooms of one of the boys for an illicit treat. The faculty decreed that the culprits should pay a heavy compensation to the widow for the loss of her hens and the damage done to her property, and that Griswold, in view of his deficient scholarship and his bad record, including firing a pistol in the College yard, should be carried on the rolls until August 15, at which time, unless he were very much improved in conduct, he was to be dismissed. Griswold apparently received the news of this judgment with poor grace, and used expressions which "implied a bad Design against the Authority of College."[26] Griswold's remarks on the occasion were carried to the administration by "Trumble" and another student with the result that Griswold was "publicly Admonished."[27] It is possible that official influence was brought to bear upon Trumbull in order to secure his testimony; nevertheless it was perhaps unfortunate that in his first year Trumbull should have laid himself open to the charge of tale-bearing, a practice which most students and some administrative officers hold in contempt.

---

spiritual purging upon this occasion may be judged from the fact that, just as he was about to leave, the boys urged him to come back and give them "one more quarter of an hour's exhortation."—Luke Tyerman, *The Life of the Rev. George Whitefield* (2 vols., New York, 1877), II, 467, 476.

[25] The college year did not close until September, when commencement occurred. The long vacation came immediately after commencement.

[26] "Judgments of the President & Tutors of Yale-College . . . 1763" (manuscript in the possession of Yale University), pp. 37-39. [27] *Ibid.*, pp. 42, 43.

JOHN TRUMBULL

Despite the many laws intended to guide the students of Yale College aright, there was from time to time a good deal of misconduct during Trumbull's day, including the circulation of lascivious books, forbidden excursions to neighboring taverns, indulgence in strong drink, and boisterous conduct in the College buildings.[28] The commencements even then were periods of great disorder, heavy drinking, the use of firearms and fireworks, and generally rowdy conduct in which the townspeople often joined. The climax of student disorder, however, followed a violent campaign of protest against the administration of President Clap.

President Clap, although an able man, was not a popular executive either within or without the College. He incurred the resentment of his extra-mural critics by thwarting an attempt to have the General Assembly of Connecticut institute a "visitation" to investigate alleged abuses in the College, particularly with respect to religious observances and disciplinary methods.[29] By the students he was regarded with hostility because of his autocratic government of the institution and because of the poor quality of commons. The first serious move against his administration occurred toward the end of Trumbull's second year, when a detachment made up

---

[28] A misdemeanor committed during Trumbull's sophomore year amusingly illustrates the disrespect the students sometimes showed for the tutors: "Whereas Yesterday at Dinner Bulkley 2d sent several Pieces of Cheese across the Hall for which indecent Action & Waste of the Cheese, he was then reprimanded by Mr. Lyman. And presently after as the Tutors were going out at the Hall-Door, the s'd Bulkley violently threw a hard Piece of Cheese at Mr. *Lyman* which passed near by his Head & struck the Side of the Door. The s'd Bulkley being sent for, said that he threw the s'd Piece of Cheese at Hunn. And Hunn being sent for said that he was at that Time at the opposite Part of the Hall. The s'd Bulkley offered nothing further in Extenuation of his Crimes."—"Judgments of the President & Tutors of Yale-College," p. 50.

[29] Thomas Clap, "The Annals of Yale-College" (manuscript in the possession of Yale University), pp. [111], [112]. The manuscript of this work differs in detail from the book of the same title referred to above, p. 27, n. 2. See also President Clap's "Reply to a Memorial for a Visitation of Yale College" (manuscript in the possession of Yale University), pp. 1-22.

of students and townspeople recorded their dissatisfaction with President Clap by "throwing great Stones against [the President's house] with violence which broke about 30 Squares of Glass damnified the Windowsashes and Clapboards broke off and carried away the Gates, and other enormities did then and there commit, whereby the President was slightly wounded."[30]

But the full tide of revolt against alleged maladministration of Yale College was not reached until the spring of 1766, when a major offensive was begun which resulted in the surrender of the President. Hostilities began on March 20 with the breaking of a tutor's windows.[31] Defiance of official discipline was further indicated by a widespread refusal to attend college exercises[32] and by the posting of "Satyrical Letters" in the College yard.[33] A formal petition of the students was followed by an unsatisfactory investigation ending in a compromise whereby the Corporation, although it remained essentially loyal to the President, granted stay of sentence to a number of offenders and allowed an unusually protracted vacation. Unfortunately two of the tutors now withdrew, as well they might from such hazardous positions, so that when the students came back from vacation there were no means of instructing them. They were therefore allowed "to go and live with what Ministers they pleased" until the fall.[34] Trumbull doubtless went home to Westbury.

President Clap now saw the handwriting on the wall; right though he conceived his administration to be, he could

---

[30] "Judgments of the President & Tutors of Yale-College," pp. 56-59.

[31] "The Diary of Joseph Bissell Wadsworth," *The College Courant*, III (September 12, 1868), 132.

[32] The extent of the breakdown of college discipline is suggested by the entry for March 28 in Wadsworth's diary: "In the After Noon I, with sundry others of my Class was sent for by the President for being absent 64 Times from Prayers this [Quarter], but we was none of us fined."—"The Diary of Joseph Bissell Wadsworth," *loc. cit.*, p. 132. [33] *Ibid.*

[34] *Ibid.* See also "Acts of the Corporation," April 22, 1766.

not with good conscience remain in office until Yale College should actually disintegrate. Accordingly, at a meeting of the Corporation in July, he handed in his resignation, pleading long service and the "State of his health."[35] Four days after his resignation, the College seemed "ready to expire,"[36] but the Corporation managed to keep it alive by accepting President Clap's resignation and proceeding to some firm measures of discipline. After one man had declined to accept the presidency on account of advanced years and a "feeble constitution,"[37] the office was settled temporarily upon Naphtali Daggett, an intrepid soul, under whose régime Yale College regained normality and, freed from the scientific predilections of President Clap, showed more favor to the arts.

It is inconceivable that Trumbull, capable of testifying against a fellow student, was active among the rioters who rendered hideous the last year of President Clap's incumbency. There is a faint possibility that he signed the petition —that being a proper mode of seeking redress—but it was doubtless as an unsympathetic spectator that he watched the violent moves of the insurgents. It would seem, from his later reactions to rebel activities upon the outbreak of the Revolution, that he was among those who, although on the side of liberty, have small stomach for the cruder manifestations of the democratic urge. During the revolution of 1766 at Yale College, he could hardly have been a participant in the seditious actions which menaced the quiet routine he evidently loved. His loyalty to the College and to his studies is suggested by his election at the end of his senior year to a Berkeley Scholarship,[38] an honor which signified

---

[35] "Acts of the Corporation," July 5, 1766.

[36] Letter from Chauncey Whittelsey to Ezra Stiles, July 5, 1766. The letter is in the possession of Yale University.

[37] "Acts of the Corporation," October 22, 1766.

[38] *The Yale Literary Magazine*, XVII (February, 1852), 152.

STUDENT AT YALE

not only his scholarly attainment but also his responsible character, for it entailed the presumably unpopular task of keeping a record of the windows broken in College and other damage to the plant, with the names of persons who caused the damage.[39]

Four years is a long time. Despite the chaos of the second half of Trumbull's junior year at Yale and other occasional disturbances, there were plenty of quiet days. A student as precocious as Trumbull probably had little difficulty in winning scholastic honors. Part of his spare time he employed in writing verse, some of which has been preserved. The poems which he produced as an undergraduate are curiously uneven in value and dissimilar in tone. Those poems which he conceived in a serious mood are almost entirely without distinction, whereas those which took a humorous turn, however trifling their subject-matter, were an earnest of the brilliant comic verse which later brought him fame. During his tumultuous junior year he produced the following smooth but lifeless ode, addressed to an unidentified youth:

From a Pastoral

To thee, oh L........, be my songs address'd,
Of friends the first, the brightest and the best;
Inspired by fancy & improved by art,
A towering genius & a social heart;
Tho' great, yet nameless, shining yet conceal'd,
Thy voice still silent & thy luster veil'd,
Rise to thyself; attend thy country's claim,
The wish of friendship & the calls of fame,
While crouding Muses court thee to be great,
And lay their harps & laurels at thy feet.

---

[39] The original character and purpose of the Berkeley Scholarship are outlined in a deed from Bishop George Berkeley to Yale College under date of August 17, 1733. The deed is in the possession of Yale University. For additional comment on the duties of a Berkeley Scholar in Trumbull's time, see *Statuta*, p. 20.

> Meanwhile attend to hear these humble lays,
> Which dread no censures, if they gain thy praise.[40]

Had Trumbull never attempted any poetry but this sort of sacrifice to the gods of respectability who guided American poetry of the period, he would not have survived his age. Fortunately, if he had the ambition to excel in the type of elegy most admired in his era, he also had the instinct to express himself in humor, frequently on subjects which were not for the drawing room.

Of course in writing humorous poems occasionally low in subject-matter, Trumbull was not setting himself apart from English poets of the neoclassical period, witness the humorous sallies of Gay, Prior, Swift, and many others; but he was writing poems for which there was very little demand on the part of the publishers and pundits in Puritan America. Indeed there was very little demand for poetry at all excepting funeral elegies, the receipt for which, as Franklin noted,[41] was in every pious poet's kit, and epic poetry, of which the nation hoped to acquire at least one example to which it might point with pride. For nearly a century and a half after the publication of a monstrous version of the Psalms (*The Bay Psalm Book*, 1640) there was very little American verse, excepting a number of Anne Bradstreet's lyrics, that could be reckoned seriously as art. The Puritans clearly felt that art, a pleasurable device, had little place in the lives of godly people unless it was hinged to use or religion. As sheer adornment of life it was just as much an invitation to the devil as was personal adornment. Persons who burned with irrepressible poetical inclinations had best marry them to theology in order to escape public censure. Humorous or satirical poetry was not to be countenanced

---

[40] Cornell MSS, p. 8. Above the word "towering" in line 4 appears the word "soaring," apparently a tentative emendation.

[41] "The Dogood Papers," No. 7, *The Writings of Benjamin Franklin* (ed. by A. H. Smythe. 10 vols., New York, 1905-07), II, 24, 25.

by proper society. A few humorous poets in the early days, whose names are now in the last degree obscure, compromised themselves with comic verse and then forswore it. Of course there was, even in Puritan times, a certain audience that relished racy humorous verse, but not many publishers were among them. Hence it is not surprising that Trumbull seems for a number of years to have regarded his comic poems as mere by-blows not to be spoken of in an age that insisted upon legitimate verse.

In retrospect it is easy to see that Trumbull did his best work only when his comic powers were in the ascendancy. The following poem, which shows that Trumbull, probably never a boisterous or uncontrolled youth, occasionally released some of his animal spirits in poetical channels, is a case in point, for it possesses a vitality (quite apart from its vulgarity) which is wanting in much of Trumbull's genteel verse. This poem, which needless to say could be circulated only privately in his time, is now first published:

POETICAL INSPIRATION

— There runs an antient story, You can
Find it, or something like in *Lucan*,
Of a strange hill, whose top, they tell us,
Puffed wind by fits, like blacksmith's bellows;
And such an odour fumed around,
Such horrid earthquakes shook the ground,
With cholic rumbling, that the hearers
Believed it near the world's posteriors.
High on the top a temple stood,
Devoted to some heathen God;
His priest (and in the days we name
A priest and poet was the same)
Fixing a sacred three-legg'd stool,
They call'd a *tripod*, o'er the hole,
And sitting down in solemn show,
Drew inspiration from below,

Which thus received he made the best on,
And by a *vicevers'* digestion,
Th' inflation rising from behind,
It came out verse, which went in wind.[42]

Another fragment from Trumbull's undergraduate days, of little value in itself, is significant as showing how early he interested himself in satire, a genre in which, with the assistance of his comic faculty, he was destined to make his only success:

Introduction to a Satirical Poem

Ye sacred Muses who did once inspire
Primeval bards with your poetic fire,
Who led great Homer to your blest abodes,
And bade him sing of heroes & of gods,
Vouchsafe to hear an humbler suppliant's prayer,
And lend assistance with propitious care.
My theme demands you all. I speak of things
Far greater than the strife of warring kings;
The dazzling charms of Homer's verse were faint,
The glories of th' illustrious Chiefs to paint,
Whose praise I sing. Thence, Oh ye tuneful Nine,
Inspire my soul and brighten every line,
That to those heights sublime I may attain,
And sound their honours with no vulgar strain.[43]

In spite of Trumbull's claim to having been the "dupe of imagination," and possessed of "the most extravagantly romantic feelings,"[44] he seems in this early verse to have had good control over his imagination. Neither was he dominated by youthful sentimentality, which sometimes presages romantic power in the adult. Rather, he appears to have been the servant of his critical propensities. The superiority of

---

[42] Cornell MSS, p. 9. The manuscript bears the dates, "1767," "1768."
[43] Cornell MSS, p. 7. The poem is dated "1766."
[44] See above, p. 18.

"Poetical Inspiration" over the ode entitled "From a Pastoral" suggests, what soon became a certainty, that Trumbull's forte even as a youngster was the sharp, brilliant, comic poem, intellectual rather than emotional in its genesis, which, with its metrical peculiarities, pointed toward his full development as a comic satirist excelling in Hudibrastic verse. This view is substantiated by the verse he produced during the three years of his graduate study.

In Trumbull's day students entered college at an earlier age than now and they stayed longer: a greater percentage of them remained to take the Master's degree. Many of them were preparing to enter the ministry; but although Trumbull with his clerical lineage must have considered the possibility of the ministry as a vocation, there is no record showing that he was ever attracted strongly by the profession. In pursuing graduate work, he was merely interested in continuing his general education. He liked academic life and, at seventeen, he was still over-young for entrance upon the world.[45] The regular period for the Master's work, which he began immediately after his graduation in 1767, was three years. This period of Trumbull's life, although superficially uneventful, was not without its significance for his career. Not only did it afford him time for a great deal of practice in poetry, but it gave him a perspective of the Yale curriculum which was extremely useful when he wrote his satire, *The Progress of Dulness.* Moreover, although Trumbull of course had then no idea of becoming a "poet of the Revolution," the incidents leading up to the war with Britain were furnishing him with the background and atmosphere for his most distinguished poem, *M'Fingal.*

If the fateful approach of the conflict with Great Brit-

---

[45] During the vacation after he received his Bachelor's degree, Trumbull, "being small in stature, . . . was sometimes seen seated in the road with other children, scraping up sand-hills with his hands."—*Proceedings of the North and South Consociations of Litchfield County,* p. 77.

ain was agitating the Colonies more with each year that passed, Yale College, having had its little revolution in Trumbull's junior year, was now settled down to a quiet, not to say soporific, routine. Confidence having been established among students, faculty, and administration, work proceeded more smoothly. Trumbull as a graduate student was still required to attend religious services and to "dispute" before the president once a week, but he was free from recitations and he apparently had few required studies;[46] for he tells us that as "master of his own time," he "devoted himself chiefly to polite letters; reading all the Greek and Latin classics, especially the poets and orators, and studying the style and endeavoring to imitate the manner of the best English writers."[47]

Trumbull, if not a radical person, was at least liberal in his tendencies as a young man, and he was anxious to promote a general interest in polite letters, particularly because he himself, as a potential poet, loved them. But the curriculum at Yale College, like that of most American colleges of the time, was shaped especially to the needs of candidates for the ministry, with little emphasis upon humane studies. Before he was through with the institution, he had done much to improve matters, and he began to work toward better things as a graduate student. The Yale curriculum was antiquated in its insistence upon "solid learning," that is, the learned languages, theology, and science, particularly mathematics and astronomy. Having been modeled upon the old scholastic curriculum of the English universities, the "back-bone of which was Theology and Logic," Yale clung to these staples long after the English universities had allowed more liberal studies a fair place in the curriculum.[48] During the period of Trumbull's graduate study the influ-

---
[46] *Statuta*, pp. 7, 11.
[47] "Memoir," p. 11.
[48] Henry A. Beers, "Yale College," *Scribner's Monthly*, XI (April, 1876), 767

STUDENT AT YALE

ence of President Clap, still felt, tended to give precedence to science. "English poetry and the belles-lettres," Trumbull said later, "were called folly, nonsense and an idle waste of time."[49]

Although Trumbull easily excelled in classical studies, he was also interested in creative writing. With the assistance of Timothy Dwight[50] and other young blood, as well as with the coöperation of the tutors, Trumbull set about trying to foster a spirit of love for art, particularly literary art. In an entirely informal way, of which the Corporation took no cognizance, these young spirits by their enthusiasm managed to arouse an interest in the English language, composition, and public speaking—forming unofficial night classes for the purpose. Thus they began to modify a régime which by this time was "almost monastic" in its dark severity.[51] Their efforts were aided slightly by a move toward democracy on the part of the Corporation, which had voted in 1766 that incoming classes should thereafter be listed in alphabetical order, thus reducing the emphasis upon social rank.[52] A synchronous reduction of the senior discipline had also a salutary effect, so that gentlemen's sons now had less advantage than before and perforce studies assumed a relatively important position. One student wrote at this period:

> There appears a laudable ambition to excel in knowledge. It is not he that has got the finest coat or largest ruffles that is esteemed here at present. And as the class henceforward are to be placed alphabetically, the students may expect marks of distinction to be put upon the best scholars and speakers.[53]

Trumbull's most potent propaganda for the relaxation of

---

[49] "Memoir," p. 12.
[50] Dwight, later a president of Yale College, was graduated two years after Trumbull.
[51] Ebenezer Baldwin, *Annals of Yale College* (New Haven, 1831), p. 98.
[52] "Acts of the Corporation," April 22, 1766.
[53] *Hours at Home*, X (February, 1870), 333.

the "monastic" method was his example. During the three years of graduate work he produced a large amount of prose and poetry which was a tacit rebuke to the system under which he labored. Much of this production has never been published and doubtless the administration was not aware of all of his activity of this kind. Of course Trumbull was no mere ignorant railer against philological studies. As a good classical scholar he had a real respect for words, and as a poet he loved the search for the *mot juste*. In later years he assisted Noah Webster by reading a "considerable portion" of the manuscript of his dictionary.[54] What he objected to in the Yale curriculum was the emphasis upon elementary linguistic studies to the exclusion of interpretation of the masterpieces of ancient and modern times and of practice in English composition. Hence he did all he could to stimulate an interest in belles-lettres both by attacking the program of "solid learning," and by engaging in purely literary exercises himself. His own wide reading in good literature is reflected in his frequent resort to parody and mock-heroic.

A number of the poetical pieces Trumbull wrote during his candidacy for the Master's degree have survived only in fragmentary form. Although in most cases this must be laid to accident, it is likely that some of the pieces were never finished by the author. Trumbull's mind was a restless, darting, nervous one, better adapted to a brief, brilliant consideration of a subject than to a sustained and thorough treatment of it. The following sketch shows his love of merry trifling in a mock-heroic vein:

> And as when Adam met his Eve,
> If good old Milton we believe,
> Pansies & violets around,
> And hyacinths bestrew'd the ground;
> 'Twas in a verdant bow'r, we learn;

---

[54] Letter from Trumbull to S. Converse, March 28, 1826, *The New York Evening Post*, May 17, 1826, p. [2].

> But what's a bower beyond a barn?
> The floor on which our Lovers lay,
> Tho' void of flowers, was strew'd with hay;
> And there on every side they saw,
> Not hyacinths, but special straw;
> And as in Eden, in amaze,
> The thronging beasts stood round to gaze.[55]

Another tiny poetical piece, a fragment, pleads for the free use of imagination in the writing of verse—a timely subject in an age when the training of a poet was likely to consist largely in imitating other poets who themselves imitated earlier models. Trumbull would have done well to profit by his own counsel more than he did:

> Mount "Fancy's horse," let loose the rein,
> Nor touch the pommel or the main,
> Clap spurs or strike a smarting blow,
> And, Hey my lads! away we go.
>   Thus, if examples we must quote,
> Bunyan, himself informs us, wrote,
> Knew not when pen in hand he took,
> "That he should make a little book,
> In such a sort, yet down he penn'd,
> And got his method by the end."
> And yet what author gain'd more fame
> Or raised more high his matchless name?
> His works where e'er they come, engage
> The looks of childhood & of age,
> Draw tears from antient matrons' eyes,
> And from their breasts heart-heaving sighs.
>   where[56]

Unmistakable prophecies of the mature satirist mark another fragment, entitled "Funeral Oration":

---

[55] Cornell MSS, p. 10. This poem and the two succeeding are dated "1768." In this and other manuscript poems by Trumbull emendations are not noted except where the author's final intention is not clear.

[56] Cornell MSS, p. 12.

Then having paused to take in breath,
He comes in course to rail at Death,
Calls him a monster, scoundrel, villain,
A knave that gets his bread by killing,
An old, illlooking, raw-boned vermin,
Enough where'er he comes to scare men;
With twenty more such ugly names—
Then smooths o'er all & mild exclaims,
"No more, my soul, why do I chide?
Death did no more than he was bid.
So let his trespass be forgiven,
For Brother Snip is gone to heaven."
   For thither every man must go,
Whose friends can make a verse below.
When Kings have run their mortal race,
Who serv'd the Devil all their days,
Ten thousand bards, right wise & knowing,
Must lend a lift, & set them going;
Ten thousand orators must say,
Nay swear, they saw them on the way;
Least they should fall or miss the track,
Six angels bearing each pickback,
                            And[57]

It is unfortunate that the remainder of this poem has not been preserved, for Trumbull reached in it a high level of satiric verse. Couplets like

      For thither every man must go,
      Whose friends can make a verse below

show that the author had a talent for witty condensation comparable to the best that eighteenth-century England could boast. Here one sees in the rhymes *villain—killing* and *vermin—scare men* early signs of a habit that was to grow on Trumbull, namely, the indulgence in the most extreme forms of Hudibrastic rhyme.

[57] *Ibid.*, p. 11.

None of these poems was included in the collected edition of Trumbull's poems in 1820, nor so far as can be ascertained have they been published elsewhere. All three are written in the octosyllabic couplet, Trumbull's favorite form throughout his career. Of no great final significance, they are illuminating as showing the author's reading of good literature and his faculty for trenchant wit. In their brevity, their bookishness, and their avoidance of substantial subject-matter they reveal their author as something of a dilettante. Indeed, the danger of dilettantism was one of the most formidable that Trumbull faced at all times. Had not the Revolution demanded his presence in more conspicuous places, he might never have come out of the closet; he might have remained a petty and obscure versifier of his age, able to turn small opportunities to small profit, but never able to interest more than a local audience. John Trumbull narrowly missed an even greater obscurity than was eventually his lot.

Two other brief poetical exercises Trumbull took time from his studies to set down. The first of these shows a common reaction to Sterne's writings, which crossed the Atlantic without delay in the 1760's, and contrary to the mandates of the moralists appear to have enjoyed a wide audience. One would have expected Trumbull, himself capable of small indecencies and given to trifling, to welcome another of his ilk from abroad, but Sterne's combination of salaciousness and sentimentality was apparently more than Trumbull could endure:

>   ON T[HE] PHILANTHROPY OF THE AUTHOR OF
>   TRISTRAM SHANDY. 1769.
>
> When *Sterne*, who could melt at the death of a Fly,
>   Declar'd he was *sorry the Devil was damn'd;*
> All his maudlin Admirers remurmur'd the sigh
>   And the Vot'ries of soft Sentimentals exclaim'd,
> "Ah! of *sweet Sensibility* this is the crown!

48 JOHN TRUMBULL

"What Philanthropy warm in this tender reflection!["]
Not *Philanthropy*, Friends—But I'm ready to own,
'Tis a striking example of *Filial Affection*.
                                    John 8. 44.[58]

Trumbull oscillated between his forte and his threatened fate. The poem on Sterne, unimportant as it is, illustrates the type of verse in which Trumbull excelled. In writing an epitaph on one Phinehas White, he was conforming more nearly to the demands of the age by producing a faultlessly rhymed poem of elevated sentiment with a gentle reminder to the reader of his own mortality:

> Here (with the dead this hallow'd ground contains)
> Of Youth & Learning dwell the sad remains;
> Of Genius bright, just opening into bloom,
> Its early flowrets with'ring on the tomb.
> Oh had kind Heav'n allowed a longer date!
> So short his warning, & so swift his fate—
> Ye young, ye gay, attend this speaking stone,
> Think on his fate, & tremble for your own.[59]

If Trumbull dabbled in piety with a view to getting practice for the elegiac verse which formed one of the staple commodities of the eighteenth century, the productions which have come down to us for this period show a happy balance in favor of the humorous and satirical poem. In August, 1769, occurred an event which suggested a poem thoroughly congenial to the poet's talent for parody and the burlesque, namely, the marriage of Tutor Stephen Mix Mitchell to a

---

[58] Cornell MSS, p. 34.—The manuscript of the poem was considerably altered, but the true reading is easily deciphered except for line 3, in which *reëchoed* was written above *remurmur'd*. The latter, however, was not deleted. "John 8. 44" contains the appropriate text: "Ye are of your father the devil, and the lusts of your father ye will do."

[59] Manuscript in the possession of the Burton Historical Collection (Detroit, Michigan), Woodbridge Papers, I, 4. This collection will hereafter be referred to as Burton MSS.

young woman of wealth. Although the poem which Trumbull wrote on this occasion was so free as to create a permanent estrangement between him and Mitchell (for Mitchell naturally resented the freedom of the nineteen-year-old lad), it need not be inferred that Trumbull had a special grudge against his superior. Rather the poem was primarily a literary exercise, a by-product of his years of classical reading, executed with such skill that the local was submerged in the universal. In a marginal note appended to a manuscript of this poem, Trumbull wrote that "in the Structure of it, & many particular Allusions, [it] is designed as a burlesque on on [sic] the ancient Epithalamia; particularly those of Spencer [sic], Claudian, &c."[60]

The poem commences with an invocation to the "nine great daughters of Jupiter" and the poet's own particular muse, whose aid he would enlist in his purpose

>To sing of bridegroom, bride, and wedding
>Of kissing fondling, love & bedding.

The persons of the action not yet having risen despite Phoebus' advancing course, the poet takes the opportunity to introduce some of his epic machinery:

>At leisure now for episodes,
>We'll introduce our set of Gods.

The supernatural beings include Hymen and Juno, mountain nymphs, dryads, and water nymphs "from swamps and flats." One absence the poet notes:

>Lucina was not there that morning,
>But ready stood at nine months warning.

---

[60] The "Epithalamium" is available in its complete form only in manuscript. Two copies exist. One of these is in the Yale University Library, and the other, which carries emendations and marginal notes, is in the Burton Historical Collection. Although a version of the poem was printed in *The Monthly Anthology and Boston Review*, May, 1805, and in the *Port Folio* (Philadelphia), October, 1805, it was even then thought too outspoken for unexpurgated publication.

Having been advised by the cock's crowing that day has returned, the bridegroom arises on his wedding morning. The poet forbears a comparison of his hero with "rogues renown'd in antient days," and places the lover before his lady's door, where he

> Address'd her with three gentle halloes
> Then read, or said, or sung, as follows . . .

The address which follows demonstrates her superiority to "all the dames above," including Venus:

> Thou'rt handsomer than all this trash
> By full three thousand pounds in cash.

In response to the lover's petition that she "cheer the world & gild the day," the bride comes forth, "array'd in all her charms & pride." Passing quickly over breakfast and the subsequent "kissing and courting" and various preparations, the poet proceeds to a description of the procession to the church shortly after midday. The "cavalcade" is described briefly except for the priest:

> In midst of these with solemn wag,
> Our priest bestrode his ambling nag.
> His dress and air right well accouter'd
> His hat new brush'd, his hair new powder'd,
> His formal band, of trade the sign,
> Depending decent from his chin;
> His threadbare coat late turn'd by Snip,
> With Scripture book & cane for whip.
> Unnotis'd [*sic*] pass'd amidst the throng,
> And look'd demure & jogg'd along.

The poet now indulges in a comparison of the powers of Hymen and the priest, much to the advantage of the latter, for a couple once "tied & hamper'd by the fetlock" can never be freed. Then he passes on to a description of the wedding, which he prefaces by an apology for the fact that he must "Pagan mix with Christian."

In the presence of a number of notable persons, including

> Venus & Cupid, (God of Love,)
> With all the rabble from above,

the priest "struck the bargain in a trice." His instructions and solemn counsel to the couple are reported and made merry over. Then, the bride and groom having given consent to "all the parson said or meant," the priest pronounces them "one flesh," whereupon a great many persons, the priest first, kiss either the bride or the groom. Now the procession returns to the bride's house, where a tremendous celebration, with bon-fires, fire-arms, shouting, singing, and bell-ringing, takes place, "for greatest joys are always shewn with greatest noise."

The bridegroom finds time an idle fellow until

> The sun when just 'twas time to sup
> Came to the sea where he puts up.

Supper takes the form of an elaborate feast with much attendant merriment, over which the poet promises not to dally long. With the arrival of "grim night," the bridegroom's "fears and griefs" are brought to an end; the maids show the bride to her chamber, where he promptly joins her.

> No Alderman—invited guest,
> To gormandize at turtle feast,
> When first he saw the dish bro't in,
> And 'gins to dip & grease his chin,
> Ere felt such raptures as our lover. . . .

The poet's "bashful muse" refuses to reveal what follows, but nevertheless reports "noises loud & ruinous" which disturb other persons in the house during the night. These noises they

> interpret as an omen
> Of something past & something coming.

The poet adds, in conclusion:

> And what that is, I'm somewhat jealous,
> A boy will come next year to tell us.

Besides Trumbull's familiarity with the classics, which he generally alludes to jocularly, this poem shows his familiarity with Butler, whose *Hudibras* he refers to twice and whom he frequently recalls by the management of his octosyllabic couplets with crazy Hudibrastic rhymes. Indeed, this poem is a more obviously successful and sustained imitation of Butler's famous work than any other poem by Trumbull, including *M'Fingal*. The Hudibrastic rhymes evidently gave their author a great deal of enjoyment, in which the reader shares; when he was riding this hobby Trumbull knew no restraint—witness such verbal unions as: *usurp—jews harp; turn he—journey; check first—breakfast; Christian—priests join; began he—Hannah.* It is thus apparent that six years before he commenced the composition of *M'Fingal*, Trumbull was imitating Butler, who was one of the models for Trumbull's best poem. Moreover, at least one passage in the "Epithalamium" was later imitated in *M'Fingal*. The following passage from the former,

> The sun who never stops to bait
> Now riding at his usual rate,
> Had scarcely pass'd the midway course. . . .

was patently the model for a couplet in *M'Fingal*,

> THE Sun, who never stops to dine,
> Two hours had pass'd the mid-way line.[61]

Standing on its own merits, the "Epithalamium" deserves moderate praise for its good structure, its able marshaling

---
[61] The couplet from *M'Fingal* occurs in Canto II.—*Poetical Works*, I, [41].

of epic machinery, and its nervous, well-knit verse. The poem is almost continuously amusing. Perhaps it errs on the side of being a little too clever occasionally—the principal sign in it of the author's immaturity. It is of course a bookish performance. Indeed, one of the major defects of Trumbull as a poet is that although he plays expertly with words and ideas, he fails to persuade the reader that he knows human nature as a whole. He knows the mind, but not the heart. He can dissect men's ideas but he is at a loss to interpret their feelings. Hence although he is capable of shrewd satirical strokes, he does not excel in characterization. Perhaps it was a realization of this deficiency which led him to deal so much in parody and burlesque, in which a comprehensive knowledge of life and character is less a desideratum and literary virtuosity is at a premium. Certainly the "Epithalamium" meets very well the requirements of its genre.

It is perhaps surprising that Trumbull could have said so many indecorous things in this poem without giving more strongly the impression that he was a profligate poet. The explanation probably is that in this matter, as in many others, Trumbull tended to be remote from reality. To him a poem was primarily an intellectual problem. Scenes involving the emotions or the passions, he tended to side-step or to treat humorously. In the latter case he seldom gave offense, for he was a master of finesse and innuendo. His indecencies are of an anaemic sort. He is often "naughty," but seldom very gross or very voluptuous. The "Epithalamium" is one of the freest poems he ever wrote; yet its literary, bookish quality prevents it from being egregiously vulgar.[62]

---

[62] In spite of the relatively harmless nature of the "Epithalamium," one Asa Bacon later testified to the interest it held for him as a boy:

"I have not seen Judge Mitchell since he left the Court in 1814. I am informed that he enjoys good health—I wonder if he ever amuses himself with

Trumbull may have lacked great original power but he had a good deal of literary initiative, in his youth at least, when he undertook a number of projects. In the same year that he produced the "Epithalamium," he commenced a series of newspaper essays, called *The Meddler*, which were published in *The Boston Chronicle* at intervals between September 4, 1769, and January 22, 1770. These essays, written mainly by Trumbull and in part by his friends, constitute one of the countless imitations of the *Tatler* and the *Spectator* written in this country in the eighteenth century. Among the first followers of Addison, so simple in style but so difficult to imitate, were James and Benjamin Franklin, who early in the century produced some essays in *The New England Courant* that were little more than paraphrases of Addison but who occasionally infused their essays with so much robust Yankee humor that they "shocked New England orthodoxy pretty thoroughly."[63] Other writers, like Thomas Prince and Mather Byles, undertook to produce imitations of the *Spectator* with no less humor than the Franklin brothers and with more decorum.[64] First and last in the eighteenth century, there were hundreds of imitations of Addison and Steele, but the heyday of the newspaper essay did not come until after 1785, when Joseph Dennie among others brought the form to a high degree of perfection.[65] Trumbull's efforts were certainly better than the average of such attempts, but they have little general interest now. Exceedingly apt in expression, they wanted sufficient originality and power to carry them very far on the road to posterity. Yet to one fol-

---

the 'Epithalamium.' When I was a boy I got hold of *that* and committed it to memory from beginning to end—without any aid, I learnt it much more perfectly than I did the 'Short catechism of the Westminster Divines,' with all my good Father's drilling."—Letter from Asa Bacon to Trumbull, April 21, 1828, Burton MSS, CXXVI, 67.

[63] *The Cambridge History of American Literature*, I, 112.

[64] *Ibid.*, pp. 113, 114.

[65] H. M. Ellis, *Joseph Dennie and his Circle* (Austin, [Texas], 1915), p. 51.

lowing the course of Trumbull's development, they are useful as showing his acute critical tendencies and as foreshadowing the views, liberal but not radical, which characterized him in mature life.

In the first number of *The Meddler*, Trumbull explains that his essays are to be "chiefly of the moral, critical and poetical kinds, upon miscellaneous and mostly unconnected subjects." In phraseology that looks backward to the *Spectator* and forward to the *Salmagundi Papers*, Trumbull congratulates himself upon being employed in "instructing the unlearned, diverting and improving the learned, rectifying the taste and manners of the time, and cultivating the fine arts in this land."[66] The "unconnected subjects" the author promised to expatiate upon included topics relating particularly to social and literary life. The foibles of the clergy, the kinds of wit and their abuses, the *double entendre*, the wiles of coquettes, the quackeries of scientists, the manners of modern gentlemen compared with ancient, political chicanery, the monotonous use of metaphors by certain poets, Milton's employment of allegory, the moral lessons contained in *Clarissa Harlowe*—these are some of the subjects which Trumbull treats with a good deal of wit, occasionally of a caustic sort. He often approaches the urbanity of Addison, but his wit is a trifle more acid than Addison's and his writing is on the whole less human. Trumbull's imitation of Addison may be seen especially in the third number of *The Meddler*, which is concluded by an "Advertisement" with the caption: "To be Sold at Public Vendue, The whole Estate of Isabella Sprightly Coquet." There follows a witty description of the several articles, including "a considerable quantity of patches, paint, brushes and cosmetics," which, since Isabella is "now retiring from business," will be for sale. Trumbull's

---

[66] *The Boston Chronicle*, II (Monday, September 4, to Thursday, September 7, 1769), 288. A complete file of *The Boston Chronicle* for the period is available in the Boston Public Library.

imitation of Addison can be seen especially in the second part of his notice:

Item. As she proposes by certain ceremonies to transform one of her humble servants into an husband, and keep him for her own use, she offers for sale, Floris, Daphinis, Cynthis, Cleanthies, and several others whom she won, by a constant attendance on business, during the space of four years. She can prove her indisputable right to them, by certain deeds of gift, bills of sale and attestations, commonly called love-letters, under their own hands. They will be sold very cheap, for they are all either broken-hearted, or broken-winded, or in a dying condition; nay, some of them have been dead this half year, as they declare and testify in the above mentioned writings.

N. B. Their hearts will be SOLD separate.[67]

In the eighth number of this series Trumbull appears in the rôle of critic of the clergy, a rôle he played more frequently in later works. This number contains an "approved and infallible receipt to make a popular Preacher. . . ." The principal factors, it appears, are "a good store of grace, or if that cannot be obtained, what is much better, an equal quantity of hypocrisy; with this a Sabbath-day face and a large grey Wig." In Trumbull's opinion the best way to attack the "affectation" which is the stock in trade of many preachers is rather "by ridicule, than by reason," for "satire strikes at the root, by shewing the man of affectation that the conduct by which he hoped to gain applause has subjected him to ridicule and contempt." It is characteristic of the future author of *The Progress of Dulness* and *M'Fingal* that he now enters upon an encomium of wit as the most efficacious agent of reform:

Wit is so powerful a weapon that it is often able to confound truth and bear down argument before it; it has been the chief engine of the enemies of virtue and religion, and has enabled

---

[67] *Ibid.*, II (October 23-26, 1769), 348.

them to support their party among the ignorant and unthinking part of mankind. How great then must be the force of wit and truth, if both are engaged on the same side, and how deserving are all attempts to reconcile them!

At the end of the essay Trumbull expresses a fervent wish that a champion may arise to espouse the cause of truth. His description of this hypothetical champion, it may be observed, would apply with considerable accuracy to Trumbull himself. Of particular interest is the fact that this leader, though liberal in tendency, will be no extremist but will seek the middle of the road:

> Oh, that some one might arise, endowed with equal powers of wit, humour and genius, to favour and support the cause of virtue; to combat vice and curb reigning infidelity; to ridicule folly and affectation, to lash indecency and immorality, and to convince the world that every extreme on either side of the golden mean is equally vile and ridiculous.[68]

The essays in *The Meddler* make good reading but they are not great literature. Their satire of social follies, the ways of literary men, the sins of the clergy and of politicians, is sharp but not deep. The wit dispensed is able and the style is polished. The chief charge against the essays is not their youthful quality but their want of personal force. Here, as often, Trumbull errs in allowing his intellectual interests to dominate him to the exclusion of things of more general appeal to humanity. Nevertheless *The Meddler* was apparently a moderately successful venture, for it was not long before Trumbull again began to conduct a "column."[69]

It is worthy of note that although Trumbull was to become one of the foremost men of letters of the American Revolution, nevertheless during the exciting days when that conflict was brewing he showed little disposition to employ

---

[68] *Ibid.*, III (December 28, 1769-January 1, 1770), p. 2.
[69] See below, pp. 79, 82 ff.

public events as topics for his writing. It must be remembered, of course, that Trumbull never became as fiery an opponent of Great Britain as Paine, Samuel Adams, or Josiah Quincy. His interest was more that of the poet or the recorder than of the protagonist or propagandist; his work naturally came later. Moreover, it was only natural that a boy in his teens, engaged in literary studies within the walls of a college, should choose themes suggested by his daily pursuits, chief of which in Trumbull's case was reading. On the other hand, it is unquestionable that during the period immediately preceding the Revolution, experience was fixing itself in his subconscious mind which was to lend a certain amount of force and authenticity to the composition of *M'Fingal*. The poet was acquiring information and impressions which he later used to good advantage. Even a bookish lad could not fail to be aware of the tension which had been increasing between the Crown and the Colonies ever since the imposition of the Stamp Act during his sophomore year. He could not help hearing of the organization of the Sons of Liberty,[70] the non-importation agreements (and their violation), and he doubtless read what all the colonists were reading with avidity, namely, Dickinson's *Letters from a Farmer in Pennsylvania*. Closer home he was able to witness the erection of a liberty-pole on the New Haven green, and he may have been a spectator of the Wilkes riot on the green and in the College yard, in 1769.[71] Within the College walls, he witnessed the appearance of the Yale seniors at commencement in their "plain coarse republican dress" of native manufacture.[72] Trumbull may not have welcomed these signs of approaching conflict, but they formed part of an experience

---

[70] There is no record showing that Trumbull was a member of the Sons of Liberty, nor is it certain that he would have approved of the radical position they represented.

[71] *The Connecticut Journal*, September 15, 1769, p. [4].

[72] *Diary of David McClure* (New York, 1899), p. 19.

which proved valuable to him when he became "the poet of the Revolution."

Trumbull's next literary production contained one spirited passage on contemporary events, but it was essentially an academic exercise, as was only appropriate, for it was an oration delivered on the occasion of his receiving the degree of Master of Arts on September 12, 1770.[73] This curious mélange, entitled *An Essay on the Use and Advantages of the Fine Arts*, was the logical result of his literary studies, ancient and modern, of the past three years. It attests both his good scholarship and his sane attitude of protest against the somewhat stuffy academic atmosphere of Yale College. The oration consisted of prose and verse. In the prose part, the author maintains the interesting thesis that the arts, which were highly venerated by the ancients, have fallen upon evil days in America. Regarded as "meer matters of trifling amusement," they are pushed aside in favor of "the more solid branches of Learning." Trumbull, himself a good scholar, does not presume to insist that the solid branches of learning should be neglected, but he does assert that, carried to extremes by men of mediocre calibre, they are stultifying and lead to absurd speculations of no moment. He then reviews the history of art in sundry countries, reaching the conclusion that those countries which have been distinguished for political or martial activities have in general been liberal toward the arts, which "polish away that rugged ferocity of manners" characteristic of uncultivated nations—witness the experience of Greece and Rome and Russia, the last merely a "cold unpolished land," until Peter took its destiny in hand. England's achievements, he finds, have been more than creditable in the past as respects art, but at the present time her literature is suffering from affec-

---

[73] The essay was promptly published: *An Essay on the Use and Advantages of the Fine Arts. Delivered at the Public Commencement, in New-Haven. September 12th. 1770*, New Haven, [1770].

tations and conventions. In a passage that derives especial significance from having been written three decades before Wordsworth led a revolt against "poetic" diction, Trumbull maintains that British men of letters are "infected with pedantry. They are great admirers of antiquity and followers in the path of servile imitation. They sacrifice ease and elegance to the affectation of classic correctness, fetter the fancy with the rules of method, and damp all the ardour of aspiring invention."

Turning to his own country, Trumbull assures his hearers confidently that America "hath a fair prospect in a few centuries of ruling both in arts and arms." This happy future he predicts for several reasons, among which are the diffusion of learning throughout all classes of people, and the love of liberty. Apropos of liberty, he launches into a passage of considerable eloquence, especially significant as one of the few known expressions of Trumbull on political liberty prior to 1774:

Many incidents unfortunate in themselves, have tended to call forth and sustain these virtues. Happy, in this respect, have been our late struggles for liberty! They have awakened the spirit of freedom; they have rectified the manners of the times; they have made us acquainted with the rights of mankind; recalled to our minds the glorious independance of former ages, fired us with the views of fame, and by filling our thoughts with contempt of the imported articles of luxury, have raised an opposition, not only to legal power, but to the effeminate manners of Britain. And I cannot but hope, notwithstanding some dangerous examples of infamous defection,[74] that there is a spirit remaining in these Colonies, that will invariably oppose itself to the efforts of usurpation and perfidy, and forbid that Avarice should ever betray us to Slavery.

---

[74] This is probably an allusion to violation of the non-importation agreements. Friction on this score had recently occurred in New Haven.—See *The Connecticut Journal*, June 15 and 22, August 24, 1770.

Returning from this vigorous digression to America's accomplishments in literature, he finds our theological writing to be "infested with the short-lived productions of controversy," but he grants that we have achieved some progress in political writings, the humorous essay, and poetry. The fame of America, however, though it remains to be established, can be prophesied. This clearly is a subject warranting an excursion into verse. Therefore Trumbull commences a one-hundred-and-twelve-line poem in decasyllabic couplets, "A Prospect of our Future Glory."

In substance "A Prospect of our Future Glory" is a promise of the coming greatness of America in commerce, science, and the arts, and of the imminent decline of Britain. This harangue, which is of a type sedulously practised by the poetasters of that day, shows that young Trumbull had more enthusiasm than discrimination: for example, Shakespeare is assigned to strange company when the young orator in one of his prognostications bids us expect to see

> Some future Shakespeare charm the rising age,
> And hold in magic chains the listning stage;
> Another Watts shall string the heav'nly lyre,
> And other Muses other bards inspire.

At the end, in deference to the occasion, Trumbull points out that in this vast evolution toward perfection in America, "fair Yalensia" shall "lead the noble train."[75]

The prose of Trumbull's essay on the fine arts is far superior to the poetry. Its matter, familiar enough today, was far from trite in his time, when it required a certain amount of courage to deliver from an academic platform an invective against "solid learning." Less can be said for the quality of the poetry. The "prospect" type of verse was little short of a blight in this period of our country's life, and Trumbull's

---

[75] This poem appears, with minor variations, in Trumbull's *Poetical Works* (II, [157]-161) as "Prospect of the Future Glory of America."

verse conformed to the specifications for such a poem. In spite of the liberal theory of poetry he had announced in his prose introduction, his own practice was conservative in the extreme. Platitudinous sentiments, bombastic diction, formal sentence-structure, elaborate circumlocutions, stock rhymes, and the rest of the neoclassical machinery for turning out "elegant" verse make this poem almost intolerable. There is not the slightest relief in the form of humor or wit. Trumbull's poetry, when he chose not to exercise his faculty for the comic, tended to be extremely dull, and of course this was not an occasion for Hudibrastic frolics.

With the perversity characteristic of many of the literary arbiters of the day, the newspaper critics chose to praise the poetical part of Trumbull's oration when it was published about two months later. At that time there appeared in *The Connecticut Journal* an eight-line poem in which Trumbull was compared with Pope. Higher praise it would then have been hard to imagine. Trumbull must have been giddy with the belief that he had now proved his powers to be of the first order:

> IMMORTAL POPE! thy SON immortal see:
> He treads the steps that once were trod by thee.
> When rules to Poets you are pleas'd to show
> As thick as starrs the bright examples glow.
> So he but copies from himself the views,
> We think are inspirations of his Muse.
> All that for future times he bids us hope,
> We see in him, as England saw in POPE.[76]

Trumbull had now spent seven consecutive years at Yale College. This practically constitutes a habit—in Trumbull's case apparently a beneficial one. To him they were probably in the main quiet years, although Yale College experienced a revolution during his undergraduate years and

---

[76] *The Connecticut Journal*, November 30, 1770, p. [3].

the nation was becoming more and more agitated by rebel activities. It is apparent from the success of Trumbull in his studies and from the frequency of his poetical sallies, as well as from his criticism of the curriculum at Yale, that he was interested more in the intellectual pursuits available to him than in any other one thing. The lust for adventure seems not to have been in him: he was by nature a recluse. Literary composition seems to have been his constant recreation. He experimented in various types of verse, alternately bowing to the conventions that made poetry marketable in eighteenth-century America, and indulging his undeniable genius for comedy and burlesque. He appears to have taken his formal efforts very seriously, and the encomium lavished upon the valedictory poem shows that he had not misgauged his public. Yet he fortunately gave his comic faculties a clandestine airing now and then, and his rollicking "Epithalamium" was the longest poem he wrote during these seven years. His prose essays too were generally couched in humor.

One would have no quarrel with the neoclassical era in America if it had produced good work of a sober variety, but it produced merely tinsel and fustian and tedious heroics. Dwight and Barlow were men of some power, but they went wrong in trying to write pretty rhymes or glittering heroics. Much of Freneau's poetry suffered from his obvious imitation of the neoclassicists. Even Trumbull, generously endowed by nature with comic force, appears to have suffered an atrophy of his normal powers as soon as he tried to adapt himself either to the elegant, mincing step of eighteenth-century elegy or to the pompous march of grandiose poetry. Much has been made of the failure of Mark Twain to write anything of consequence without his cap and bells, but Trumbull was an even clearer example of a humorist who failed utterly when he attempted serious things. Trumbull strove to become a writer of odes and elegies; his comic poems were the easy expression of his natural genius. At this stage in his career—he was now twenty years old—one looks anxiously for his future. His fate hung in the balance. Evidently he himself was unable to guide his own destinies wisely: the force of literary example in Augustan England and Puritan America was too perplexing. Would circumstance lend him a hand by stimulating his satirical and humorous powers to a sustained effort? Ultimately, yes, but in the meantime he was to engage in efforts of a less important kind before proceeding to the composition of the two longer poems which showed his full powers.

CHAPTER IV

TEACHER AND ESSAYIST

TRUMBULL did not see the eulogy comparing him to Pope in *The Connecticut Journal* when it appeared in New Haven on November 30, 1770, but his friend Buckingham St. John sent a copy of it to him at Wethersfield, Connecticut,[1] whither he had gone after receiving his Master's degree.[2] Of his occupation at Wethersfield no direct record remains, but the probability is that he studied law or, like many of the Yale graduates of the time, taught school, the latter being the more likely.[3] Away from home and away from Yale and away from New Haven, where he had been a "sad rogue" to one Miss "MT,"[4] Trumbull may have found his life in Wethersfield a bit lonely. The cold winter, he complained, interfered with his literary productivity.[5] In May of the next

---

[1] Cornell MSS, p. 19. Letter from St. John to Trumbull, December 4, 1770. —St. John was the subject of an elegy that Trumbull wrote later in the year. See below, p. 67.

[2] Stiles, "Itinerary," IV, [205].

[3] He could have studied law, of course, in New Haven. It is a fair guess that he acted as principal in the school at Wethersfield, a position assumed a year later by his friend, David Humphreys.—Frank Landon Humphreys, *Life and Times of David Humphreys Soldier-Statesman-Poet "Belov'd of Washington"* (2 vols., New York, 1917), I, 39.

[4] Letter from St. John.

[5] In a fragment dated January, 1771, addressed to "Mr. H...." (probably David Humphreys) he wrote:
> "Dear Friend,
> A little leisure time
> I'll spend to make a Page of Rhyme:
> So from your Servant to command,
> Pray take it as it comes to hand.
> The verse will have but little form in 't;

spring, he heard the mournful news of the death of his dear friend and former roommate, Buckingham St. John. These considerations do not suggest a happy year for the twenty-year-old Trumbull. At all events, he returned to New Haven, a day's journey by horseback, at the end of twelve months.

Although Trumbull complained of the untoward effects of Wethersfield weather upon his muse, he wrote a few things during his exile which have been preserved. He now had a reputation, albeit a local one, to sustain. Shortly after he left New Haven, St. John suggested that he write a "piece in the Hudibrastic" as a retaliation against a young lady in New Haven who had made "very free" with his name.[6] Whether or not Trumbull produced this piece, the request is worth noting, for it shows that among Trumbull's friends, at least, his talent in comedy was recognized. The only poem for the year 1770, other than those already referred to, is a fragment which apparently had nothing to do with the voluble lady mentioned by St. John. It is of little intrinsic value, but it shows that Trumbull continued occasionally to mine his vein of satire and burlesque:

>   Join too the hooting Owl in chorus,
>   And croud his verse with Sol & Boreas.
>   For him all Phoebus' rays inspire,
>   To wield the pestle, & the lyre.
>   Phoebus, you know, in antient times,
>   Was God of Physic and of Rhymes;
>   So long my Muse has rested dormant:
>   Nor does the season or the Clime
>   Assist the growth of sprightly rhyme.
>   In Summer's warmth the genial Hours
>   Can ripen Wits as well as Flow'rs;
>   And warm the dull & barren brain,
>   Till gayest Fancies spring amain."
>   —Burton MSS, CIII, 5.

[6] Letter from St. John.

For verses & cathartics tend
To reach at last the selfsame end;
Their nature as their use conjoin'd;
Verse is the physic of the mind,
And oftentimes, as readers rue,
'Tis physic for the body too.
For who, that hears such lays pathetic,
Would need cathartic or emetic,
Or fear from ague, cramp or pain,
Lull'd by these anodynes of brain?
So Bards may prove of mighty use
The price of opium to reduce,
Lull Pegasus amidst his capers,
And cure th' Aonian Maids of vapors,—[7]

If Trumbull's poetical faculties slumbered for a time at Wethersfield, they were awakened to a heavy duty in May, 1771, when the death of his friend St. John called forth the *Elegy on the Death of Mr. Buckingham St. John*. St. John was drowned off the shore of Fairfield, Connecticut, while on a voyage from New Haven to New York.[8] Sorely stricken as Trumbull must have been by the loss of one of his "earliest and most intimate friends,"[9] he set about composing a poem in honor of St. John's memory. Here was an opportunity worthy of a Milton. If it had ever been in Trumbull to become a first-rate elegiac poet, he could have shown it now. He evidently took his task seriously, for part of his "first sketch" shows that he originally wrote the poem in a form quite different from the final form. This fragment, the only available example of Trumbull's blank verse, does not show great originality, but it is at least fairly melodious:

---

[7] Cornell MSS, p. 10. There is no proof that this poem was not written before Trumbull left New Haven; it is dated merely "1770."

[8] *The Connecticut Journal*, May 10, 1771, p. [3].

[9] *Poetical Works*, II, [187], n. For two years St. John was Trumbull's roommate.—*Ibid.*

JOHN TRUMBULL

1771
Part of my first sketch of an Elegy on the death of Mr. St. John

— And lo, as here I roam, among the dead,
The realm of horror; mid these cypress shades,
This death of sound, this sad funereal gloom,
Mid empty forms of fleeting shapes of night
Slowly I view a whiterobed shade ascend,
That says, 'I once was St. John.' From the seas,
From the dark caverns of the watry world,
Where ever-restless floods, in endless wave,
Roll nightly o'er my head; from bursting glooms,
That cloud the portals of eternity,
Permitted I return. My warning voice
Sound, from the caves of death. Oh thou attend,
Now flushed with all the bloom of vernal years,
Who build'st on airy dreams, thy proud hope trusting.[10]

These fourteen lines correspond roughly with lines 21 to 44 of the completed poem as it appeared in the original broadside, 1771.[11] Much of the same phraseology is used in both versions, but a number of changes were necessarily made for the sake of rhyme, into which, according to the best eighteenth-century practice, the poem was finally cast. The elegy in its final form was the most ambitious poem of a serious nature yet essayed by Trumbull. Largely undistinguished as it is, it suggests, what later became a certainty, that high seriousness was not Trumbull's forte; when he attempted the sublime, he attained the banal. Yet this poem, with its unquestioned elevation of sentiment, its adequate

---

[10] Cornell MSS, p. 13, *verso*.

[11] A copy of this broadside is in the possession of the New York Historical Society. In 1915 Oscar Wegelin brought out an edition of the poem with a facsimile of the broadside and a preface (New York, 1915). He observes that the *Elegy* is "without doubt Trumbull's first separate publication." This statement is erroneous, for, as has already been noted, Trumbull's *Essay on the Fine Arts* was published in 1770. See above, p. 59, n. 73.

melancholy, and its obvious reminiscences of Gray's *Elegy*, undoubtedly went far toward establishing Trumbull's extra-academic reputation, for Elihu Smith printed it in his *Columbian Muse* (1794) as among those poems he believed to have won a secure place in American literature.

The next theme which evoked Trumbull's muse was of a different order. Having attempted to defend the reputations of certain young ladies who had been subjected to slanderous remarks, Trumbull "became in consequence implicated in the quarrel."[12] The details of the quarrel are not available, but it appears that some of those persons responsible for the slander were ladies far more advanced in years than Trumbull. With the intention of bringing the whole matter to a conclusion, the intrepid Trumbull, now but twenty-one years old, composed a poem entitled *Advice to Ladies of a Certain Age*. The poem, though written in July, 1771,[13] does not appear to have been published until 1820, but Trumbull's assertion that it "was written (to use a mercantile phrase) to close the concern" seems to imply that it was put to service, probably in manuscript form. The advice is of a caustic nature; in brief, Trumbull unequivocally advises the ladies concerned to act their age, to avoid envy and slander, and to accept their decline gracefully, realizing that physical charms are not the sum of happiness, for

> Within the mind a glory lies.

These precepts he enforces by examples from the lives of two unfortunate ladies introduced conventionally under the names of Eliza and Sophia. Generally Trumbull's satire works hand in hand with humor; but although this poem is witty, it is by no means mirthful, and the lessons the author intends are conveyed pitilessly. Trumbull uses his favorite verse form, the octosyllabic couplet, eschewing, however,

[12] *Poetical Works*, II, [171], n.
[13] *Ibid.*

70   JOHN TRUMBULL

for the nonce, Hudibrastic rhymes. In his management of the couplet, he recalls Gay rather than Butler. In one passage it is clear that he is looking to Pope for inspiration;[14] and at least one passage presages the mastery of epigram he later showed in *M'Fingal*:

> Thieves heed the arguments of gibbets
> And for a villain's quick conversion,
> A pillory can outpreach a parson.

During 1771 Trumbull wrote another poem on the subject of slanderous remarks entitled "Epistle Addres[s]ed to Mr. I. J.,"[15] which may have been related to the same case as the *Advice to Ladies*. Conceived apparently in a mood of anger, it is stilted and unconvincing. It has the technical finish of all of Trumbull's poems, but curiously enough Trumbull seems to have been unable to express himself well when his feelings were genuinely concerned. In high indignation he was no more at home than in deep-toned elegy. His best work generally has an air of detachment, as if the author were an interested spectator. Strong personal emotion is largely absent, of course, from his two major poems, *The Progress of Dulness* and *M'Fingal*. In this "Epistle" he is relatively ineffective, as an example will show:

> And didst thou think the world would tamely hear,
> Nor check thy Slanders in their mad career!
> Shall Truth turn dastard at thy wrathful eye,
> Or hast thou licence uncontroll'd to lie;
> And safe from vengeance, as from conscience free,
> Point thy black rage at innocence & me?
> And yet, so long for vanity renown'd,

---

[14] "Now at tea-table take thy station,
Those shambles vile of reputation,
Where butcher'd characters and stale
Are day by day exposed for sale."—*Poetical Works*, II, 175. Cf. Pope, *The Rape of the Lock*, Canto III, ll. 7-18.

[15] Cornell MSS, p. 36, *verso*. The poem has remained unpublished.

TEACHER AND ESSAYIST

Can sense affect thee, or can Satire wound,
Touch thy sear'd soul, or pierce thy guarded side,
Wrapt in the baseborn dignity of pride?
Tho' long despised, the mark of known disgrace,
What blush e'er changed thine impudence of face?
Hath shame once taught thy coward steps to fly,
Or thy tongue faulter'd to pronounce a lye?

Nothing in Trumbull's life suggests that he was endowed with the spirit of an adventurer; rather he appears to have been designed for a life of cloistered retirement and lettered ease. Consequently, although he had already spent seven years at Yale College, one imagines that he was glad to be called back, after a year of exile in bleak Wethersfield, to his alma mater to assume the position of a tutor,[16] a position which, though it had been a peculiarly dangerous one in President Clap's time, was normally sedentary. He assumed his position with mixed feelings, for it was understood that he was appointed "in the Room of Mr. St. John, deceased."[17] Nevertheless he looked forward to renewing old friendships and returning to favorite haunts. His friend Timothy Dwight was appointed to a similar position a short time after Trumbull, and the two young men probably took together the oath of office.

Trumbull's special charge was evidently the sophomore class, for the president generally took the seniors and Joseph Howe by reason of priority in the tutorship doubtless had the juniors, with Timothy Dwight, the latest adjunct to the staff, presumably in charge of the freshmen. According to the college laws, each tutor was to instruct his own class "in tribus Linguis edoctis, et Artibus ac Scientiis liberalibus."[18] As special tutor for the second-year students, Trumbull was called upon to teach rhetoric, geometry, and geography. In

---

[16] "Acts of the Corporation," September 11, 1771.
[17] *The Connecticut Journal*, September 20, 1771, p. [4].
[18] *Statuta*, p. 5.

addition to the president and the three tutors, the faculty included at this time Professor Nehemiah Strong, who gave special instruction in mathematics and natural philosophy.

Trumbull's duties were not confined to hearing recitations. It was his business to coöperate with other tutors and the president in detecting and curbing "crime," maintaining discipline and decorum, and administering justice. The laws stipulated that he reside in College and dine at commons, where he frequently asked the blessing and returned thanks. He was expected to observe the conduct of the students upon all occasions and to visit their chambers daily "ut omnia Delicta supprimantur." He had certain specific powers and responsibilities; for example, he was empowered to give liberty to students who wished to go out of town or to go sailing or fishing; to approve the steward's quarterly bills; and to impose fines of one shilling or less.[19] In general, of course, the chief authority was vested in the president, and the staff acted in an informal advisory capacity.

The lot of a tutor, as has been observed, was not easy when the students were rebellious. Fortunately the college year 1771 to 1772 was relatively uneventful. Nevertheless at any time to enjoy the good will of the students while living at such close quarters with them without neglecting one's duties to the College must have tested one's discretion to the utmost. The tutors were apparently seldom free from the proximity or actual company of the students. One evening in January, 1772, while writing a letter to Silas Deane, Trumbull complained good humoredly that he was hampered by the number of people around him. "I scarcely know what I am writing," he wrote; "I have a number of Letters to write, & a roomfull of people round me . . . I cannot write sense or english, with all the help of conversation I have round me—I am no Caesar, to write letters, give orders

---

[19] *Ibid.*, pp. 11, 13, 14, 16, *et passim*.

TEACHER AND ESSAYIST

& hold familiar conversation all at once."[20] Outside of chambers, too, the tutors mingled with the undergraduates and the bachelors. Oliver Wolcott, who visited the Yale campus about two years after Trumbull became a tutor, described in vivid fashion what he saw there. It appears from his account that Trumbull's rank was indicated by a black silk gown with a band on it:

> Men in black robes, white wigs, and high cocked hats; young men, dressed in camblet gowns, passed us in small groups. The Men in Robes and Wigs, I was told, were Professors; the young men in Gowns were Students. There were young men in black silk Gowns, some with Bands, and others without. These were either Tutors in the College, or resident Graduates, to whom the title of *Sir* was accorded.[21]

Evidently Trumbull was both happy and useful in his new work. His high social standing, his wit, and his reputation as a poet and essayist favored his having a good time.[22] His enthusiasm for belles-lettres, which was matched by that of Dwight, was in large part responsible for a renascence of cultural studies in Yale College. It has already been observed[23] that even as undergraduates and bachelors, Dwight and Trumbull kindled an unusual interest in liberal studies in the college. Trumbull's valedictory address[24] had pleaded for less emphasis on solid learning and more on polite letters. While he was in Wethersfield, the good work of encouraging the students to study their own language and literature and to practise public speaking was carried on by Joseph Howe,

---

[20] Letter to Silas Deane, January 8, 1772, manuscript in the possession of the Reverend Anson Phelps Stokes.

[21] Samuel Wolcott, *Memorial of Henry Wolcott* (New York, 1881), p. 225.

[22] A chapter in James Eugene Farmer's romance, *Brinton Eliot From Yale to Yorktown* (New York, 1902), fancifully represents Trumbull as drinking (moderately) with a group of students and reading portions of his compositions to them to their great delight.

[23] See above, pp. 43, 44.

[24] See above, p. 59.

a man of unusual gifts in oratory.[25] When Trumbull and Dwight joined forces with Howe in 1771, the three men worked in the direction of liberalizing the curriculum at Yale—breeding an interest in writing, speaking, and acting —to such good purpose that the "period from 1771 to 1777, will ever be considered as forming an era in the history of the College."[26] Their methods were informal. Instead of attempting to change the official curriculum, they proceeded by encouraging extra-curricular activities, such as evening exercises in composition, oratory, and histrionics. They not only criticized the forensic efforts of their protégés, but they went upon the platform and illustrated correct methods.[27] Trumbull's prolific writing and his growing reputation must have been an inspiration: his literary activity during the period of his tutorship was astonishing.

The results of this campaign were salutary if not of long duration.[28] The Corporation, generally a conservative body, took no immediate action in regard to these activities, but it is noteworthy that three years after Trumbull left, the Corporation cautiously granted a petition of the senior class that Dwight be allowed to instruct them in the "Branches of polite Literature . . . provided it may be done with the

---

[25] Joseph Howe (Yale, 1765) later entered ministerial work in Boston, where he rendered Trumbull important assistance in connection with the sale of *The Progress of Dulness*. When he died (in 1775) he was engaged to Elizabeth Whitman of Hartford, whose subsequent tragic history provided the theme for one of the earliest American novels, Hannah Foster's *The Coquette* (Boston, 1797).

[26] Timothy Dwight, "Memoir of the Life of President Dwight," in *Theology Explained and Defended in a Series of Sermons* (4 vols., New York, 1858), I, 9.

[27] *Ibid.*

[28] It is probably true that throughout the years Yale has steadily maintained a slight preference for the scientific training as opposed to the "cultural." "There has always been in the training given at Yale a certain severity. Discipline, rather than culture; power, rather than grace; 'light,' rather than 'sweetness,' have been, if not the aim, at least the result of her teachings. Her scholars have been noted for solid and exact learning. . . ."—H. A. Beers, "Yale College," *Scribner's Monthly*, XI (April, 1876), 781, 782.

TEACHER AND ESSAYIST 75

Approbation of the Parents or Guardians of said Class."[29] Even better evidence of the success of this movement in which Trumbull was the leader is to be seen in the plight of Nehemiah Strong, Professor of Mathematics and the Natural Sciences. Apparently as a consequence of a misunderstanding with the Corporation, Professor Strong, who thought he had been appointed on the basis of permanent tenure, made a bitter complaint when in 1781 the Corporation, ostensibly at least because of lack of funds, found it expedient to dispense with his services. In an elaborate address to the Corporation, Professor Strong voiced his distress at the idea that the Corporation should abolish the professorship in "those more Solid Branches" of learning which he represented. He granted that a new spirit in the College had rendered his work unpopular with the students, but he regarded as pernicious the new interest in the more "Showy & superficial parts of Learning" and the "rapturous transporting Displays of the *Stage*."[30] In 1777, a former tutor of the College, Jonathan Wells, complained to President Stiles that the students had "left the more solid parts of Learng & run into Plays & dramatic Exhibitions chiefly of the comic kind & turn'd College . . . into Drury Lane."[31] It would have grieved President Clap mightily could he have known that during the period of Trumbull's tutorship at Yale, the Linonian Society's list of productions included: Steele's *Conscious Lovers*, *The Beaux Stratigems* [sic], and "a Farce call'd the Toy Shop."[32] Yet even granting possible abuses in this crusade of letters, there can be no doubt that the new spirit of inquiry into belles-lettres and the freer use of the comic, which Trumbull did his part to foster, provided a wholesome lesson

[29] "Yale College Register," I, 211.
[30] Nehemiah Strong, "An Address to The Reverend Corporation of Yale-College" (manuscript in the possession of Yale University), pp. [8]-[10].
[31] *The Literary Diary of Ezra Stiles*, II, 230.
[32] "Records of the Linonian Society: 1768-1790. Manuscript in the possession of Yale University.

for phlegmatic Yale College, which up to this time had lagged behind Harvard in attention to English literature and composition.[33]

Trumbull was a brilliant example of devotion to literature in an environment none too friendly toward art, for the period of his tutorship (1771-1773) was as fertile as any of his life. In it he produced a number of short poems, a great many essays, and *The Progress of Dulness*. His capacity for application to mental tasks may be judged from the fact that in addition to all his other activities he was now studying law and was to take his bar examinations just after completing his tutorship. His writing during this period is of mixed sorts. His point of view appears not to have changed very much, for his favorite subjects continued to be the clergy, the college, the quack, the fop, against whom he continued to direct shafts of satire, at times merrily, at times a bit maliciously. He continued to be progressive with respect to modes of learning, and he reiterated his belief that although it ought to be freed from useless theological speculation, religion should not countenance the brazen contentions of the deists. His prose improved in conciseness and brilliance. His poetry, put to the test in a long poem, *The Progress of Dulness*,[34] showed him to be slightly deficient in organization of his materials but quite capable of shrewd argumentation accompanied by a constant flow of witty commentary. Personally he was beginning to show a strain of caution, for although he had begun criticizing society with all the pertness of youth, he now realized the flattering but disturbing truth that his warfare upon antiquated methods of teaching and shams in church and medicine was cre-

---

[33] For a discussion of the improvement of the Harvard curriculum by placing greater emphasis upon "Elocution, Composition in English, Rhetoric, and other parts of the Belles Lettres," see Benjamin Peirce, *A History of Harvard University* (Cambridge, 1833), p. 246.

[34] *The Progress of Dulness* is discussed below, in Chapter V.

ating enemies for him. After all, he had his way to make in the world, and John Trumbull was never one to be reckless of personal consequences. Yet the net result of all his literary enterprises was profitable, for his *Progress of Dulness* substantially increased his reputation even outside his own state.

The two principal shorter poems written by Trumbull during his tutorship show him practising the orthodox verse of his day and also keeping his penchant for humor alive—parallel efforts on his part which, of course, could never touch each other. In December, 1771, he wrote an elegy of the sort which satisfied the criteria of the age—a flawlessly rhymed poem of proper sentiments, agreeable melancholy, and perfect technical finish. This poem, whose content is sufficiently suggested by its title, *On the Vanity of Youthful Expectations*, is an exceedingly dreary piece of work, woven thinly of shreds and patches from Milton, Goldsmith, Johnson, and Young; but because it represented a species of verse that was in favor at the time, it was reprinted in Mathew Carey's popular repository, *The American Museum*,[35] and was accorded a place in Elihu Smith's carefully selected anthology, *The Columbian Muse*.[36]

This poor poem was fortunately compensated for by a brighter piece called *The Owl and the Sparrow*,[37] a fable which, although probably unimportant, was a more useful exercise of Trumbull's talents than its sober companion above described. A note on the first page of the 1820 text explains the genesis of the poem: "In the course of a poetical correspondence with a friend,[38] having received a very humor-

---

[35] *The American Museum, or Repository of Ancient and Modern Fugitive Pieces*, II (August, 1787), 206-203 [*sic*].

[36] In *The Columbian Muse* (New York, 1794) the poem was printed under the title, *Ambition, An Elegy*.

[37] *Poetical Works*, II, [149]-154.

[38] The "friend" is almost certainly David Humphreys, for in the last line of the poem Trumbull employed asterisks to the exact number of the letters in Humphreys' full name. It may be that the "Epistle to M^r. H...." quoted on

ous letter in ridicule of Love, &c. I sent him this fable in return." The thread of action in the fable is slight. A sparrow who has foolishly laid his affection at the feet of a bird of more aristocratic lineage, a thrush, without declaring his passion consults an owl in order to learn

> If love were worth a wise one's care.

The owl replies at some length to say that the sparrow would be wise to relinquish love, for

> Each woman is at heart a rake.

In this poem Trumbull apparently followed the more sprightly, if still jacketed, tradition established by Pope, Gay, and Prior, with the result that *The Owl and the Sparrow* is as captivating as the ode on *The Vanity of Youthful Expectations* is dull. A few lines from the opening of the poem will illustrate the crystalline quality of his verse:

> In elder days, in Saturn's prime,
> Ere baldness seized the head of Time,
> While truant Jove in infant pride,
> Play'd barefoot on Olympus' side, . . .

Written in rapid octosyllabic couplets, the poem abounds in puns and Hudibrastic rhymes. The subject-matter is trivial, but the verse shows that Trumbull was now approaching mastery of his craft. Certainly *The Owl and the Sparrow*, notwithstanding its slenderness of substance, was better practice for Trumbull than the elegies later approved by the anthologist Elihu Smith, for it was in a direct line with *The Progress of Dulness* and *M'Fingal*, soon to be written.

Trumbull is known almost exclusively as a poet; yet the body of his prose writing is large, and its quality is such that

---

p. 65, n. 5, is a part of the same "poetical correspondence." Humphreys had a very high opinion of Trumbull's wit.—See *The Miscellaneous Works of Colonel Humphreys* (New York, 1790), p. 96.

if he had been fortunate enough to expend his energies on more important questions, he might have made a permanent reputation as a prose writer. The *Meddler* and the *Essay on the Fine Arts* have already been considered.[39] During the intervals of studying, teaching, reading law, and writing poetry, Trumbull produced, in addition to these, some forty-five essays, most of which were published in the local newspaper. In the third year of his graduate study (1770), he inaugurated a series of essays under the pen name, "The Correspondent." During his tutorship he wrote seven essays entitled "Speculative Essays." In 1773, during his second year as tutor, he resumed *The Correspondent* and carried the series to its thirty-eighth number. The "Speculative Essays" have remained unpublished;[40] but the essays comprising *The Correspondent* were printed in *The Connecticut Journal*, where they were read with avidity.[41] However outmoded these essays may seem today, some knowledge of them is essential to a full understanding of Trumbull. Moreover, they exemplify one popular type of the newspaper essay of the late eighteenth century in America.

The "Speculative Essays," seven in number, are competently written; but they could never have a wide popularity, for they deal largely in abstractions. Six of the essays are devoted to philosophical and religious inquiries with related controversial matter; the other is a purely literary study treating the rules of description. The philosophical essays reflect the profound and widespread interest in theological and philosophical speculation of that time. The air was thick

---

[39] See above, pp. 54-57, 59-62.

[40] They are in the Cornell University Library, Cornell MSS, p. 24. Although Trumbull in later years affixed a note to the manuscript in which he stated that the essays were "Begun anno 1773," it is clear from internal evidence that they were written in part at least by August, 1771. They were probably completed by January 8, 1772.—See below, p. 82.

[41] The only file of *The Connecticut Journal* which approaches completeness is available in the Yale University Library.

with pamphlets expounding, refuting, and reiterating opinions, not only on questions of broad importance, but upon the smallest points of doctrine. A minister at New Haven would produce a pamphlet minutely analysing a problem in metaphysics. This would be answered by a minister at Saybrook, who would print a reply, headed by the most prodigious title, in which he "exposed the dangerous errors and heresies" of his brother in New Haven. With increased warmth, the New Haven minister would write an answer to the answer, captioned still more formidably, in which he "examined" the orthodoxy of his competitor's doctrines, only to find them, of course, full of "false propositions." Other pamphleteers would enter the lists from Maine to New Jersey and before long the air would be networked with the most elaborate analyses of problems ranging from freewill to the order of the service.[42] Trumbull regarded most of this speculation and controversy as harmful. He found that the controversialists were likely to be of two sorts—the skeptics and the dogmatists. First of all, Trumbull feared those "metaphysicians" who, relying upon the use of reason, dispensed with revelation entirely. The confusion and error into which man may be plunged by such practices is apparent in the works of the deists Bolingbroke, Shaftesbury, Voltaire, Rousseau, and Hume, names which were always anathema to Trumbull. Secondly, he thought most of the speculation on theological matters entirely unnecessary, for although he granted that there are knotty problems which cannot be easily explained without undermining the idea of a benevolent God, he believed that when one's thinking reached an impasse one should give up thinking and resort to faith. Trumbull was a keen but not a daring thinker.

---

[42] Among the more eminent theologians of the period were: Nathanael Emmons, Stephen West, William Hart, Joseph Bellamy, and Samuel Hopkins. In addition, of course, Jonathan Edwards' *Inquiry into Freedom of the Will* continued to be a lively center in this war of the pamphleteers.

He was not at home in the larger reaches of thought and imagination; he had no desire to "pursue . . . reason to an *O altitudo!*" His thinking was clear but confined. Yet he did not speak of these subjects without some knowledge, for it is obvious that he read Locke and Berkeley, as well as the deists he so much detested. His own belief lay in the middle ground. He accepted the Calvinistic doctrines of foreknowledge and foreordination; yet he did not wish to press their logical implications too far lest they make men out to be "meerly mechanical Agents."[43] In case of logical difficulty he would take leave of reason, for it is "no objection against the System of Religion, any more than against Revelation, that there are things contained in it, inexplicable by human reason."[44] He granted the existence of evil in the world, but he denied the ability of any human being to explain its purpose. Thus Trumbull was hardly more opposed to deism than to the scholastic treatment of religion. The position which he took in these essays, and which he maintained substantially throughout life, was that a simple acceptance of revelation with such exposition of Scripture as any divine can readily give is sufficient for all mankind; and to quarrel over fine and incomprehensible points of doctrine is to encourage heresies within the church and to prepare the way for the encroachment of deism. Trumbull thus tolerated very little latitude in religious matters. He could not approve of the incessant hair-splitting of the theologians, but neither would he brook the slightest tendency toward deism. Both the *cymini sectores* and the deists he attacked either by scorching satire or lively ridicule not only in the "Speculative Essays" but also in *The Correspondent* and *The Progress of Dulness*.

Trumbull's curious anti-metaphysical mania was so urgent that he even planned to produce an extended work exposing

---
[43] "Speculative Essays," p. 15.
[44] *Ibid.*

these pests, as may be noted in his letter to Silas Deane, January 8, 1772. It is a matter of regret, he writes to Deane, that Swift never carried out a project (mentioned in the preface to *A Tale of a Tub*) which he had formed of "writing a Satirical work, in ridicule of Deism & the Deistical writers of his day." He adds:

Such a work, executed in his severe way, would have done the world more service, than all his other Productions. . . . No men so much deserve Satire, as those who would unsettle our minds, with regard to every point of Philosophy or Religion, & make us doubt, if possible, even our own existence. If this be not the Design of Hume, Voltaire, Rousseau, & their followers, I cannot see that they have any.[45]

Swift having abandoned the project, Trumbull suggests that he himself might execute such a work, for which, he vouchsafes, he has sketched out several chapters—probably some of those essays discussed above as "Speculative Essays." For such a project Trumbull was equipped by his training in scholarship, his conservative point of view, and his command of satire. Yet in his letter to Deane he very naturally expresses a doubt as to whether he will complete the work, for he "never can keep [his] thoughts long on any one Subject." In fact he soon gave over his plan in favor of two other projects he had in mind, *The Correspondent* and *The Progress of Dulness*, in both of which he managed to satirize the metaphysicians occasionally.

The Correspondent consists of thirty-eight essays averaging about twelve hundred words apiece. The series was begun in 1770, when it ran for eight numbers, but it belongs principally to the year 1773, when thirty numbers were printed between February 12 and September 3 in *The Connecticut Journal*, a four-page weekly published at New Haven. Probably all but eight of the essays were of Trumbull's author-

---

[45] Letter to Silas Deane, January 8, 1772.

ship, the remainder having been written wholly or in part by Trumbull's friends, including, doubtless, Dwight and Humphreys.[46] Before the series had advanced very far, Trumbull's satiric shafts began to draw reprisals. Although some of his earliest critics may have been "planted," a number of the later expostulations and replies have every appearance of being genuine. Trumbull replied in kind to his more vituperative critics with the result that by the end of the summer *The Connecticut Journal*, which generally printed *The Correspondent* on its front page, was enlivened by a controversy in which courtesy played a very small part.

Although *The Correspondent* was one of scores of literary enterprises which drew their inspiration from Addison, it is clear that if Trumbull imitated Addison in a number of minutiae, he was essentially different from Addison in being more sharply satirical. In traditional fashion he promised amusement and instruction, invited correspondence, organized a club, and indulged in social satire on a variety of topics. But whereas Addison was so genial that he generally remained on good terms with the subjects of his satire, Trumbull lashed his victims with such a heavy whip that he found himself before long embroiled in a somewhat undignified controversy.

Trumbull treated many of the ills of society, but the main objects of his scorn were three: "metaphysical" writers, incompetent or hypocritical clergymen, and medical quacks. The first of these, the metaphysical writers, he assails in passages of withering sarcasm for their senseless and irreligious philosophical inquiries as well as their needless examination of Scriptural difficulties. Frequently employing irony he

---

[46] The detailed evidence for ascribing certain essays to Trumbull and others to his friends is not given here. In a few cases, such are the difficulties of conducting research in the early years of our literary history that a decision had to be made on the basis of little more than conjecture. Trumbull, however, was of course generally responsible for the whole series.

ridicules them for their conceit, their absurd terminology, and their inconsistencies. Professing themselves able to explain all problems, they easily "stride over infinity and eternity, those stumbling blocks to a weaker understanding." If indubitable physical fact embarrasses their arguments, they simply deny the existence of matter. In order to lend elegance and mystery to their discourse they invent an elaborate terminology. Their speculations are useless, but they pride themselves upon their discoveries so much that Trumbull is moved to congratulate mankind, for

> the sluices of knowledge will be now opened, and our dry, thirsty land watered with the copious stream of metaphysics. What great difficulties will now be removed! What mighty controversies will now be brought to a point! The great questions whether there is any such thing as *matter?* Whether one infinite line is longer than another? Whether eternity is an infinite now? Whether it be most like a strait line or a circle? with many others which have puzzled our progenitors the schoolmen, and the rest of the grave writers of all ages, will now be solved with the utmost facility. . . .[47]

Of course Trumbull would have had little quarrel with the metaphysical writers if their arguments had not had practical results. Unfortunately most of these writers were divines who might have served their charges better if they had expounded Scripture in the old ways without trying to read into it new subtleties. In engaging in wordy debate not only with their confrères but also with secular philosophers[48] these pastors did little but unsettle the minds of their flocks, open the way for heresies in the church, and give encouragement to deism and other varieties of free-thinking. Trumbull ap-

---

[47] *The Connecticut Journal*, June 1, 1770, p. [1].

[48] Trumbull does not specify the participants in this ignoble movement, but it is clear not only from *The Correspondent* but also from the "Speculative Essays" that most of the ideas he despised and feared were derived from the doctrines of such men as Hobbes, d'Holbach, Helvetius, Locke, and, oddly enough, Berkeley.

parently believed with Bacon that "a little philosophy inclineth man's mind to atheism." He may also have believed that "depth in philosophy bringeth men's minds about to religion," but he did not approve of running needless risks.

The metaphysical writers were not the only members of the clergy upon whom Trumbull vented his disapproval. There were also the incompetents and the hypocrites. In later numbers of *The Correspondent* he contended that, on account of the inadequate training for the ministry, the profession attracted candidates with low motives and inferior intelligence. Perhaps the greatest storm of criticism evoked by any of the Correspondent's statements centered around an unequivocal observation he made regarding college graduates: "In every class, that is graduated, some of the best scholars and a great part of the worst undertake the work of the ministry. And such is the tenderness of examinations, that the worst pass as smoothly and become as reverend as the best."[49] This comment created all the more consternation because it could not fail to be applied to Yale College. Trumbull's remedy for the evil, of course, was a more thorough course of study and a more rigorous examination.[50]

A similar laxity, Trumbull thought, characterized the training and examination of medical students and resulted in an enormous number of practising quacks. The subject of quackery Trumbull treats in three essays that combine serious discussion of the evil with ludicrous commentary. In connection with itinerant quacks, for example, he writes:

Happy then is the Patient, who lives in the neighbourhood of some advertising Quack, that cures diseases by miracle; some seventh son of a seventh son to the first man, that discovered the virtues of powder-post; whose very aspect frightens away sickness, and whose touch alone is good for warts and the king's-

---
[49] *The Connecticut Journal*, July 9, 1773, p. [1].
[50] In *The Progress of Dulness* Trumbull iterated these strictures on the clergy. —See below, pp. 102, 103.

evil; who hath the sense of feeling, as critically as hounds have, that of smelling, and by the mere movement of your pulse, can distinguish the very spot, where your pain lies, though it be no greater than the pricking of a pin; who is so well accustomed to all the properties of urine, that he can tell by the colour, odour and flavour of it, the habit, constitution, age and diseases of a person he never saw, and by putting a bottle of it into a course of physic, can cure the patients an hundred miles distant, without administering to him a single drop of medicine.[51]

In a later essay on the subject of quackery Trumbull makes humorous use of Addison's "Club of Duellists"[52] by remarking that entrance into the "honorable Society of Physicians" is as easy as into the duellists' club, "in which it was only required of every Candidate to certify that he had killed his man."[53] In concluding, as a measure designed to correct what was doubtless a real abuse in his day, Trumbull recommends that the examination of commencing practitioners be controlled by the General Assembly.[54]

A youthful satirist is never at a loss for subject-matter: he has only to look about him to see how defective the social structure is. Among the other objects of Trumbull's ridicule in *The Correspondent* are the fop and the coxcomb, whom he regards not only as useless but also, because of their tendency to consort with free-thinkers and deists, as a menace to society.[55] Another theme which engages his pen with surprising frequency is slander, apparently a contemporary vice of great virulence.[56] Occasionally he considers subjects relating to literature. For example he deplores the lack of literary initiative in New Haven.[57] He cautions writers against the

---

[51] *The Connecticut Journal*, March 19, 1773, p. [1].
[52] *Spectator*, No. 9.
[53] *The Connecticut Journal*, April 30, 1773, p. [1].
[54] *Ibid.*
[55] *Ibid.*, May 21, 1773, p. [1].
[56] *Ibid.*, March 2, 1770, p. [1]; March 12, 1773, p. [1]; June 25, 1773, p. [2].
[57] *Ibid.*, February 12, 1773, p. [1].

dangers of a too constant imitation of a single model.[58] In an analysis of the state of the arts and sciences in America he reports that although we acquired "*Sense* and *Genius* . . . with the first European Settlers" and are now beginning to exhibit "*Fancy* and *Invention*," we have not yet made appreciable progress in "*Humour* and *Satire*."[59] Contemporary biographies, he finds, are absurdly prone to eulogy, and obituaries are so steeped in panegyric that "Dying is certainly the most expeditious way of gaining a reputation."[60] To press the latter point home, he writes a delicious bit of parody in connection with the death of one Samuel Snip, a cobbler:

. . . So great was the fame of his honesty and integrity, that he was often appealed to in disputes between his neighbours, & made arbitrator of several considerable wagers at the tavern & ale-house. With all this reputation both for abilities and piety, the reader will not be surprized to hear, that he sustained many honorable offices in this town. In the forty-sixth year of his age, he was solemnly set apart to the ecclesiastical office of a Sexton, which he exercised with much care and fidelity to his dying day. He kept the church in the utmost neatness, dug graves with great alacrity, and rang the bells with peculiar harmony and modulation. Nor was he neglected on the civil, or military list. He was for many years one of the School-committee for a certain district in the town; in which office, in conjunction with two Blacksmiths and a Barber, he was always particularly frugal of the public money, and engaged the cheapest school-master that offered himself for sale. . . .[61]

Political affairs it was no more Trumbull's purpose to discuss than it was Addison's; yet a few times he glances at the state of the Colonies. One essay, possibly called forth by the

---
[58] *Ibid.*, June 4, 1773, p. [1].
[59] *Ibid.*, July 2, 1773, p. [1].
[60] *Ibid.*, February 26, 1773, p. [1].
[61] *Ibid.*

appearance in 1773 of Phyllis Wheatley's poems, constitutes a vigorous if somewhat general attack upon slavery in a brilliantly ironical manner which recalls Franklin's *Edict of the King of Prussia*. Its conclusion is irresistibly amusing:

I would just observe that there are many other nations in the world, whom we have equal right to enslave, and who stand in as much need of Christianity, as these poor Africans. Not to mention the Chinese, the Tartars, or the Laplanders, with many others, who would scarcely pay the trouble of christianizing I would observe that the Turks and the Papists, are very numerous in the world, and that it would go a great way towards the millenium, if we should transform them to Christians.

I propose at first, and by way of trial, in this laudable scheme, that two vessels be sent one to Rome, and the other to Constantinople, to fetch off the Pope and the Grand Signior; I make no doubt but the public convinced of the legality of the thing, and filled to the brim, with the charitable design of enslaving infidels, will readily engage in such an enterprise. For my part, would my circumstances permit, I would be ready to lead in the adventure and should promise myself certain success, with the assistance of a select company, of seamen concerned in the African trade. But at present, I can only shew my zeal, by promising when the affair is concluded, and the captives brought ashore, to set apart several hours in every day, when their masters can spare them, for instructing the Pope in his creed, and teaching the Grand Signior, to say his Catechism.[62]

Another number calls attention to the almost incredible ignorance and apathy displayed by his countrymen in the days when "many of the encroachments on our liberties still continue,"—an ignorance so great that "not one in twenty" knows the nature of the Writs of Assistance.[63] Although Trumbull was a patriot, it is characteristic of him that he was disgusted by the grosser manifestations of the

---

[62] *Ibid.*, July 6, 1770, p. [3].
[63] *Ibid.*, April 2, 1773, p. [1].

patriotic spirit such as the mob demonstration in favor of John Wilkes.[64] Like many another patriot, too, he soon learned that frequently "patriotism and self-interest" go hand in hand.[65]

Trumbull thus wrote on a variety of topics in *The Correspondent*. Although despite his humor he often exhibits the extreme tenseness of juvenile critics, on occasion he relaxed. Two poems of more than a hundred lines apiece appeared among the later numbers of his venture, one of them probably written by Humphreys, and the other, a reply to the first, by Trumbull. The second part of *The Progress of Dulness* having by now appeared, Humphreys jocosely warns Trumbull that he may as well give over trying to reform the world by satire, for the world is too set in its ways.[66] Trumbull replies philosophically, saying that although he hopes to ameliorate conditions, he does not expect to see "fools and knaves" disappear completely. Nor would it be to his advantage if they did:

> As Doctors thrive by patients ills
> And sickness aids their weekly bills,
> The Poets trade and fame increases
> By intellectual diseases.
>
> . . . .
>
> Were there no fools beneath the skies,
> What were the trick of being wise?
>
> . . . .
>
> And yet we've not a dunce to spare.
> These make our wits appear so fine,
> As darkness makes the glow worm shine.
> As he, that hath one eye, we find
> May serve for king among the blind,
> While fools and knaves are nine in ten,
> We'll pass for wits and honest men.[67]

---

[64] *Ibid.*, February 12, 1773, p. [1].
[65] *Ibid.*
[66] *Ibid.*, July 23, 1773, p. [1].   [67] *Ibid.*, July 30, 1773, p. [1].

Of course this attitude was pertinent not only to the poet but to the prose satirist, as Trumbull probably began to realize toward the end of his enterprise when the strength of his enemies must have proved to him that he had not succeeded in reforming all his readers.

Striking right and left over a period of months, Trumbull naturally reached his mark on several occasions. His diatribes against free-thinkers and incompetents proved their applicability to the times by their power to draw answers. As his enemies multiplied, Trumbull conceived the idea of organizing them, and for this purpose he created a club,[68] into which he amusingly consigned his critics severally as they appeared. As the summer advanced, the controversy grew warmer. Trumbull kept his head admirably in the face of terrific attacks from various calumniators and even threats of physical violence. The chief charges brought against him were his insufficient knowledge concerning things of which he spoke, his want of reverence for the cloth, his vanity, and his cocksure manner. Particularly his opponents seemed to resent the fact that the social order should be so confidently attacked by one so young—for apparently Trumbull's authorship was guessed before many months. Despite his youth, however, Trumbull was able to defend himself spiritedly against any antagonist who opposed him; few American authors have shown greater skill in dialectic. Nevertheless toward the middle of the summer, Trumbull, who had plans of moving to Boston after the commencement in September, announced the imminent decease of "the Correspondent." After much elaborate "settling of accounts" and other preparation, Trumbull reported his death, which he attributed to the attack of a certain opponent

---

[68] The club may be seen taking shape in *The Correspondent*, No. 23, May 21, 1773. The progress of the quarrel between Trumbull and his enemies may be traced in subsequent issues of *The Connecticut Journal*, May 21, 1773—September 3, 1773, *passim*.

whom he despised: the lion, he said, having been insulted by various beasts, was finally dispatched by the kick of an ass. The degree of heat generated by this controversy may be judged from an epitaph inserted in *The Connecticut Journal* by one of Trumbull's enemies:

> Sacred to the Memory
> of that pattern of Learning,
> The
> RENOWN'D CORRESPONDENT:
> Who with a noble Firmness,
> undaunted by Opposition,
> Continued for the Space of near Nine Months
> the sole Director of the Press, the Supporter
> of Virtue, and the Darling of the Muses,
> The Standard of Wit, the Master of Repartee,
> The Dread of Coquets,
> And the chief Favourite of the Ladies.
> But Alas!
> Nor his Wit, nor his Humour, nor the Charms
> of his Person, nor the Sweetness of his
> Voice, could keep him hence;
> He fell,
> A Victim to a lingering Disorder, resembing [*sic*]
> a Catarrh, or dripping of the Brains,
> And died of an empty Scull,
> In the Tenth Year of his Age—Anno Dom.—[69]

Trumbull, however, had still a number of parting shots to deliver, which he embodied in his "last Will and Testament," aimed at his principal calumniators.

There can be no doubt that *The Correspondent* was a successful venture for Trumbull and for *The Connecticut Journal*, whose readers could not fail to enjoy the animated quarrel spiced with personalities which filled the columns of the

---
[69] *The Connecticut Journal*, August 20, 1773, p. [3].

paper during the summer of 1773. If the series has small interest today, it must be remembered that the undertaking was an exceedingly difficult one: most of the English imitators of the *Spectator* have also found their way to oblivion. Moreover, the literary skill displayed in *The Correspondent* is so great that, were the essays not so heavily freighted with local allusion and so marred by laborious logomachy between persons no longer to be identified, they would be worthy of being better known today. What had been too formal and florid in Trumbull's prose style was toned down so that the prose of these essays is concise, firm, nervous, brilliant—admirably suited to the controversial business Trumbull had in hand. Almost every essay shows his familiarity with a long line of English essays sired by Addison. Yet Trumbull differed radically from Addison (and even more from Steele) in that his manner was not genial and expansive but urgent and intense. Like Addison, he had the purpose of reform, but where Addison gently chided, Trumbull acidly ridiculed. Where Addison was tolerant, Trumbull was uncompromising, impatient. Addison cajoled his readers; Trumbull's readers were discomfited. Trumbull had a great deal of humor but not enough good humor; indeed, he had more in common with Swift, whom he greatly admired, than with the authors of the *Tatler* and the *Spectator*. Hence although he dispensed his own ideas liberally in *The Correspondent*, Trumbull cannot be considered as a personal essayist par excellence; he was too critical, too ironical. The satirist in him overcame the informal essayist.

Trumbull's two exceedingly active years as a tutor at Yale College had now drawn to a close. During his tutorship, far from being an inert schoolmaster of the traditional type, Trumbull was a leading spirit in a movement to liberate the curriculum from the shackles of the old "solid learning" with its overemphasis on science, theology, and the learned languages. Such time as he could snatch from his duties as tutor and his law studies he devoted to writing. If his prose studies, the "Speculative Essays" and *The Correspondent*, showed him to be less liberal in theology than in theories of education, they also exhibited a keen mind, a facile pen, and an apparently inexhaustible wit. His poetical faculty he exercised at the same time by writing a number of shorter pieces, already discussed, as well as his extended satire on outmoded educational methods, *The Progress of Dulness*. The plan for the latter was apparently conceived in 1772, but its publication in three parts took place during approximately the same period as the publication of most of *The Correspondent* in 1773. The same attitude toward ignorance and cant in the learned professions characterizes both works, but the *Progress of Dulness* is almost exclusively a study of education.

CHAPTER V

THE PROGRESS OF DULNESS

POSTERITY is generally just in its judgments on the major productions of literature, but the works of smaller men it frequently pigeonholes without due cause. The inevitable labor involved in orienting oneself in the period in which a work was written in order to understand the author's purpose too often persuades the readers of a later generation to dismiss a minor work impatiently or casually with a disparaging comment. One cannot quarrel with a person who is not interested in literary history, but one deplores the tendency to fix values on works not sufficiently examined. *The Progress of Dulness* is not a diverting book to the average reader of today, nor is there any reason why the average reader should bother to dissect the dead issues implicit in it. Nevertheless the historian of literature has an obligation to examine the material he appraises. *The Progress of Dulness* has too often been relegated to that class of books which the hurried historian or anthologist must say a word about but hasn't time to read. Consequently the poem has been underrated—not grossly underrated but still appreciably so. Another reason why the poem has been so easily dismissed is that for several generations Americans, affected by a provincial fear of seeming to claim too much merit for their own productions, have silently damned the poem while they have paid homage to English poems of even less merit. A few critics have been more discerning. The eighteenth century was a century riddled with satires both here and in England; yet W. B. Otis was not far from the truth when he asserted (in 1909) that *The Progress of Dulness* is "superior to the average satire of the eighteenth century, either American or British."[1] The proof of course is in the reading. Yet this statement contains a salutary hint for those American scholars (and they are many) who patiently pore over the text of a mediocre English poet until they have wrested from it the last grim footnote but who, upon the mere mention of early American poetry, either scoff openly or politely change the subject. The few who actually read *The Progress of Dulness* are likely to express genuine surprise not only because of its literary merit but because of its entertaining quality.

The Progress of Dulness, written during the two years of Trumbull's tutorship, was published in three separate parts between December, 1772, and September, 1773. It is evident that for some years Trumbull had looked upon the Yale curriculum with dissatisfaction. As a student, he had had experience of the hard walls of tradition; but, more agile than the average, he had learned to vault them. Nevertheless, other students of less stature and enterprise were still immured. How to help them? Evidently not only must the students be encouraged by example to seek freedom for themselves but also an attack must be made upon the strong system which enslaved them. This attack Tutor Trumbull now made in the form of a poem which, far from being the dull tirade of a dogged reformer, depended for its effect largely upon the free use of satire and humor. Lest the more literal readers should be misled into thinking that his purpose was to give vent to malice or merely to entertain, he supplied the poem with prose prefaces which directly revealed his aims. The reaction to this attack proved its power. At the same time, the generous reception accorded the poem by more impartial observers showed that its literary value was promptly perceived. In *The Progress of Dulness*, John Trumbull approached the peak of his poetical ability.

---

[1] *American Verse 1625-1807* (New York, 1909), p. 131.

When it was completed, he was but twenty-three years of age.

The poem had its origin in the antiquated modes of instruction at Yale College in the Colony of Connecticut. Yet although its theme arose out of a local problem in the new world, the poem is primarily British in spirit. The desire for literary independence is of slower growth than the demand for political independence. To be sure, Trumbull occasionally expressed himself with vigor in behalf of colonial rights, but he had no quarrel with his literary heritage from the mother country. As a man of letters he was instinctively conservative. Hence, although the subject-matter of *The Progress of Dulness* is largely American, Trumbull's models must be sought in English poetry, particularly that of the eighteenth-century satirists whom Trumbull resembled in temper and talent.[2] Furthermore, such was his proneness to read life through books that, although for *The Progress of Dulness* he had only to draw his characters from living persons in his own community, the second and third parts of the poem too often give the impression that the author had his eye on types of fops and coquettes that had long been familiar figures in English poetry. In short, imitation might have been fatal to this poem had it not been for Trumbull's peculiar comic genius. This, together with the unquestionable freshness of Part First, gives the poem considerable claim to originality, notwithstanding a number of "sources."

The Progress of Dulness is written in the only verse-form Trumbull ever mastered, the octosyllabic couplet. Here, as elsewhere, he employed many amusing Hudibrastic rhymes. In his "Critical Reflections" (1778),[3] Trumbull mentioned a number of poets who excelled in Hudibrastic verse, and

---

[2] American models for *The Progress of Dulness* there appear to have been none. In these early days the only American poet Trumbull apparently had a high opinion of was Timothy Dwight.

[3] Cornell MSS, pp. 30, 31.

he evaluated their work. Among these were Prior, whom he praised for his "easy elegant and natural description," and Swift, whom he characterized as a "Hogarth among writers." Apropos of Swift's poems in the octosyllabic couplet, he wrote that Swift's excellence lay partly in his "strong descriptive painting." Moreover, despite cousin Dryden's dictum in regard to the Dean's poetic ability, Trumbull added that "Many of his little Poems are in this way superior to any writing of their kind in the world."[4] Although Trumbull's debt to other writers is inclined to be more general than specific, occasionally he writes a passage which bears a close analogy to Swift's work. In particular, he appears to have been familiar with *Cadenus and Vanessa* and *The Furniture of a Woman's Mind*. The following bit of innuendo in the former may have been in Trumbull's mind when he wrote a similar passage in *The Progress of Dulness*:

> . . . What awkward thing
> Was that last Sunday in the ring?
> I'm sorry Mopsa breaks so fast:
> I said her face would never last.
> Corinna, with that youthful air,
> Is thirty, and a bit to spare:
> Her fondness for a certain earl
> Began when I was but a girl!
> Phillis, who but a month ago
> Was married to the Tunbridge beau,
> I saw coquetting t'other night
> In public with that odious knight![5]

Trumbull's lines, if similar to Swift's, are even superior in witty condensation:

> "And did you hear the news? (they cry)
> The court wears caps full three feet high,

---
[4] "Critical Reflections," Cornell MSS, pp. 3, 4.
[5] *The Works of Jonathan Swift* (19 vols., Edinburgh, 1814), XIV, 452.

98   JOHN TRUMBULL

And were you at the ball last night?
Well, Chloe look'd like any fright;
Her day is over for a toast;
She'd now do best to act a ghost.
You saw our Fanny; envy must own
She figures, since she came from Boston.
Good company improves one's air—
I think the troops were station'd there.
Poor Cœlia ventured to the place;
The small-pox quite has spoil'd her face,
A sad affair, we all confest:
But providence knows what is best.
Poor Dolly too, that writ the letter
Of love to Dick; but Dick knew better;
A secret that; you'll not disclose it;
There's not a person living knows it.
Sylvia shone out, no peacock finer;
I wonder what the fops see in her.
Perhaps 'tis true what Harry maintains,
She mends on intimate acquaintance."[6]

The other two writers whom Trumbull alludes to as having excelled in Hudibrastic poetry are Churchill and Butler. Butler, however, Trumbull admits having found hard to imitate.[7] Churchill he apparently had less in mind as a model for *The Progress of Dulness* than for *M'Fingal*, but there is much similarity between his handling of material and Churchill's even here. Among the poems not confessed by Trumbull as models for his Hudibrastic writings are one or two that may have had a share of influence both as to style and as to substance, namely, J. D. Breval's *The Progress of a Rake*,[8] and Thomas Warton's briefer poem entitled *The*

---

[6] *Poetical Works*, II, 73, 74.   [7] "Critical Reflections," Cornell MSS, p. 30.

[8] *The Progress of a Rake: Or, The Templar's Exit* (London, 1732).—The hero of this poem, named Dick, goes through a cycle of experience similar to, though even more sordid than, Dick Hairbrain's in *The Progress of Dulness*, Part Second.

Progress of Discontent[9]—two of the almost innumerable eighteenth-century poems which bore the word "progress" in the title. It may be confidently added that in *The Progress of Dulness* Trumbull had one other poet as a model, namely, Pope, a writer whose accents persistently echo through Trumbull's verse.[10] Trumbull's general imitation of Pope is obvious—despite the fundamental difference that Trumbull used the octosyllabic couplet in his best works whereas Pope preferred the decasyllabic couplet. Whether he definitely had in mind any part of Pope's works when he wrote *The Progress of Dulness* is not sure, but it is a reasonable conjecture that he received some inspiration, direct or indirect, from Pope's treatment of the "Empire of Dulness" in *The Dunciad*. Although close parallels between Trumbull and Pope are not available, it is perhaps worth observing that in the fourth book of *The Dunciad* Aristarchus, representing the universities, delivers in the presence of the Goddess of Dulness a farcical harangue which reveals some of the same weaknesses in educational procedure that Trumbull satirizes in *The Progress of Dulness*:

> Avaunt—is Aristarchus yet unknown?
> Thy mighty scholiast, whose unwearied pains
> Made Horace dull, and humbled Milton's strains.
> Turn what they will to verse, their toil is vain,
> Critics like me shall make it prose again.
>
> . . . .
>
> 'Tis true, on words is still our whole debate,

---

[9] *The Progress of Discontent*, written 1746, was first printed in 1750. See Chalmers, *English Poets*, XVIII, 123. Warton satirizes, among other things, the practice of admitting to college poorly prepared candidates for the ministry. This and other resemblances to *The Progress of Dulness* mark Warton's poem definitely as a possible source for the first part of Trumbull's poem.

[10] Trumbull is reported to have said late in life that whereas "Milton was an Architect," Pope was "a mere Cabinet Maker."—*New York Commercial Advertiser*, May 30, 1831, p. [2]. Yet Trumbull was much closer to Pope in spirit and technique than to Milton.

Disputes of *me* or *te*, of *aut* or *at*,
To sound or sink in *cano*, O or A,
Or give up Cicero to C or K.

. . . .

In ancient sense if any needs will deal,
Be sure I give them fragments, not a meal;

. . . .

'Ah, think not, Mistress! more true dulness lies
In Folly's cap, than Wisdom's grave disguise.
Like buoys, that never sink into the flood,
On learning's surface we but lie and nod.
Thine is the genuine head of many a house,
And much divinity without a νοῦs.

. . . .

See! still thy own, the heavy Canon roll,
And metaphysic smokes involve the pole.
For thee we dim the eyes, and stuff the head
With all such reading as was never read:
For thee explain a thing till all men doubt it,
And write about it, Goddess, and about it:
So spins the silkworm small its slender store,
And labours till it clouds itself all o'er.
'What tho' we let some better sort of fool
Thrid ev'ry science, run thro' ev'ry school?

. . . .

With the same cement, ever sure to bind,
We bring to one dead level ev'ry mind.[11]

These names by no means exhaust the list of poets to whom Trumbull may have been indebted in greater or less degree. Yet although Trumbull was an imitator, it was not his practice to borrow entire passages outright from other writers; rather he used his sources more subtly, and he reflected his extraordinarily wide reading more generally than specifically.[12] The result is that although *The Progress of*

---

[11] *The Dunciad*, Book IV, ll. 210-68.
[12] For further comment on Trumbull's reading, see below, pp. 147 ff.

THE PROGRESS OF DULNESS

Dulness was indirectly influenced by a great many other poems, Trumbull fused his material and tempered his style so as to create a poem which possesses a considerable amount of individuality.

The Progress of Dulness, like *M'Fingal*, was not created in its entirety at first but grew by accretion. Trumbull, who was probably a less resolute person than has generally been believed, apparently relied for encouragement upon Silas Deane. Deane it was also who later assisted at the conception and publication of *M'Fingal*. The first reference to *The Progress of Dulness* occurs in a letter which Trumbull wrote to him on January 8, 1772. By this time, as will appear, some part of the poem had been written. In the letter, Trumbull replies to a suggestion Deane had evidently made that Trumbull should enlarge the poem. It is interesting to note that although Trumbull has been commonly regarded as a reckless radical in spirit, he did not pursue the writing of *The Progress of Dulness* without misgivings as to its possibly injurious effect upon his career:

... [Of] the Progress of Dulness, I know not what to say. I am [sen]sible the subject affords opportunity for a great deal of Satire; but there are many things which I am a little afraid to speak my mind freely on. The method of education at College, the proceedings of the Clergy with many other topics, I have passed over slightly. I am certain that any thing of that kind would be charged on me & I do not want to make a new set of Enemies. I have fought my way thro' the world thus far, & have now pretty well got rid of my enemies, & I imagine it will tend much to my peace, not to do any thing to raise any more. I will however consider of what you propose, & if I dare venture any enlargement of it, perhaps I may, & send it to you.[13]

---

[13] Letter to Silas Deane, January 8, 1772. The enemies alluded to probably included Stephen Mitchell, whom Trumbull had very imprudently satirized in 1769, as well as those persons who took umbrage at *The Correspondent.*—See above, pp. 49, 90, 91.

Since the draft of the poem referred to is not extant, it is not possible to say how far Deane encouraged Trumbull to go in the direction of satire, but that the additions which Trumbull made were considerable is likely, inasmuch as "The method of education at College, the proceedings of the Clergy with many other topics," which Trumbull says he has "passed over slightly" in the draft referred to, form the subject of a very severe invective in the first part of the poem as published.

Probably at the time when he suggested additions to *The Progress of Dulness*, Deane also urged Trumbull to think seriously of publishing the poem. Over a year later, Trumbull wrote that "though the subject was not undertaken at first with a view to publication, yet the author sees no reason to be sorry that he gave in in [*sic*] to the request of his friends. . . ."[14] In the letter to Deane already quoted, he wrote: "The piece will want some alterations, as in some parts the humor is a little local, & suited to college affairs:—I mean if it be printed at Hartford." The poem was not printed at Hartford but the changes were apparently made, for the satire contained in the poem as published is by no means merely local. The first part of the work appeared at New Haven, not in August, 1772, as the *Poetical Works* would have it, but later in the year, probably in December.[15]

Part First of *The Progress of Dulness* was provided with a preface which, although severely critical, was expository rather than controversial in tone. It shows the poet's aims to be two-fold: to criticize the selection and training of candidates for the ministry and to demonstrate the weaknesses of collegiate education in general. It is his intention to show that "a fellow, without any share of genius, or application to study may . . . be admitted to the right hand of fel-

---

[14] *The Connecticut Journal*, February 5, 1773, p. [1].

[15] It probably came off the press late in December, for on January 1, 1773, it was referred to as "Just Published."—*Ibid.*, January 1, 1773, p. [3].

THE PROGRESS OF DULNESS

lowship among ministers of the gospel."[16] Trumbull mentions no names of institutions, but it is clear that Yale College is not alone as an object of his attack, for "in numberless instances throughout these colonies, sufficient care hath not been taken to exclude the ignorant and irreligious, from the sacred desk."[17] It appears to Trumbull that "this tenderness to the undeserving, tends to debase the dignity of the clergy. . . ." Finally, he enters objection to the many "virulent controversies" of the day on religious subjects, which, having arisen out of "vanity and ostentation, . . . have done more hurt to the cause of religion, than all the malice, the ridicule, and the folly of its enemies."[18]

Trumbull's strictures on college education are severe. A tutor of Yale College, he is speaking, partly at least, from observation when he makes the drastic criticism that "except in one neighbouring province, ignorance wanders unmolested at our colleges, examinations are dwindled to mere form and ceremony, and after four years dozing there, no one is ever refused the honors of a degree, on account of dulness and insufficiency."[19] As an advocate of liberal studies, he feels that "the *meer* knowledge of antient languages, of the abstruser parts of mathematics, and the dark researches of metaphysics, is of little advantage in any business or profession in life." He speaks warmly, too, of his long cherished belief that "it would be more beneficial, in every place of public education, to take pains in teaching the elements of oratory, the grammar of the English tongue, and the elegancies of style, and composition."[20]

This admirably lucid and dignified preface is followed by

---

[16] *The Progress of Dulness*, Part First ([New Haven], 1772), Preface, p. [v]. The preface in the first edition differs from that in the *Poetical Works*.
[17] *Ibid.*, p. vi.
[18] *Ibid.*
[19] *Ibid.*, p. [v]. The "neighbouring province" is unquestionably Massachusetts. See above, p. 76.
[20] *The Progress of Dulness*, Part First, Preface, pp. [v], vi.

a poem of 452 lines on the "rare adventures" of Tom Brainless. Convinced on no very good grounds that their son will make a "special preacher," the parents of Tom Brainless, a farmer and his wife, send the boy to a clergyman to prepare him for college. After a year's study under a man who

> . . . in his youth before,
> Had run the same dull progress o'er,[21]

Tom succeeds in gaining admission to college, where he is promptly attacked by the "college evil," a malady which prevents one from studying for fear of injuring the health. Now the poet embarks upon a digression against the curriculum of the unnamed college. He objects to a system whereby the students,

> . . . plodding on in one dull tone,
> Gain ancient tongues and lose their own.

He inveighs against his ancient aversions, mathematics, astronomy, and metaphysics. Of the last he says:

> For metaphysics rightly shown
> But teach how little can be known.

It is not that he wants the classics abolished; he merely longs for the day which will

> Give ancient arts their real due,
> Explain their faults, and beauties too

and

> From ancient languages well known
> Transfuse new beauties to our own.

Graduated from college, Tom, by the advice of his father, enters a school

> To teach what ne'er himself could learn.

---

[21] The quotations from the poem are taken from the text of the *Poetical Works*.

A year later, under the tutelage of a famous preacher, he

> ... settles down with earnest zeal
> Sermons to study, and to steal.

He learns to hold to the tried and the orthodox in idea and expression; particularly must he

> ... shun, with anxious care, the while,
> The infection of a modern style.

After a term of training under his master, Tom becomes a licensed preacher:

> What though his skull be cudgel-proof!
> He's orthodox, and that's enough.

Now commences an address to the "fathers of our church" in which Trumbull tries to make it clear that he is writing in the interest of religion and the clergy. He, too, objects to the enemies outside the church, but he thinks the "deist's scoffs" less subversive of real religion than those abuses within the church which he has already exemplified in the career of Tom Brainless.

Tom Brainless, a specimen of a hundred "fools" like him, now commences to preach with all the assurance of those in whom "impudence is yoked to dulness." Ultimately he settles in a small place where he "does little good, and little harm."

Part First of *The Progress of Dulness*, here briefly summarized, contains a severe indictment of the mode of filling the ranks of the clergy and of the principal faults of collegiate education. Notwithstanding the author's constant resort to humor, the study is basically serious in intention. For the most part it is dignified in tone, and, although severe, it nowhere falls into the sin of ranting. Perhaps the least urbane couplet occurs just after Tom has received his license to preach:

Perhaps with genius we'd dispense;
But sure we look at least for sense.

Yet most of the poem is free from the irritation inherent in this couplet and the whole is not so much a malicious as a virile attack.

Trumbull did not delay long after the publication of the first part of his poem before offering the second part, dealing with Dick Hairbrain of "finical Memory." By the time this part appeared in January, 1773,[22] however, it is clear that the author had been rebuked for his sins in Part First. In the preface to the second installment, Trumbull acknowledged that the "first part of this Poem met with very kind reception" from many readers, but he made it plain that a number of representatives of the clergy took umbrage at it. They apparently did not publish their grievances but voiced them—perhaps in a clerical conference. Trumbull wrote: "I had the pleasure, . . . on the first publication of my poem, to hear the remarks made upon it by a cluster of your fraternity, who might each of them have sate for the picture of Tom Brainless."[23] Thus the young man who had but a year before written that he did not "want to make a new set of Enemies"[24] found himself in the very center of a hostile attack. From the nature of his retaliation it is evident that if he tried to beware of entrance to a quarrel, he was quite capable of making the opposed beware of him.

The preface to *The Progress of Dulness*, Part First, is a plain statement of Trumbull's purpose. It is fearless in tone but measured and cool withal. The preface to Part Second is probably the most vituperative work from Trumbull's pen that has been printed. Perhaps encouraged by influential

---

[22] Part Second was announced as "Now in the Press" on January 8, 1773, and as "just published" on January 15. See *The Connecticut Journal* for these dates, pp. [1] and [3] respectively.

[23] *The Progress of Dulness*, Part Second ([New Haven], 1773), Preface, p. vi.

[24] See above, p. 101.

friends, Trumbull for once throws all caution to the winds and indulges in an orgy of abuse. Instead of beginning with conventional courtesy, Trumbull, "being an enemy to ceremony and circumlocution," promptly addresses his critics, whom he typifies as "*the Envious and Malicious Reader.*" He first congratulates himself on the signs that his "medicine" is working:

Satire is a medicine very salutary in its effects, but quite unpleasant in its operation; nor do I know a more evident symptom that the potion has taken its proper effect, than the groans and distortions of the Patient.[25]

Then he recites the strictures made on Part First. These are:

that the whole piece was low, paltry stuff, and both scurrilous in the sentiments and dirty in the style; that it was evident, the Author knew nothing of language, or versification, and was incapable of writing wich [*sic*] any degree of elegance; that he was an open reviler of the Clergy, and an enemy to truth and learning; that his apparent design was to ridicule religion, disgrace morality, sneer at the present methods of education, and in short, write a satire upon *Yale-College* and the ten commandments; that he treated the subject in the most partial and prejudiced manner, and must certainly be either a Separatist, or a Sandemanian.[26]

He pertinently adds that the defamers of his poem have spent more time in criticizing his intention than in attempting to meet the issues raised.

In rebuttal of these charges Trumbull exhibits skillful tilting. His critics do well, he says, to defend the system which made it possible for them to reach their positions unchallenged. It is only natural that they should "despise the study of those finer Arts and Sciences, of which . . . [they] never once knew the want, or perceived the advantages

---
[25] *The Progress of Dulness*, Part Second, Preface, p. vi.
[26] *Ibid.*, p. vii.

..." They are also shrewd, the author adds, in asserting that a general condemnation of the clergy was intended, for by so doing they lessen the chances of their being thought to be the special objects of the author's satire. And yet the satire was intended to be particular instead of general, for "the Author hath the highest veneration for the ministerial robe, or he would never thus trouble himself about the spots that defile it." He intimates that he would be pleased if the gentlemen at whom the satire is chiefly aimed would reply to the author's charges, for then he would have the right to be "more particular" in his satire. This invitation is extended with especial cordiality to "the haughtiest Dullard, and the most impertinent Coxcomb of this age. . . ." That the objects of his shafts are not merely subordinate parts of the system he abhors, Trumbull suggests when he writes of "those, *however dignified in station*, who rail at the Progress of Dulness. . . ."[27]

The extremes of abuse to which Trumbull's warmth urged him in this clever, youthful, impudent preface may be judged from two passages not yet referred to. The author deprecates the charge of unreality in his work:

. . . if the good people, who sate for the painting, have the ill hap to find themselves drawn with a wide mouth, a long nose or a blear eye, he begs of them to get a little acquainted with their own faces, and see whether these be not their real defects of nature, before they begin to rail at the Painter, for the badness of their resemblance.[28]

Again, when rebuking those reactionaries who will not admit new studies into the curriculum, he says:

justly should you undervalue them [that is, liberal studies] in comparison with that antient Learning, which from experience you rightly term *Solid*, as your own wits were never able to penetrate it.[29]

---

[27] *Ibid.*, pp. viii, ix.   [28] *Ibid.*, p. viii.   [29] *Ibid.*, pp. viii, ix.

Thus it may be seen that if Trumbull was cautious by nature, he could become, when once aroused, a formidable and ruthless antagonist, with little apparent respect for age or position. If his attacks seem juvenile and unnecessarily personal, it should be recalled that the author was at this time but twenty-three years old, and that he was living in an age when literary controversy was carried on in a manner which is now associated chiefly with politics.

Nevertheless there is reason to believe that upon cool deliberation, Trumbull regretted his impetuosity. Written hastily while he was still smarting from the lash of adverse criticism, the preface must have seemed to him too unrestrained at a later period, for it was omitted from the 1794 (Exeter) edition and the 1801 (Wrentham) edition of *The Progress of Dulness* as well as from the 1820 edition of the *Poetical Works*. Moreover, in the preface to Part Third, Trumbull once more adopted the dignified judicial tone that had characterized the preface to Part First.

Introduced by the roar of Trumbull's angry preface, *The Progress of Dulness*, Part Second, seems incongruously mild. Satire it does contain, but the satire is for the most part differently applied from the criticism in Part First. Unable or unwilling to sustain his philippic, Trumbull lapses into a "literary" manner that vitiates the reality of his work. In this part the author's criticism is almost constantly focused on Dick Hairbrain instead of on his environment; consequently Yale College is no longer a chief point of attack. Moreover Trumbull tries to make it perfectly apparent that he is on the side of religion against infidelity. There is less specific narrative in this part than in the preceding one. The progress of Dick is reported chronologically, but his character is so highly generalized that the total effect of the poem is more expository than narrative.

Dick Hairbrain, unlike Tom Brainless, is the son of "the wealthiest farmer of the town." Realizing, however, that

Dick is but a raw product, his father destines him for college, "to make a man of DICK." After three years spent at school, Dick prepares to enter college, and he indulges in a long, characteristically eighteenth-century "meditation" on the prospect. It is clear from this prevision of academic life that Dick has no stomach for the "long fatigue of turning books," but expects to prove the joys that money can bring. He has no doubt that he can fashion his own course of pleasure without let or hindrance, for he intends to enter one of the colleges

> Where kind instructors fix their price,
> In just degrees, on every vice,
> And fierce in zeal 'gainst wicked courses,
> Demand repentance, of their purses;
> Till sin, thus tax'd, produces clear
> A copious income every year,
> And the fair schools, thus free from scruples,
> Thrive by the knavery of their pupils.

At college Dick is transformed from a clown to a fop. Through sedulous imitation and impudence, he gradually acquires the "pert address and noisy tongue" of the true fop. The tailor does his part for Dick:

> For now, by easy rules of trade,
> Mechanic gentlemen are made!
> . . . .
> To taylors half themselves they owe,
> Who make the clothes, that make the beau.

The tailor's art is supplemented by those of the barber and the dancing master. From France, Dick acquires a "set of compliments for show," and he even patronizes learning for the sake of providing himself

> With double meanings, neat and handy,
> From Rochester and Tristram Shandy

as well as the "blund'ring aid of weak reviews." One mark of his perfection as a fop is that he must jest at orthodox religion and proclaim himself a free-thinker after the style of Hume, Bolingbroke, and Voltaire. After tracing the evolution of Dick from clown to coxcomb, the author tells briefly of his college career, which includes practically no study but much gaming, nocturnal revel, and drinking. The accomplished fop

> Drank wine by quarts to mend his sight,
> For he that drinks till all things reel,
> Sees double, and that's twice as well.

Nevertheless after a riotous and profane course, Dick receives his diploma *"Pro meritis"*!

His father having died about this time, Dick uses his legacy to take a trip abroad in order to study

> The levities of other climes.

Among his chief amusements is the pursuit of women, who, he has been convinced by Pope and Mahomet respectively, are rakes at heart and destitute of souls. His amorous excesses stamp him as a complete fop; but no sooner has he reached his zenith than he begins to decline toward a miserable fate brought on by "lewdness, luxury and wine." Having declined into a wretched and lonely old age, he is fit subject for the moralist:

> The coxcomb's course were gay and clever,
> Would health and money last for ever,
> Did conscience never break the charm,
> Nor fear of future worlds alarm.

From this slight summary it is obvious that Part Second of *The Progress of Dulness* was a distinctly less offensive production from the point of view of a conservative educator or clergyman than Part First. Although it may be held that the college was culpable for graduating men of the type of Dick, still the poet's satire is directed less against the college for its laxity than against Dick and others of his ilk for their dissoluteness. Indeed, Trumbull is highly indignant when Dick presumes to criticize his alma mater:

> The praise of other learning lost,
> To know the world is all his boast,
> By conduct teach our country widgeons,
> How coxcombs shine in other regions,
> Display his travell'd airs and fashions,
> And scoff at college educations.
> Whoe'er at college points his sneer,
> Proves that himself learn'd nothing there. . . .

The last couplet quoted above is the core of the matter, for in it Trumbull virtually admits that a good man can secure a good education at college—too generous an admission for a consistent satirist of college curricula. Perhaps the witty asperities of Part First had called down upon the author more wrath than he cared to face again. Certainly he had as much reason for satirizing the college for graduating Dick as for graduating Tom Brainless. He chose to lay the responsibility largely upon Dick. Tom was represented as worthless but harmless and not to be held responsible: the system that produced him was bad. Dick is represented as worthless and vicious; but it is not the fault of the system so much as of himself. This is a new emphasis and it suggests a chastened Trumbull.[30]

---

[30] Commentators on *The Progress of Dulness* have generally failed to note the difference in tone between the first two parts. M. C. Tyler, for example, writes as follows in regard to the whole poem: "No wonder that a notable stir was made by these three satires, so fresh and ruddy with the tints of real life, so fearless in their local tone and color, so pungent with contemporary and local criticism. . . ."—*The Literary History of the American Revolution*, I, 220. Tyler's phrases describe Part First with a fair degree of accuracy, but they are hardly applicable to Part Second, which is, in comparison, mild and conventional.

A similar change of tactics characterizes the treatment of religion in Part Second. Whereas in the first part of the poem he has openly bombarded the slacker members of the clergy, he now suspends his barrage upon those delinquent persons and commences fire upon coxcombs of the stamp of Dick Hairbrain, who make petty war upon true religion and good clergymen. In Part Second, then, we see Trumbull not as the critic of an incompetent clergy, but as a champion defending religion against free-thinkers and deists. When the poet says of Dick that

>Of pious Hume he'll learn his creed,

and

>Take arguments, unvex'd by doubt,
>On Voltaire's trust, or go without,

he is writing with irony and with the utmost scorn. Indeed, he makes his own position unequivocally orthodox by the many lines he devotes to condemning Dick and the "thousand fools" who have railed at religion. A few incisive couplets will illustrate:

>Alike his poignant wit displays
>The darkness of the former days,
>When men the paths of duty sought,
>And own'd what revelation taught;
>Ere human reason grew so bright,
>Men could see all things by its light,
>And summon'd scripture to appear,
>And stand before its bar severe,
>To clear its page from charge of fiction,
>And answer pleas of contradiction;
>Ere miracles were held in scorn,
>Or Bolingbroke, or Hume were born.

On the whole, then, Part Second is so mild and so orthodox as to constitute a partial recantation. A few attacks

Trumbull indirectly makes upon the administration of the college, but these are not pressed home; moreover, they are over-shadowed by his attack upon free-thinkers. The clergy, so far from being censured in individual cases, are defended en masse. One would expect such a work as this, bolstered by an unexceptionable moral at the end, to be secure from criticism, at least from the conservative party. Nevertheless shortly after the appearance of Part Second a public rebuke was administered to Trumbull in the form of a communication to *The Connecticut Journal* by one who signed himself "A Lover of Virtue and Good Manners."

This communication, an anonymous one, purporting to incorporate the views of many persons who had been outraged by Trumbull's satire, particularly in Part First and in the preface to Part Second, constitutes a stinging criticism of Trumbull set forth in the form of a series of queries. The writer takes Trumbull to task for treating serious subjects with ridicule in order to exhibit his wit; for upbraiding the metaphysicians unduly; for implying that all those who have criticized him have done so out of envy or malice; for making poor men's sons the object of satire; and for casting offensive personal reflections.[31] Despite his temperamental caution, Trumbull found the writer of this letter too tempting game to forego. It is just possible that he knew or guessed the author of the communication and realized that in setting him down he would not be indiscreetly opposing an important personage. A week later he replied to his inquisitor in detail with a combination of dialectic and wit that must have rendered his critic exceedingly uncomfortable. Not in the slightest did he retract but he iterated his points with more acumen than before, evidently deriving considerable exhilaration from the encounter, for he loved to exercise his gift for argumentation.[32] It is worth observing, however,

---

[31] *The Connecticut Journal*, January 29, 1773, p. [2].
[32] *Ibid.*, February 5, 1773, p. [1].

that the third part of *The Progress of Dulness*, still to be published, was the least obnoxious of the three to his local critics.

In the meantime, the poem was becoming favorably known elsewhere; shortly after his reply to "A Lover of Virtue," Trumbull learned of the welcome that *The Progress of Dulness* received in Boston, where at least no one could have felt himself to be the personal butt of Trumbull's ridicule. His friend Joseph Howe, who had resigned his tutorship in September, 1772, was given a call to Boston which entailed a visit there at a time when Trumbull's poem was a topic of great public interest. What Howe heard there he soon reported to Trumbull in a letter. Trumbull, it will be seen, was still astonishing people on the score of his precocity; but although more than two years before, he had been compared to Pope,[33] he could hardly have been more gratified than by the analogy now drawn between him and Swift and Butler:

. . . But what I mean to rally you for, is for being a good poet, a great Wit & a Satirist.—Nay, do not flinch. The story is got all over Boston. The other day a Gentleman came to me, and said *I am told you are acquainted with Mr Trumbull, the Author of the Progress of Dulness.* Sir, Said I, stroking my Face down with an Air of Satisfaction, I have the Honour to be particularly acquainted with him. *Pray of what Age is he?*—About 24. *Twenty four?* replied he with some Surprize, *I should have Thought he had been Sixty. His Prose is equal to Swift's & his Poetry to Butler's.* I had not the Temerity to Contradict him. Nor indeed an Inclination for it. If I had, I suppose it would not have been of any Avail. For he was none of your Second Edition People, but undoubtedly, the first Classical Scholar in Boston.[34]

Even before he could have heard of the approval accorded

---
[33] See above, p. 62.

[34] Letter to Trumbull from Joseph Howe, February 26, 1773, Burton MSS, CIII, 6. This letter has never before been printed, nor does any biographical or critical notice of Trumbull refer to it.

116   JOHN TRUMBULL

Parts First and Second in Boston, Trumbull was sanguine enough about the success of *The Progress of Dulness* to set about the composition of a third part, to be published considerably later. On the verso of the last page of the first edition of Part Second, in accordance with a common custom, he entered an advertisement of the forthcoming part. The composition of this section of his work may have been completed by July, 1773,[35] but publication was deferred until early September, doubtless for the sake of synchronizing the appearance of the book with the arrival of commencement guests.[36] In conformity with a common advertising practice of the time, the elaborate title-page of the poem, greatly abridged in subsequent editions, was printed in full in the newspapers:

The Progress of Dulness. Part Third, and Last: Sometimes Called, The Progress of Coquetry, or the Adventures of Miss *Harriet Simper,* Of the Colony of Connecticut. Containing Advice of the Ladies to Harriet's Mother concerning education, Address to Parents, Harriet's studies, skill in fashions, scandal and romances; with the consequent occurrences of her life by way of illustration of the moral of the work. *For the use of the Ladies and their Parents.—Quæq; ipse miserrima vidi, Et quorum pars magna fui.* —Virgil, New-Haven; Printed by Thomas and Samuel Green, near the College, 1773.[37]

In the preface to Part Third of this trilogy on education, Trumbull expressly states that his "design . . . is to shew, that all the foibles we discover in the Fair Sex arise principally from the neglect of their education, and the mistaken notions they imbibe in their early youth." These foibles it is his intention to "laugh at with good humour" and "expose without malevolence." The need for this work arises from

---

[35] Trumbull so dated the preface in his *Poetical Works* (1820).

[36] On September 10, the work was announced as "*Just Published.*"—*The Connecticut Journal,* September 10, 1773, p. [2]. Commencement this year occurred on September 8.

[37] From the title-page of the first edition of *The Progress of Dulness,* Part Third.

two facts. First, most of the writers who have treated the subject of women have been either too censorious or too complimentary to arrive at the truth. Second, although "Mankind in general seem sensible of the importance and advantages of learning," the education of women "hath been most neglected."[38]

It is plain from the tone of this preface that Trumbull has no intention of writing such a poem as will bring a "new set of Enemies" (and these female) down upon himself. His first sentence is a disavowal of any such purpose: "Nothing gives more convincing proof of deficiency in judgment or malevolence of heart in an Author, than general, undistinguishing satire, levelled at an order of men, at a sex, or at human nature." Again he says, "I have endeavoured to avoid unseasonable severity, and hope, in that point, I am pretty clear of censure." Rendered somewhat nervous by his previous experiences, he fears that although his purpose will probably not be subject to "general misrepresentation," still by some people it will be "ignorantly or wilfully misunderstood." For that his consolation will be "the consciousness that a desire to promote the interests of learning and morality" is his chief motive. Even in the matter of style, the author is willing to make a concession to his readers, for, having learned that many readers thought the style of Part Second too heavy, he promises to adopt a more lively manner and to conduct his narrative with "a perpetual drollery."[39] Thus the preface to Part Third is of a very different order from the savage outburst of the preface to the second part.[40] Indeed its whole effect suggests that Trumbull realized his past indiscretions and was now determined that his behavior should be unimpeachable.

---

[38] *The Progress of Dulness*, Part Third (New Haven, 1773), Preface, pp. vi, vii.
[39] *Ibid.*, pp. [v]-vii.
[40] This preface was retained in later editions except for the somewhat tedious first paragraph.

The Progress of Dulness, Part First, had related the progress of a dunce; Part Second, of a fop; Part Third describes the life of a coquette. This last part, consisting of 708 lines, is the largest unit of the trilogy. The coquette, Harriet Simper, presumably an American girl, but suspiciously similar to coquettes in contemporary and earlier British literature, is unfortunate in her parents: her mother has been a toast in her own day, and her father is not inclined to go to any trouble over his daughter's education. Consequently, upon the advice of her former friends, it is easy for Harriet's mother to give up such simple instruction as she has conscientiously begun and to proceed to train the young lady upon fashionable models. The primer is put away:

> 'Tis quite enough for girls to know,
> If she can read a billet-doux.

Having introduced the narrative, the author soon digresses in order to address those parents, who, bowing to "ancient rule," deny their daughters training in all but trifles and vanities. Thus schooled, a girl

> . . . values only to be gay,
> And works to rig herself for play.

She sews, to be sure, but she works six weeks to produce a useless article which could be purchased for a nominal sum. She is sent to a city, whence she returns "prouder than she went" but only "half-genteel." Her entire life is dedicated to idleness and folly.

Harriet shortly commences her novitiate as a toast, and soon she can

> . . . tell, exact to half a minute,
> What's out of fashion and what's in it.

On Sundays, she is

> Deck'd in her most fantastic gown,
>
> . . . .
>
> For, like the preacher, they [coquettes] each Sunday
> Must do their whole week's work in one day.

She learns to bandy gossip and scandal. She reads romances, and, believing herself "a young Pamela," she "hopes a Grandison, or Lovelace." Her conquests are transient matters: she "fish'd for hearts to throw away." When merely earnest suitors offer their hands, she spurns them, for she has other objectives:

> In purse of gold, a single stiver
> Beats all the darts in Cupid's quiver.

Yet, when Dick Hairbrain returns from abroad, Harriet, with poetic justice, falls truly in love—only to learn that Dick is "too gallant to marry."

After her day as toast is over, Tom Brainless, "six years a rev'rend Pastor," appears upon the scene in the rôle of a suitor, having been told that Harriet

> Had left her levities of youth,
> Grown fit for ministerial union,
> And grave, as Christian's wife in Bunyan.

Harriet accepts Tom's proposal and shortly the "tag-rag gentry" in Tom's town welcome her home. They

> Greet her at church with rev'rence due,
> And next the pulpit fix her pew.

In Part Third of *The Progress of Dulness*, as in the two preceding parts, the story-writer is frequently submerged by the essayist. A certain amount of time is lost, too, because the author, not content with telling a story, digresses from the action to comment directly upon the characters and to drive home his moral. Yet the story is slightly less recessive in this part because of the reappearance of Tom Brainless and Dick Hairbrain. Harriet's character, although mainly a type, is brilliantly etched. As in most of Trumbull's finer work, the salient virtues of Part Third are timely brevity and quick turns of thought. The author is not more adept at piercing the rottenness of old modes of education than he is in perceiving innuendoes of apparently guileless gossip.[41] His satire in this part, however, bears very little on controversial matters. Having promised to write in a lighter manner, Trumbull frees himself from all inhibitions and indulges in an orgy of unmitigated Hudibrastic verse. Indeed toward the end of the poem his whole manner becomes so close to that of burlesque that the story and the satire are correspondingly weakened.

Viewed as a whole, *The Progress of Dulness* has obvious defects which are overlooked in a study of any one part. The method of presentation wavers between narrative and exposition or description, with frequent interludes of straight argumentation. Moreover, as a story it suffers from the fact that the characters are so highly generalized as to be chiefly types. The attempt in the third part to throw the three narratives into a common relationship is largely abortive, despite the devastating criticism implied in the marriage of Tom Brainless to Harriet Simper. The burlesque tone adopted at the very end tends to deprive the characters of the little reality with which they have been endowed. Of course the story is but a flimsy bait which the satirist uses to catch his readers; but charges must also be brought against the satirist. Although there can be no question of the essential sincerity of Trumbull's criticism of the social order, his satire occasionally slips out of focus. Beginning as a staunch critic of college and church, he is transformed into a satirist of conventional types of character, the rake and the coquette. His prefaces, too, are wanting in homogeneity; the first one

---

[41] See the example quoted above, pp. 97, 98.

is dignified and severe; the second one, savagely vindictive; and the third, apologetic. Thus the effect of the work as a whole is that of a gradual diminuendo—not a happy condition in satire.

On the other hand, the organic defects which mar the structure of the poem are unnoticed upon a close view, for then one is impressed by the perfection of the smaller parts. If Trumbull sometimes reckons his larger dimensions badly, he is a master of the details of fretwork, inlay, frieze—fine tooling of many sorts—with perhaps an undue fondness for gargoyle and grotesque. Line for line, the poem is so brilliantly executed that one experiences a constant pleasure in following the detail; and the rapid intellectual pace at which the author urges the reader on, prevents the latter from rebelling at what in less skilled hands might have become tedious elaboration. Indeed, since the extended prefaces clearly convey the points of the author's satire, the very *raison d'être* of the whole poem is its perfection of detail and its humorous commentary. Trumbull's courage flows and ebbs, but his language is always at flood. If he occasionally loses the course of his story, his wit at least never wanes. *The Progress of Dulness* shows him to be a brilliant (if discursive) satirist, but even more clearly it shows him to have been possessed of a gift for sustained comic or burlesque commentary equaled by few poets of any period.

Despite the high degree of poetical merit which it possesses, and its considerable original success, *The Progress of Dulness* has had a somewhat unfortunate fate. Two major factors have tended to diminish its popularity. First, the problem which gave rise to the poem was of passing interest; second, Trumbull soon wrote another poem, *M'Fingal*, the subject of which was more generally interesting and the style at least equally pleasing. The Revolution, which commenced two years after *The Progress of Dulness* was published, quickly dwarfed all other subjects. Literature in general did not thrive in America during the Revolution, but such literary interest as there was, centered upon those productions, chiefly prose essays, which were related to the great struggle. After the war for a number of years also, literature dealing with national themes was naturally much favored. *M'Fingal* soon replaced *The Progress of Dulness* as Trumbull's most popular poem. The latter seems to have languished until near the end of the century, when it enjoyed a renascence of interest signified by three editions published between 1794 and 1801. Thereafter it appears never to have been accorded much general attention. In 1831, the year of Trumbull's death, *The American Annual Register* probably recorded the history of the poem correctly when it asserted that although *The Progress of Dulness* "was successful as a satire," "its reputation was eclipsed by [Trumbull's] subsequent poems."[42] At the present time the poem is little known. V. L. Parrington doubtless voices the opinion of many when he states, "Trumbull's reputation rests exclusively on *M'Fingal*."[43] Now and again the poem has had its advocates. William Cullen Bryant preferred it to *M'Fingal*.[44] Samuel Kettell, the anthologist, apparently believed it to possess as much value as *M'Fingal*.[45] A few modern critics have read the poem and have tried to do it justice, among them H. M. Ellis, in whose opinion it "deserves probably at least equal credit with *M'Fingal*. . . ."[46] But of course critical approval is quite a different thing from popularity; and there is no question that *The Progress of Dulness* is a very obscure poem today.

Trumbull had now written one of the two poems for which posterity values him most. The fruit of his nine years' ex-

---

[42] VII, 383 (Appendix).
[43] *The Colonial Mind* (New York, 1927), p. 250.
[44] *The North American Review*, VII (July, 1818), 201.
[45] *Specimens of American Poetry* (3 vols., Boston, 1829), I, 178.
[46] *Modern Language Notes*, XXXVIII (December, 1923), 499.

perience at Yale College and of his constant practice in octosyllabic verse, it was actually written and published in about two years, while Trumbull was holding the office of a tutor. When the first part of the poem appeared, his friends in New Haven congratulated him upon his genius and his daring, but conservative observers were enraged at his impudence. At Boston, the home of Harvard College and one of the two chief arbiters of literary taste at the time, there is no record that the poem received anything but warm approval in a period when scant recognition was generally accorded native literary productions. Yet the consternation Trumbull created at home seemed to cool his ardor, for the second and third parts of the poem were distinctly more restrained and his satire was directed into less dangerous channels. These parts contained less original matter and leaned more heavily than the first part upon literary models. Although the progress of the poem is marked by a decrease in local satire, its literary vitality remains unimpaired.

There is no direct record of the attitude taken by the fellows of Yale College toward the gratuitous criticisms of their administration offered by a twenty-three-year-old tutor. One can only conjecture with what embarrassment Trumbull's father, a clergyman and a member of the Yale Corporation, viewed the first broadsides of his son. Yet as has been shown, Trumbull soon moderated and shifted his attacks, so that such enemies as he had made by Part First and the preface to Part Second of *The Progress of Dulness* were undoubtedly mollified by the increasingly orthodox tenor of the poet's message. At all events, Trumbull had evidently not done irreparable damage to his reputation in official quarters, for only three years later the Corporation chose him to be treasurer of Yale College.[47]

In the meantime, shortly after the last part of his poem

---

[47] "Yale College Register," I, 212.

was published, Trumbull moved to Boston, where, in the troubled days immediately preceding the Revolution, his somewhat volatile interests became thoroughly grounded in national problems. Here he produced his first patriotic poem, *An Elegy on the Times*, which was but an earnest of the larger service he was to perform a year later in the composition of *M'Fingal*.

CHAPTER VI

THE EVE OF THE REVOLUTION

ABOUT two months after concluding *The Progress of Dulness* Trumbull set out for Boston, where he remained almost a year. His life in Boston may best be regarded as a preparation for the production of *M'Fingal*, for although that poem was not yet thought of, Trumbull's principal activities during this period bore upon it directly or indirectly. As a law student, he became intimately acquainted with John Adams, who was the prototype for one of the major characters in *M'Fingal*. Through his association with Adams, he became acquainted with a number of Revolutionary leaders, among them probably those men who later suggested that he write *M'Fingal*. Most important of all, he became thoroughly acquainted with the *mise-en-scène* of the approaching conflict between the Colonies and the Crown, and he was witness to its prologue. His chief poetical production of the year arose out of an unforgivable act of tyranny, the Boston Port Bill, which virtually determined the outbreak of the Revolution in the following spring. This poem, *An Elegy on the Times*, served to bring Trumbull to the fore as a national spokesman. At the same time, although the work was accounted a fair success, the tedious heroics and arid diction which stifled its life provided another proof that Trumbull was not fitted to write a great elegy. Hence *An Elegy on the Times* may be said indirectly to have influenced Trumbull to return to the genre of which he was master, that is, the comic poem. During the period from September, 1773, to September, 1774, Trumbull also wrote a number of shorter poems, some serious and some humorous. The former have added little to his fame; but the latter, although exceedingly light in substance, were good practice for the future creator of *M'Fingal*.

Like many another artist who has excelled in comedy, Trumbull was anxious to prove his abilities in more serious work; hence the *Ode to Sleep*, a pretentious but mediocre poem of 145 lines.[1] This piece is a hybrid derived from seventeenth-century metrical practice crossed by pseudo-classical diction. Trumbull's chief model was clearly Milton, and indeed in certain parts of his poem he showed how well he had studied Milton's manner. In the third stanza, for example, he writes:

> Descend, and graceful in thy hand,
> With thee bring thy magic wand,
> And thy pencil, taught to glow
> In all the hues of Iris' bow.
> And call thy bright, aerial train,
> Each fairy form and visionary shade,
> That in the Elysian land of dreams,
> The flower-enwoven banks along,
> Or bowery maze, that shades the purple streams,
> Where gales of fragrance breathe th' enamour'd song,
> In more than mortal charms array'd,
> People the airy vales and revel in thy reign.

Yet the simplicity and chastity of diction in Milton's *L'Allegro* and *Il Penseroso* are wanting in Trumbull's poem. Its stereotyped phraseology and too-brilliant gloss betray the author as a pupil primarily of the eighteenth century. M. C. Tyler's comment that the *Ode to Sleep* makes "a nearer approach to genuine poetry than had then been achieved by any American, excepting Freneau"[2] is startling. Neverthe-

---

[1] *Poetical Works*, II, [113]-120. The title-page bears the date "1773." Whether it was completed before or after Trumbull left Boston cannot be determined. It was apparently not published until 1820.

[2] *Op. cit.*, I, 211.

less in view of the paucity of "genuine poetry" in American verse of the eighteenth century, this appears to be very moderate praise. The poem is now interesting biographically and historically. Probably a love-poem in its inception,[3] it contains Trumbull's nearest approach to the lyric expression of "the most extravagantly romantic feelings."[4] In its prayers for untrammeled flights of "th'ethereal wing," the ascent of the author's soul to "nobler themes of . . . sublimer strain," and other celestial privileges in "realms of endless glory," it reflects the taste of the age. Indeed the *Ode to Sleep* is a thoroughly competent poem of its type; but it bears the stamp of the journeyman rather than of the master.

Trumbull's odes and elegies were the labored results of persistent practice; his humorous poems flowed easily from his pen. Hence there is less of true art in the *Ode to Sleep* than in the fragmentary poem entitled "To a Lady on Returning Her Thimble."[5] Trumbull did not publish this trifle in his *Poetical Works*, doubtless because it is not thoroughly integrated and because it is wanting in significance and general interest. Written apparently under the inspiration of Pope's *Rape of the Lock*, it is not worked out with enough attention to unity of structure and tone to bear comparison with that poem. Yet the author's deftness, his amusing drollery, and a certain elastic quality in the verse, make the poem stimulating. It opens brightly in a jocular vein that Trumbull often employed in allusions to the Papists :[6]

---

[3] In a stanza treating of love Trumbull refers to a young woman as to his betrothed. His use of five asterisks in place of her name leads to the conjecture that he had already become engaged to marry *Sarah* Hubbard, to whom he was wedded three years later.

[4] See above, p. 18.

[5] Cornell MSS, p. 27. The manuscript bears the date "1773."

[6] Trumbull also made game of Popery in *The Correspondent* (*The Connecticut Journal*, July 6, 1770, p. [3] and in *M'Fingal* (See below, pp. 177, 204). The French Catholics, never popular in early New England, became increasingly odious to the colonists during the next year (1774) after the passage of the Quebec Act.

As pious Papists, who adore
Some twenty thousand Saints or more,
And many a league their burdens carry,
To bow before the Virgin Mary;
Though their devotion wish in vain,
The Virgin or the Saint to gain
Yet gladly boast to get a relic
Once own'd by persons Evangelic;
A tangled lock of hair adore,
Which once the blessed Virgin wore;
Bow to St. James's Beard, forsooth,
Or hymn an Apostolic tooth;
Or praise in strains of pious metre
A finger's end of holy Peter;
And boast those gifts with honest pride
Which touch of Saints hath sanctified;
The relic prize however small,
'Tis all they gain, but 'tis their all;
'Tis all they hope; the Priest alone
Can claim the Saint to be his own.

The want of reverence manifested in the preceding poem is not unique in Trumbull's writings, as two frolicsome and indecent manuscript pieces of 1773 remain to attest. The first of these, "An Epitaph to be Inscribed on the Marriage Bed of Miss S . . . W . . ." is a somewhat labored satire of no great value except in a few places where it is redeemed by wit.[7] The other is a brief poem celebrating the marriage of Daniel Lyman and Statira Camp in New Haven. For some reason, perhaps because Lyman showed Loyalist proclivities, Trumbull took this union amiss; and he gave vent to his disapproval in a scurrilous little poem entitled "On the Marriage of Two Special Friends of the Author."[8]

---

[7] Burton MSS, CIII, 21.

[8] Cornell MSS, p. 13. Trumbull evidently dated this manuscript from memory, for the date he affixed to it, 1769, is obviously incorrect. The marriage referred to took place on November 15, 1773.—*The Connecticut Journal*, November 19, 1773, p. [3].

THE EVE OF THE REVOLUTION 129

For obvious reasons, the poem has remained unpublished:

> What whims has Love! See joined by Cupid
> A Rake so vile, a Dolt so stupid!
> They're One, and tell, for pity's sake,
> What mongrel creature do they make?
> What creature? See on Cupid's plan
> They just form *Whitfield's natural Man;*
> A motly [sic] mixture, both parts evil,
> The one half, Beast; the other, Devil.

Literature, whether in the serious vein or the comic, had not of course yielded Trumbull a livelihood; and it was not to be expected in those days that a man with his special talents should support himself by his pen. Hence for a few years past Trumbull had been preparing himself for a more profitable profession by pursuing a course of legal studies. These were formally completed on November 12, 1773, when he was admitted to the bar of Connecticut by the New Haven County Court.[9] He then prepared to carry out the plan conceived during the preceding summer of going to Boston, there to further his legal knowledge in the office of John Adams. Despite the hospitable reception which Boston had accorded his *Progress of Dulness* several months earlier,[10] Trumbull evidently had no serious literary intentions when he changed his residence to Boston. In any case, not Boston but Philadelphia was the principal literary center of the country at this time. Hence although he was to reach the meridian of his poetical career in a very short time, Trumbull composed a farewell to letters in the form of an "Epistle" to a friend.[11] Though but a trifle, the "Epis-

---

[9] [New Haven] County Court Records (1767-1776), VII, 538. See also *The Connecticut Journal*, November 19, 1773, p. [3].

[10] See above, p. 115.

[11] The name of the friend is not divulged; the title on the manuscript reads, "Epistle to .... 1773." Cornell MSS, p. 14.

tle" shows flashes of Trumbull's best talent. He introduces the subject with his usual vivacity:

> Dear Friend, this verse would let you know,
> I've turn'd philosopher, or so;
> Forsworn all wild poetic fancies,
> Took leave of novels & romances,
> Bade nonsense, sighs & love, goodbye,
> And turn'd a stoic—or I lye.

He then bids farewell to various forms of the "muse's theme" and finally

> To Heroes famed in epic story,
> And all Apollo's Inventory.

He addresses himself to his new profession:

> I turn my looks, with deepest awe,
> Toward Sages learned in the law.
> In solemn coif before my eyes,
> I see the awful Coke arise. . . .

He has no illusions concerning the profession he is about to enter, for he calls upon the "Lawyers" to assist him in acquiring

> The conscience mild that sleeps at ease,
> Nor trembles at the touch of fees.

The poem is evidently a fragment, for it ends abruptly. Trumbull did not include it in his *Poetical Works* and neither has it been published elsewhere except for excerpts quoted by M. C. Tyler.[12] Yet it has more poetical value than a number of carefully polished poems which Trumbull chose to include in his collected works.

Arriving in Boston about the middle of November,[13] Trum-

---

[12] *Op. cit.*, I, 427, 428.
[13] After being admitted to the bar, he "immediately went to Boston."—"Memoir," p. 15.

bull took quarters in the home of Thomas Cushing, Speaker of the Massachusetts Assembly; and, although he had been admitted as a practising attorney before the bar in Connecticut, he "entered as a student" in the office of John Adams.[14] Nothing could have been more fortunate for his future as a poet (as well as for his career as attorney and judge) than his close association with these men since, because of their prominence in colonial affairs, Trumbull "was now placed in the centre of American politics."[15] Impartial political winds blew upon the youth at this period, for if Adams was an alert, even bloodthirsty, guardian of American rights, Cushing, who later opposed the Declaration of Independence, was a conservative statesman, sometimes regarded even as a lukewarm patriot. Trumbull was now in a position to study the background of his most admired poem, *M'Fingal*,[16] and to become acquainted personally with a number of men who later figured in that poem.

Within a month after Trumbull's arrival in Boston, an event occurred which was fraught with great significance for him as a poet, and yet, an instinctive conservative, he was slow to approve of the action—if, indeed, he ever did. This event, the Boston Tea Party (December 16, 1773), evoked the Boston Port Bill, which in turn furnished the theme for Trumbull's major poem of the year, *An Elegy on the Times*. It was, in fact, an action which practically committed Massachusetts (and therefore the Colonies) to rebellion. Yet Trumbull passed over the subject in silence in his elegy, and he made but little of it in *M'Fingal*. The day after the Party occurred, John Adams was jubilant over this "most magnificent movement of all."[17] The same evening, Trumbull dropped in to talk the matter over with his mentor,

---
[14] *Ibid.*   [15] *Ibid.*

[16] The scene of most of the action of *M'Fingal* is a small town near Boston.

[17] *Works of John Adams* (ed. by Charles Francis Adams. 10 vols., Boston, 1850-56), II, 323.

but Adams's diary records merely that Trumbull had learned of the Tories' attitude in the matter.[18] The probability is that Trumbull, always an advocate of law and order, was among those who were shocked by the violation of private property. His failure to glorify this act of independence in the poem which indirectly grew out of it, the *Elegy*, was tantamount to an expression of disapproval. Indeed in that poem he sounded a warning against the injudicious or unseasonable use of force.[19]

In the midst of the excitement that thrilled Boston in December, 1773, and January, 1774, Trumbull, the scholar-poet, was collected enough to pursue the paths of pure literature. During these months, despite his recent farewell to letters, he produced two poems which bore no relationship to current affairs. In the first of these, *The Prophecy of Balaam*,[20] a free paraphrase of Chapters 23 and 24 of the book of Numbers, one sees Trumbull attempting to create for himself the name of a "sublime" poet, but he was not equal to the flight he essayed. Nature intended Trumbull to be a merry, chattering ground-bird, frequenting the haunts of men; but a perverse ambition often led him to attempt to soar as with the wings of an eagle. The other poem, *The Destruction of Babylon*,[21] is a kindred piece. An imitation of "sundry passages" in Isaiah and Revelation, it consists of 108 stalwart lines in iambic pentameter couplets. Although the poet invests his lines with considerable dignity at times, still the bright couplets of the neoclassical school in which Trumbull had been trained were not adapted to suggest the dark grandeur of his theme. It is difficult to believe that the simple Scriptural line, "How art thou fallen from Heaven, O Lucifer, son of the morning!" is improved by being smartly clothed in the eighteenth-century mode:

---

[18] *Ibid.*, p. 324.
[19] See below, pp. 134, 137, 138.
[20] *Poetical Works*, II, [141]-146.   [21] *Ibid.*, II, [195]-201.

What sudden fall hath dimm'd thy boasted ray;
Son of the morn! bright Phosphor of the day!

Trumbull's next poetical composition, *An Elegy on the Times*, was his most pretentious literary effort of the year 1773-1774. It was called forth by the Boston Port Bill. Anxious to punish Boston for her bad behavior on the occasion of the Tea Party, King George hit upon the plan of locking her up commercially until the inhabitants of Boston should have made satisfactory reparation for the damage to the goods of the East India Company. The news of the passage of the Port Bill was greeted in America with storms of protest. Before the Bill went into effect, Josiah Quincy boldly published over his own name his brilliant prose tract, *Observations on . . . the Boston Port Bill*, in May, 1774. Trumbull's poetical treatment of the subject, *An Elegy on the Times*, did not appear, however, until the Bill had been in operation more than three months.[22] It was printed late in September in two successive issues of *The Massachusetts Spy*.[23] Like all of Trumbull's authorized publications prior to 1820, *An Elegy on the Times* appeared anonymously.

The Colonies were now more nearly united than they had ever been. The King's frequent interference with local government had given rise to the formation of the committees of correspondence, those powerful cementers of colonial thought and feeling. The recent clashes over East India tea had stirred the Colonies from Boston to Charleston. When the King angrily rebuked Massachusetts by closing the port of Boston, not only Massachusetts but colonial America felt the force of his attack. Thus in writing *An Elegy on the Times*, Trumbull was acting for the first time (albeit anonymously) as a spokesman for the entire country.

---

[22] Trumbull later stated that the poem was composed "at Boston, during the operation of the Port Bill, August 1774."—*Poetical Works*, II, [205].

[23] September 22, 1774, p. [4]; September 29, 1774, p. [4]. The original printing of this poem has hitherto remained undiscovered.

The poet first pictures the happy condition of Boston before she was stricken by the blight of the Port Bill, when her "splendid mart with rich profusion smiled"[24] and in the harbor

> Tall groves of masts arose in beauteous pride.

But after the operation of the Bill he sees "each friendly vessel" fly the "interdicted strand." This is the work of the "factious nobles" of Britain, who

> Guide the blind vote and rule the mock debate.

We have been humble, the poet says, and have sought redress of our wrongs by petition, but our petitions have been scorned even when offered by a Franklin. Now we can expect no recognition of the merits of our case:

> O'er hallow'd bounds see dire oppression roll,
>   Fair Freedom buried in the whelming flood;
> Nor charter'd rights her tyrant course control,
>   Tho' seal'd by kings and witness'd in our blood.

Rather

> 'Tis strength, our own, must stem the rushing tide,
>   'Tis our own virtue must command success.

Yet the poet cautions his countrymen against untimely violence:

> But oh my friends, the arm of blood restrain,
>   (No rage intemp'rate aids the public weal;)
> Nor basely blend, too daring but in vain,
>   Th' assassin's madness with the patriot's zeal.[25]

---

[24] *Poetical Works*, II, [205]. Although the version of *An Elegy on the Times* in Trumbull's *Poetical Works* differs from that which appeared in *The Massachusetts Spy*, the former is quoted in this study because it had the benefit of the poet's final revision.

[25] When the poem was reprinted in 1775 this stanza seemed so incongruous with the spirit of the times that a footnote was added to explain its moderation. See below, p. 137.

THE EVE OF THE REVOLUTION

Rather by the "manly firmness of the sage" and by unity in peaceful measures of combating oppression shall we gain our end. Chiefly, it appears, we must repel Britain economically by refusing to import or consume British goods, for otherwise we shall fall into a condition of commercial vassalage, a type of slavery that would betray the memory of the fathers of the country. It was not for this that they

> Dared the wild horrors of the clime unknown.

Addressing North, who was a focal point for many a stormy literary effusion from the Colonies, the poet assures the minister that he might as sensibly

> Bid the broad veil eclipse the noon-tide hour

as to hope to make the great hearts of our leaders submit to slavery.

Continuing his mocking address to North, the poet calls upon him to acknowledge the rights of a new and great power, and the imminent decline of Britain:

> Then tell us, NORTH: for thou art sure to know,
>   For have not kings and fortune made thee great;
> Or lurks not wisdom in th' ennobled brow,
>   And dwells no prescience in the robes of state?
>
> Tell how the powers of luxury and pride
>   Taint thy pure zephyrs with their baleful breath,
> How deep corruption spreads th' envenom'd tide,
>   And whelms thy land in darkness and in death.
>
> And tell how rapt by freedom's sacred flame,
>   And fost'ring influence of propitious skies,
> This western world, the last recess of fame,
>   Sees in her wilds a new-born empire rise—
>
> A new-born empire, whose ascendant hour
>   Defies its foes, assembled to destroy,

> And like Alcides, with its infant power
>   Shall crush those serpents, who its rest annoy.

Then in one of those patriotic passages so dear to young poets of the eighteenth century, Trumbull views the future career of America and Great Britain. He requests North to

> . . . look through time, and with extended eye,
>   Pierce the dim veil of fate's obscure domain.

What North will see the poet describes at length. In brief, he will look upon the rising glory of America and the collapse of Britain—a frequent, if somewhat vague image in colonial writings. The American shores again will smile, but a melancholy fate is in store for England:

> And where is Britain? In this skirt of day,
>   Where stormy Neptune rolls his utmost tide,
> Where suns oblique diffuse a feeble ray,
>   And lonely streams the fated coasts divide,
>
> Seest thou yon Isle, whose desert landscape yields
>   The mournful traces of the fame she bore,
> Where matted thorns oppress th' uncultur'd fields,
>   And piles of ruin load the dreary shore?
>
> From those loved seats, the Virtues sad withdrew
>   From fell Corruption's bold and venal hand;
> Reluctant Freedom waved her last adieu,
>   And devastation swept the vassall'd land.
>
> On her white cliffs, the pillars once of fame,
>   Her melancholy Genius sits to wail,
> Drops the fond tear, and o'er her latest shame,
>   Bids dark Oblivion draw th' eternal veil.

Less than a year after its publication in Boston, *An Elegy on the Times* was reprinted in New Haven. The author's name was not given in the new edition, but the work was described as "A piece possessed of too much merit to need an encomium."[26] It is to be surmised that Trumbull's authorship was known and that the printers expected to profit by Trumbull's local reputation. The poetical merit of the work was evidently considered to be so great that the poem was reprinted, notwithstanding the fact that its subject matter had been rendered relatively obsolete by the rapid events which had taken place since April, 1775. A preface therefore accounted for the fact that such a temperate poem should be reprinted in such stirring times. Moreover, it was deemed wise to provide a footnote to the stanza in which Trumbull had asked his countrymen to restrain "the arm of blood":

To this passage on its first publication at *Boston*, the Author subjoined the following note, viz. "This is not meant as a caution against defending our rights with our blood, if we should be driven to that extremity; but only against the impolitic zeal of those, who seem desirous to let loose the rage of popular resentment, and bring matters immediately to a crisis in this Province." As the state of the times is now changed, the Author would undoubtedly, with every other Friend to his country, rejoice in that animated Spirit of Heroism, which now rouzes every man to arm in defence of our invaded Privileges.[27]

Probably in 1774 *An Elegy on the Times* was considered by many people to be an excellent poem and a valiant stroke in behalf of freedom; now it seems to be an inferior poem and a very tame revolutionary document. It is not hard to understand why it had a considerable measure of popularity. In the first place, its mere length was impressive; and its sixty-eight four-line stanzas, rhyming flawlessly *a b a b* and set forth in language of glittering formality, were calculated to win the respect of Puritan readers, who were

---
[26] *The Connecticut Journal*, July 5, 1775, p. [4].
[27] *An Elegy on the Times* (New Haven, 1775), p. 8 n.

inclined to set a high value upon obvious technical display. The poem offered an orderly survey of the subject treated. It described, in general terms at least, local and contemporary conditions. It also glanced at parts of the country other than Massachusetts. The state of California was not then dreamed of, but the poet was using an "extended eye" when he looked as far as "cold Ontario's icy waves" and "Altama's silver waters." These references, as well as the mention of Philadelphia, New York, Virginia, and Charleston were interesting and serviceable in the days when one of the chief problems of the colonists was to create a feeling of unity. The position which Trumbull took in the poem was not extremely radical, but the moderate liberals were comforted by the sane counsel it offered. And indeed in 1774 who should say that Trumbull was wrong to advise caution when such men as Dickinson, Hancock, and Franklin were among those who deprecated a premature resort to force?

On the other hand, the more ardent advocates of early independence and the better critics of poetry must have seen many weaknesses in the poem. It made no mention of the gallant act which provoked the Boston Port Bill. It was Trumbull's error that he thought the time not yet ripe for action. Massachusetts had been notably restrained in her reaction toward the various injustices and penalties which the King had inflicted on her, even pardoning the soldiers who fired upon unarmed men in the Boston Massacre. When legal measures of redress fail, it may be necessary for a nation to use force. Undoubtedly it was illegal to destroy the tea, but the very act was intended as a warning to England that legal tyranny can be countered only by violence. Consequently Trumbull's counsel of arbitration was a trifle tardy. Indeed his error was so obvious upon review a year later, that, as has been observed, when the second edition of the *Elegy* was published, the printers felt it necessary to apologize for its mildness.

Not only was the thesis of the poem inappropriate, but its vitality was impaired by Trumbull's insistence upon neoclassical decorum. Enough has been quoted to show that its verse is quite as bombastic as that of Trumbull's valedictory exercise, "A Prospect of our Future Glory."[28] Moreover, despite Trumbull's genius for clarity, the many contractions, elliptical expressions, and inversions, in conjunction with the formal and abstract diction, make this a rather annoying poem to read. It was polished; but what it needed was less refinement and more robustness, more crude colonial strength. Hence it is hard to imagine that the British ministry was seriously annoyed by the pompous periods of this closet exercise.[29] One has only to call to mind the fiery utterances of an Otis, a Samuel Adams, a Tom Paine, or a Freneau to realize fully the bookishness of *An Elegy on the Times*.

It is obvious from Trumbull's careful revision of this poem and the documentation with which he provided it before printing it in his *Poetical Works* in 1820, and from the prominent position he accorded it in this collection, that he set great store by it. But posterity's verdict has not agreed with his. The foreword which Messrs. Green felt it necessary to prefix to the 1775 edition of the poem was a presage of its fate. Its relatively mild tone and its unseasonable counsel of deliberation prevent its being included among the nation's classic poems of patriotism; and its poetical value has depreciated rapidly since the rise of the romantic poets. Even its historical value is insufficient to give it permanent interest. It lost ground rapidly. To be sure Elihu Smith, with

---

[28] See above, pp. 61, 62.
[29] The poem was made available to British readers through the publication of a London reprint in 1775 by John Almon.

an unerring sense for Trumbull's poorer poetry, included it in his anthology in 1794.[30] Interest in the poem gradually fell off, however, and critics and anthologists since the middle of the nineteenth century generally have had no more than a word for it. Reading the poem at this distance from its setting in time, one finds it illuminating as a mirror of contemporary taste; but it is impossible to take it very seriously either as art or as propaganda. Had Trumbull never done more than this for his country, he would never have earned the sobriquet, "Poet of the Revolution."

An Elegy on the Times, then, Trumbull's first conspicuous service in the cause of colonial freedom, was a poem not distinguished by the blind fury of youth or the lust for combat, but by a reasoned message of prudence arising out of Trumbull's innate conservatism. One must admire the good taste displayed in the poem and the dignity of the attack upon America's foe, but one feels that the time had come for a bolder remonstrance—for less style and more fervor. Trumbull's formal stanzas were not adapted to inflame the populace, but neither could they convince a large part of the intelligentsia. It was therefore a sound instinct which led his friends to advise him in his next effort to write in mirthful vein.[31] Once more Trumbull had proved that unless acted upon by the exciting force of humor, his poetry was impotent. When next he espoused the cause of the Colonies in poetry, he did so with a gaiety and abandon which made the work, *M'Fingal*, infinitely more effective than *An Elegy on the Times*.

In private also Trumbull expressed conservative views touching the rebel preparations for violent action. When on August 10 John Adams left Boston with Cushing for a leisurely progress toward Philadelphia, there to attend the sessions of the Continental Congress in September, 1774, the poet remained in Boston a few weeks longer. Ten days after

---

[30] *The Columbian Muse*, pp. 51-61. [31] See below, pp. 158-60.

THE EVE OF THE REVOLUTION

Adams's departure, Trumbull wrote him a letter regarding a critical situation in Worcester, where the populace was irate over the order that the salaries of judges be paid by the Crown. Wrote the judicial Trumbull:

> It is to be hoped, however, that no violent measures will be taken, till the sense of the whole continent is known; as the people have great dependence upon the determinations of congress, and expect them to chalk out the line for their conduct.[32]

The rest of the long letter which Trumbull wrote Adams at this time is devoted to an amusing episode of military camp life near Worcester, involving a sergeant who, in an attempt to arrest a number of deserters from the British ranks, not only failed to recover his men but found that the remainder of his force were so attracted by the position of the deserters that they left him on the spot and joined the renegades.[33] Trumbull's evident enjoyment of this tale, which he passed on to Adams, was proof that no matter how seriously he might weigh the respective rights of the Crown and the Colonies, his ears were always cocked for incongruous anecdote involving the comic. In *M'Fingal*, fortunately, he suppressed his judicial interests and gave full indulgence to his appetite for the incongruous.

Additional proof that Trumbull's comic powers were not slumbering in disuse is to be found in a few literary performances relating to this period. One of these, a bagatelle he turned off before leaving Boston, is entitled "On some Ladies joining to hiss M^r. Q......s oration at the Commencem^t. at Harvard College":

> When Damon in a smart oration,
>   Exposed those faults the fair would hide,
> Railed at their love of dress & fashion,
>   And tax'd their Coquetry & pride;

---

[32] H[ezekiah] Niles, *Principles and Acts of the Revolution in America* (Baltimore, 1822), p. 323. [33] *Ibid.*

142   JOHN TRUMBULL
>   Some laugh'd, while others hiss'd, as loud,
>   As love or reason proved the weaker.
>   [Bu]t most exclaim'd 'twas low and rude,
>   That ladies join'd to hiss the speaker.
>   Damon cried, in each sweet Miss,
>   ['T]was nature all—be not so sharp on't;
>   [No]r think it strange the fair should hiss:
>   [Th]eir earliest league was with the serpent.[34]

There also remains an amusing "Advertisement" of "Poems on Several Occasions" which indicates that the author of *The Meddler* and *The Correspondent* again contemplated entering the journalistic world, this time under the emblem of poetry. He writes that he has "undertaken to revive the Art of composing Poems on Several Occasions, & hath prepared a very extraordinary collection, suited to all possible circumstances, that can occur in the polite world."[35] Although Trumbull was well qualified for this sort of project, nothing came of it, or, if the poems were actually written, none has been preserved. Perhaps Trumbull or his publishers felt that political embroilments rendered such follies untimely.

A number of poems by Trumbull are, perhaps characteristically, addressed to ladies: Trumbull does not give the impression of having been a "man's man." One of these, relating to the latter part of his stay in Boston or to the days immediately following his return to New Haven, is entitled *To a Young Lady . . . A Fable*.[36] The content of the poem is of little significance except for one autobiographical passage which seems to show that Trumbull was aware of the kind of reputation he was acquiring by dabbling con-

---

[34] Cornell MSS, p. 34. The manuscript is dated "1774," but, as it happened, public commencement exercises were omitted at Harvard that year on account of the confusion of public affairs.—Albert Matthews, *Harvard Commencement Days 1642-1916* (Cambridge, 1916), pp. 352, 353. The probability is that the poem refers to some other academic occasion of the year.

[35] Cornell MSS, p. 27.

[36] *Poetical Works*, II, [123]-128.

THE EVE OF THE REVOLUTION   143

stantly in the crude oil of satire. The young lady having requested the poet to "draw her Character," the poet warns her that she need expect no gentle treatment:

> From me, not famed for much goodnature,
> Expect not compliment, but satire.

The poem is not extremely unpleasant in content, but, wanting the airy manner characteristic of Trumbull at his best, it is somewhat grim in tone. Yet it was better practice for Trumbull than boudoir trivia or sleek elegies, for the lifeblood of *M'Fingal*, soon to be written, was "not compliment, but satire."

It is to be inferred that when Trumbull went to Boston in November, 1773, he intended to stay longer than he actually did and that his departure was hastened by unforeseen developments. He later gave his reasons for returning to New Haven: "Every thing then verging towards hostility in Massachusetts, the session of the courts being suspended, and Mr. Adams absent at the Congress in Philadelphia, he returned to New-Haven. . . ."[37] He left Boston between September 22 and September 30, 1774.[38] In November of that year, he "successfully commenced practice at the bar" in New Haven.[39] Thenceforth he was to be a resident of Connecticut until, in his seventy-fifth year, he journeyed to Detroit, where he spent the last quiet years of his life.

Trumbull had now completed another important stage of his career. During the year 1773, he had moved to Boston to perfect his education in the law. Here, besides studying law, he had oriented himself in the setting which he was to employ later in *M'Fingal*, and he had studied in the life a number of men whose portraits were to appear in that poem.

---

[37] "Memoir," p. 17. V. L. Parrington incorrectly states that when Trumbull left Boston, he "withdrew to Hartford."—*The Colonial Mind*, p. 249.

[38] "Memoir," p. 17. See also Stiles, "Itinerary," IV, [205].

[39] "Memoir," p. 17.

He had also written a moderate number of poetical pieces, some humorous and some serious. In the former, he showed many flashes of his true genius for comedy and satire; but in them the comedy spent itself largely upon trivial or indecent subjects, so that Trumbull included only one of them in his *Poetical Works*. The serious poems he apparently valued more highly, and yet these added little or nothing to his fame. An obstinate ambition to become known as a writer of odes and elegies led him to produce such showy but sterile poems as the *Ode to Sleep*, *The Destruction of Babylon*, and *An Elegy on the Times*. The last of these, a sustained effort at formal composition, brought him before the public as more than a Connecticut poet. Despite its fair contemporary success, it is now interesting chiefly from a biographical point of view. It showed Trumbull struggling with a genre which he was destined never to master. It also revealed his temperamental aversion to violence. His friends later rescued him from his false estimate of his elegiac powers, and upon the outbreak of the Revolution they virtually conscripted him into the literary service of the nation. Trumbull resented British tyranny, but he deplored violent reprisal except as a last resort. There appears to have been in his nature more of the critic than of the agitator. As a Revolutionist, Trumbull was not born but made. Indeed, had not his friends advised him wisely at crucial moments in his career, he might have gone down into history as a petty versifier of the age, a facile writer of ponderously correct elegies and of clever but ephemeral lampoons. It was Silas Deane who lent Trumbull much of the moral support necessary to push *The Progress of Dulness* to completion. The same person, in conjunction with certain other men of prominence, was in large part responsible for the production of *M'Fingal*. Within less than a year after his return from Boston, Trumbull began the composition of the poem which has given him the rank of the first comic poet of the Revolution.

CHAPTER VII

M'FINGAL, COMIC LIBRETTO OF THE REVOLUTION

TRUMBULL was now upon the threshold of an enduring fame. When he returned to New Haven in September, 1774, he intended to devote himself to the practice of law; but before a year had elapsed, he had begun the composition of a poem, *M'Fingal*, which not only brought him immediate recognition, but ultimately made him one of the most popular American poets before Longfellow. It also proved him one of the greatest comic satirists in the history of American poetry. Undertaken upon the instigation of friends, it was first intended to be an auxiliary weapon for use against Tory propaganda and the British arms. At the end of the war, however, Trumbull amplified it and revised it, principally with a view to giving it permanent literary value. From that time forward, *M'Fingal* enjoyed a broad and enduring popularity which can be understood now only if the poem is seen in its perspective through a study of its derivation, the circumstances of its composition, its public reception, and its intrinsic character.

The ultimate success of *M'Fingal* was based less upon its value as a political document than upon its importance as a contribution to American belles-lettres. Although Trumbull's genius for ridicule made the poem useful in its day, it was by no means a flaming Revolutionary manifesto comparable to Freneau's *British Prison Ship* or Paine's *Common Sense*. Indeed, it was later found to contain seeds of conservatism. There was in Trumbull's nature a strain something akin to malice which caused him to take pleasure in making his enemies smart; yet his essentially moderate and judicial temperament prevented him from being a Revolutionary writer *par excellence*. It is significant that even from the beginning *M'Fingal* won high praise for its literary quality. Its merits were immediately acclaimed by those British reviewers whose political faith did not dictate their literary judgments. At home it promptly earned the gratitude of the patriots; but gradually after the Revolution gratitude gave place to simple affection, and *M'Fingal* became one of the most cherished poems of the American people, who enjoyed its comic portraiture, its lively episodes, and its shrewd Yankee wit delivered in bright epigrammatic couplets that lodged easily in the memory. Cool critical examination after the smoke of battle had cleared away also proved that it had many merits independent of utility. To be sure, its patriotic content was never forgotten; but if it had possessed no other claim to attention, it would not have become a household poem. *M'Fingal* was evoked by a political emergency, but it endured as literature.

The permanence of Trumbull's fame depends principally upon *M'Fingal*. Hence he must be regarded as heavily indebted to those friends who virtually insisted that he exert his comic powers in the cause of American liberty. Throughout his career up to this point, Trumbull appears to have looked upon himself as a potential writer of odes and elegies with a regrettable knack for comic verse. The production of *M'Fingal* proved indisputably to himself, as well as to the public, that his genius was not for ode and elegy but for comedy and satire. Nearly forty editions of *M'Fingal* appeared between 1782 and 1922. At the present time, almost one hundred and fifty years after its first publication, critics are less enthusiastic about it, and the general reader, impatient of its historical content, no longer enjoys it as he once did. Yet, when read by the discerning, the poem still commands respect and admiration. Indeed, excepting Lowell's *Biglow Papers*, it is difficult to point to another political satire in the history of American poetry which can bear comparison with *M'Fingal* for the happy union of satire and wit.

Although Trumbull's capacity for wit was undoubtedly born in him and his critical flair seems also to have been native, yet his equipment as a satirist was clearly augmented by his extremely wide reading. His bookish habit, which perhaps militated against the development of lyric powers, stood him in good stead when the business was satire. His early sessions of reading in Westbury and his nine years of academic life familiarized him with many classical and modern writers who unquestionably reinforced his satirical works. The authors whom he mentions familiarly in his relatively brief "Critical Reflections" (1778) indicate a catholic appetite in reading: Swift, Aristophanes, Lucian, Erasmus, Pope, Arbuthnot, Sterne, Homer, Vergil, Butler, Dryden, Addison, Cicero, Prior, Churchill, Young, La Bruyère, Gay, Steele, Richardson, Marmontel, Thomson, Gray, Shenstone, Goldsmith, Beattie, Mason, Isaac Hawkins Browne, Whitehead, Johnson, Brooke, Tickell, Spenser, Cibber, Phillips, Shakespeare, Cervantes, Tasso, Isocrates, Horace, Juvenal, Ovid, Pliny, Tacitus, and Cowley.[1] The works of these authors may be regarded as part of the general background for Trumbull's poetry. Some of them he mentions in the footnotes to *M'Fingal* as having been definitely used for that poem in point of substance or style.[2] Among the English writers, he was inclined to use as models chiefly poets of nearly his own era, although one occasionally notes the influence of Chaucer, Butler, Cowley, Milton, Dryden, and other earlier English poets. The main contemporary British poets in vogue in America at this period included Prior,

---

[1] "Critical Reflections," Cornell MSS, pp. 30, 31, *et passim*.

[2] These include the writings of Homer, Aristophanes, Plato, Claudian, Juvenal, Vergil, Ovid, Livy, Rabelais, Shakespeare, Milton, Bunyan, Tickell, Blackmore, and Gray.—*Poetical Works*, I, *passim*.

Collins, Gay, Gray, Young, Goldsmith, Macpherson, Thomson, and Pope.[3] Pope and Goldsmith were the favorite exemplars of the heroic couplet; Young and Thomson, of blank verse. Trumbull, who used the octosyllabic couplet, could not, of course, imitate any of these closely in his metrics. Pope he did study, however, for his compact wit and the neat embellishment of his verse. Trumbull saw in Pope a kindred spirit capable of malicious thrusts of satire delivered with a minimum loss of energy. As models for the use of octosyllabic couplets overlaid with occasional Hudibrastic rhymes, Trumbull used principally four writers: Butler, Churchill, Swift, and Prior.

Among the innumerable comments passed upon *M'Fingal*, perhaps the most trite and the least considered is that *M'Fingal* is primarily an imitation of Butler's *Hudibras*. From June, 1776, when *The Monthly Review* (London) dubbed it "An American Hudibrastic,"[4] until 1887, when Lowell described it as being "as near its model as any imitation of the inimitable can be,"[5] the criticism was parroted incessantly, for the most part in complimentary vein. This was natural enough. The many English imitations of *Hudibras* in the eighteenth century served to keep Butler's poem before the public eye.[6] Moreover, Trumbull's own references to Butler's work invited the comparison between *M'Fingal* and *Hudibras*.[7] Yet the similarity between the two poems has

---

[3] Advertisements in colonial newspapers at this time support the view that there was a quick market in America for eighteenth-century British works. One New Haven dealer, for example, offered this list in November, 1770: "Pope's Works; with Cutts"; Johnson's *Idler;* Sterne's *Sentimental Journey;* Goldsmith's *Citizen of the World;* Pope's *Essay on Man;* Thomson's *Seasons;* Milton's *Paradise Lost;* Le Sage's *Gil Blas;* and Smollett's *History and Adventures of an Atom.—The Connecticut Journal*, November 16, 1770, p. [4].

[4] First Series, LIV (June, 1776), 504.

[5] Horace E. Scudder, *James Russell Lowell, a Biography* (2 vols., Boston, 1901), II, 362.

[6] A list of imitations of *Hudibras* between 1674 and 1755 may be found in *The Retrospective Review*, Vol. III (1821), Pt. II, p. 318.

[7] *Poetical Works*, I, 92, 135 n.

M'FINGAL, POEM OF THE REVOLUTION

been over-emphasized. The use of octosyllabic couplets with crazy rhymes does not necessarily make a poem "Hudibrastic" in a true sense. Other metrical characteristics, the diction, the allusions, and the texture of the poem as a whole must be considered before such a judgment may be safely pronounced.

Some truth there is in the statement that *M'Fingal* contains Hudibrastic elements. This fact was brought out most capably by *The Monthly Review* in 1793:

> M'Fingal attends the town-meeting, which was held in a church; where we are entertained with an altercation between him and a whig, which is carried on whimsically enough, like the snip-snap argumentative dialogues between Sir Hudibras and his 'squire, Ralph; among other things, we have a humourous apology for political lying, in the genuine spirit of Butler. . . .[8]

This reviewer quotes the "humourous apology for lying" which occurs in *M'Fingal*, Canto I.[9] He does not cite an analogous passage in *Hudibras*, but a comparable disquisition on the violation of oaths occurs in Part Second, Canto II, of Butler's poem.[10] *The Monthly Review* adds that "this Tory 'squire [M'Fingal] is not much inferior to the fanatical knight, in the use of tropes and figures." It further affirms that when M'Fingal harangues the Whigs in the market-place before the liberty-pole,[11] he does so "as Hudibras does the bear-baiters, and to as good a purpose." These two speeches are roughly similar throughout; and at one point they reach a parallel as close as any that can be found be-

---

[8] Second Series, X (January, 1793), 37.

[9] *Poetical Works*, I, 35-37.—The *Review* of course quotes an early edition of *M'Fingal*, which shows minor variations from the 1820 text. The many editions of *M'Fingal* disclose numerous discrepancies, most of them relatively unimportant. For the sake of uniformity in this study, the 1820 text, which was prepared under the eye of the author, is used for all quotations and citations unless a different edition is specified.

[10] *Hudibras* (Cambridge, 1905), pp. 132-34.

[11] *Poetical Works*, I, 87-101.

tween Trumbull and Butler. In the midst of his oration to the bear-baiters Sir Hudibras satirizes those tradesmen who meddle in "reform";

> When *Tinkers* bawl'd aloud, to settle
> *Church Discipline*, for patching Kettle.
> No *Sow-gelder* did blow his Horn
> To geld a Cat, but cry'd *Reform*.
> The *Oyster-wom[e]n* lock'd their Fish up,
> And trudg'd away to cry *No Bishop*.
> The *Mouse-trap* men laid *Save-alls* by,
> And 'gainst *Ev'l Counsellors* did cry.
> *Botchers* left old *Cloaths* in the lurch,
> And fell to turn and patch the *Church*.
> Some cry'd the *Covenant* instead
> Of *Pudding-pies* and *Ginger-bread*,
> And some for *Broom*, *Old Boots*, and *Shooes*,
> Baul'd out to *purge* the *Commons House:*
> Instead of *Kitchin-stuff*, some cry
> A *Gospel-preaching-Ministry;*
> And some for *Old Suits*, *Coats*, or *Cloak*,
> No *Surplices*, nor *Service-Book*.
> A strange harmonious inclination
> Of all degrees to *Reformation*.[12]

In a like manner Squire M'Fingal ridicules the rude proponents of democracy who engage in politics unwarrantedly:

> While every clown, that tills the plains,
> Though bankrupt in estate and brains,
> By this new light transform'd to traitor,
> Forsakes his plough to turn dictator,
> Starts an haranguing chief of Whigs,
> And drags you by the ears, like pigs.
> All bluster, arm'd with factious licence,
> New-born at once to politicians.
> Each leather-apron'd dunce, grown wise,

---

[12] *Hudibras*, Part First, Canto II, p. 42.

M'FINGAL, POEM OF THE REVOLUTION

Presents his forward face t'advise,
And tatter'd legislators meet,
From every workshop through the street.
His goose the tailor finds new use in,
To patch and turn the Constitution;
The blacksmith comes with sledge and grate
To iron-bind the wheels of state;
The quack forbears his patients' souse,
To purge the Council and the House;
The tinker quits his moulds and doxies,
To cast assembly-men and proxies.[13]

Nevertheless, in spite of these and other resemblances between *Hudibras* and *M'Fingal*, it is a mistake to press the analogy too far. Trumbull himself refuted the charge that his poem was merely an imitation of *Hudibras*. In his unpublished "Critical Reflections" he wrote:

The Critical Reader will discern, that I have rather proposed to myself Swift & Churchill as models in my Hudibrastic writings, than the Author of Hudibras. I have sometimes had Butler's manner in my eye, for a few lines, but was soon forced to quit it. Indeed his kind of wit & the oddity of his Comparisons was in my Opinion never well imitated by any man, nor ever will be.[14]

In 1785 he reverted to the subject in his reply to a letter from the Marquis de Chastellux. On this occasion he called attention to the major distinction between the two poems:

. . . In the style, I have preferred the high burlesque to the low, (which is the style of Hudibras) not only as more agreeable to my own taste, but as it readily admits a transition to the grave, elevated or sublime. . . .[15]

An apt student of contemporary literature, Trumbull was quick to discern in the poetry of Churchill a model of style

---
[13] *Poetical Works*, I, 90, 91.
[14] "Critical Reflections," Cornell MSS, p. 30.
[15] *Poetical Works*, Appendix, II, 232-33.

which he could easily imitate to advantage. The principal poem of Churchill which he seems to have studied for this purpose is *The Ghost*. Whereas Butler's verse frequently loiters, Churchill's verse is rapid; and it is the easy onward motion of the latter's verse which Trumbull's most resembles. A passage from *The Ghost* will illustrate:

> Hence, ev'ry place and ev'ry age
> Affords subsistence to the Sage,
> Who, free from this world and its cares,
> Holds an acquaintance with the Stars,
> From whom he gains intelligence
> Of things to come some ages hence,
> Which unto friends, at easy rates,
> He readily communicates.[16]

The substance of *M'Fingal* is of necessity largely original; yet *The Ghost* contains a surprising amount of cognate material. A major theme common to both poems is the satire of the Scottish ministers, Bute and Mansfield.[17] Much is made by both poets of the Scottish disposition to rebel and of the Scotsman's gift of second-sight.[18] Moreover, Churchill uses a number of details which also appear in Trumbull's poem. For example, Churchill twice alludes to Fingal; he puns on the name of North; he uses as an illustration the danger of allowing children to play with knives; he refers to bagpipes as connoting din or confusion; he employs once an illustration which later was a favorite of Trumbull, namely, Balaam's ass; and he twice uses a phrase, ". . . or seemed to . . .," which was also affected by Trumbull.[19] In substance the greatest influence of Churchill on Trum-

---

[16] *Poems by C. Churchill* (2 vols., London, 1769), I, 162.

[17] *Ibid.*, pp. 254, 289, 319, 322, 340. Cf. *Poetical Works*, I, 5, 99, 128, 167.

[18] Churchill, *op. cit.*, I, 167, 168, 271, 280. Cf. *Poetical Works*, I, 5, 6, 7, 77, 118, 123, 126, 128.

[19] Churchill, *op. cit,*, I, 197, 352, 358, 232, 251, 288, 298, 313. Cf. *Poetical Works*, I, 4, 73, 61, 81, 11, 54, 124.

M'FINGAL, POEM OF THE REVOLUTION   153
bull is seen in the emphasis Trumbull placed upon the Scottish element in *M'Fingal* by making both the hero and his chief henchman Scotsmen—an emphasis not wholly desirable in a satire treating of New England Loyalists.[20] With respect to style, however, Trumbull could not have derived anything but benefit from Churchill's swift, smooth, well-trimmed verse.

Trumbull's imitation of Swift and Prior was more general than specific. Despite Trumbull's statement that he "proposed" Swift to himself as a model in his "Hudibrastic writings,"[21] direct parallels between Swift's poetry and *M'Fingal* are not discoverable. The probability is that when he made this statement, Trumbull had *The Progress of Dulness* in mind.[22] Nevertheless Trumbull's study of Swift's octosyllabics was undoubtedly an indirect preparation for the writing of *M'Fingal*. Among the poems of Swift written in octosyllabic couplets which may have served as general models for Trumbull are: *A Grub-Street Elegy; The Answer; A Libel; Dean Smedley's Petition;* and *Cadenus and Vanessa*. A quotation from the last-named poem has been given in order to show to what extent Swift's management of his verse is like Trumbull's.[23] Swift also occasionally expresses political views not unlike those voiced by Squire M'Fingal. The following passage from *To Mr. Lindsay* is comparable in theme and manner to the Tory squire's vituperation of the Whigs in the third canto of *M'Fingal:*

> 'Tis hard, where dulness overrules,
> To keep good sense in crowds of fools.
> And we admire the man, who saves

---
[20] On this account "a certain local genuineness is lost to the poem," for Trumbull's "satiric venom . . . really belonged to Loyalists of the pure American type, like Hutchinson, and Leonard, and Oliver."—M. C. Tyler, *op. cit.*, I, 445.
[21] See above, pp. 96, 97.
[22] Trumbull's indebtedness to Swift in connection with *The Progress of Dulness* is discussed above, pp. 97, 98.
[23] See above, p. 97.

JOHN TRUMBULL

His honesty in crowds of knaves;
Nor yields up virtue at discretion,
To villains of his own profession.
Lindsay, you know what pains you take
In both, yet hardly save your stake;
And will you venture both anew,
To sit among that venal crew,
That pack of mimic legislators,
Abandon'd, stupid, slavish praters;
For, as the rabble daub and rifle
The fool who scrambles for a trifle,
Who for his pains is cuff'd and kick'd,
Drawn through the dirt, his pockets pick'd;
You must expect the like disgrace,
Scrambling with rogues to get a place.[24]

As his fourth literary creditor in this connection Trumbull named Prior. Prior employed the octosyllabic couplet with greater finesse and grace than Swift and he wrote with a jaunty insouciance which appears at times also in Trumbull's verse. Among his humorous poems in the octosyllabic couplet are: *An Epistle to Fleetwood Shephard, Esq.; Hans Carvel; An English Padlock; Paulo Purganti; The Ladle;* and *Alma: or, the Progress of the Mind*. Some of these, notably *An Epistle to Fleetwood Shephard* and *Paulo Purganti*, occasionally carry Hudibrastic rhymes. On account of the radically different materials treated by Prior and Trumbull few close parallels between their poetry are available. Nevertheless that a literary kinship existed between the two men is suggested, for example, by their facetious manner of alluding to Homer. In his *Epistle to Fleetwood Shephard* Prior wrote:

> Thus, of your Heroes, and brave Boys,
> With whom old HOMER makes such Noise,

---

[24] *The Works of Jonathan Swift* (Edinburgh, 1814), XIV, 229-30. Cf. Trumbull, *Poetical Works*, I, 88, 94, 95. Apropos of Trumbull's use of Swift, it may be added that on two separate occasions in *M'Fingal* Trumbull refers to Brobdignag.—*Ibid*., I, 85, 107.

M'FINGAL, POEM OF THE REVOLUTION

> The greatest Actions I can find,
> Are, that they did their Work, and Din'd.[25]

This may be compared with a passage from the opening of Canto II of *M'Fingal*:

> And now expired the short vacation,
> And dinner o'er in epic fashion,
> While all the crew, beneath the trees,
> Eat pocket-pies, or bread and cheese,
> (Nor shall we, like old Homer, care
> To versify their bill of fare). . . .[26]

These four men—Butler, Churchill, Swift, and Prior—appear to have been the principal British poets whom Trumbull set before himself in the composition of *M'Fingal*, primarily of course as models of style. They do not, however, tell the complete tale of his indebtedness to earlier writers, for Trumbull was a learned man as well as a wit, and his tenacious memory was stored with the literary plunder of the ages. What he borrowed he made his own to such an extent that the poem has a considerable degree of originality. Yet it remains fundamentally a literary performance. The literary background of *M'Fingal* perhaps lessened its immediate effect as American propaganda, but it doubtless favored the probability of its surviving as a work of art.

It is a commentary upon the slow development of American poetry that Trumbull's American sources for *M'Fingal* are negligible. After the imposition of the Stamp Act, native writings on the subject of the conflict with the mother country were legion; but whereas many prose writers of real distinction appeared, most of the poetical production was unprofitable—either sentimental or bombastic or doggerel. The prose was mainly of a utilitarian sort which could have aided Trumbull but little in preparation for his bur-

---

[25] Matthew Prior, *Poems on Several Occasions* (3 vols., London, 1733-34), I, 16.
[26] *Poetical Works*, I, [41].

lesque epic. Francis Hopkinson's allegory, *A Pretty Story* (1774), a prose satire, showed a fine imagination, but it was by no means a source for *M'Fingal*. The anonymous *First Book of the American Chronicles of the Times* (1774-75) offered a humorous account of events down to the Battle of Lexington in the form of a parody of Scripture, but there is no evidence that Trumbull used it even for the first parts of his poem. Verse satire of genuine merit was almost wholly lacking. The almanacs were probably instrumental in developing a taste for humorous verse by printing comic bits here and there between astronomical tables and household remedies,[27] but native production of this sort was for the most part lamentable. A few ballads stood out above the low average of many patriotic attempts, among them *The Liberty Song* (1768) and *Virginia Banishing Tea* (1774). Bob Jingle's versified report of the proceedings of the First Continental Congress (1774) contained a rough and ready humor that Trumbull may have enjoyed but probably did not attempt to imitate. More formal attempts at political satire were not encouraging. These included Benjamin Church's *The Times* (1765), "a rather toothless satire,"[28] and James Allen's *Lines on the Massacre* (1772), a mediocre poem that gained some reputation for its celebration of the Boston Massacre. Trumbull's *Elegy on the Times* (1774), of small absolute value, seemed a poem of respectable stature when it rose against a background of such verse as this. It is obvious from the obscurity of these titles that *M'Fingal* did not grow out of a rich American poetical tradition, but appeared as a little-heralded pioneer work. The only American poet who was producing work comparable to Trumbull's upon the outbreak of the Revolution was Philip Freneau.

Freneau, much more naturally an agitator than Trumbull, rose quickly to prominence in 1775 by writing eight

---

[27] *The Cambridge History of American Literature*, I, 161.
[28] M. C. Tyler, *op. cit.*, I, 185.

rather long poems during the space of about six months between the outbreak of the Revolution and November.[29] He needed no goading to express his contempt of the British cause and his hatred for its protagonists.[30] Among his several diatribes is one which resembles in a small way Trumbull's *M'Fingal*. This poem, *A Voyage to Boston* (later known as *The Midnight Consultation*), made game of a man whom Trumbull also found to be excellent shooting, namely, the proclamation-vendor, General Thomas Gage. Moreover, there is at least one passage in this poem, a passage in which the author satirizes Lord Percy for his adeptness at flight, which is surprisingly similar to a passage in *M'Fingal* on the same subject.[31] The almost simultaneous composition of the two poems, however, indicates that neither poet probably influenced the other.[32] In this instance, too, Freneau used a longer (pentameter) line, while Trumbull used the eight-syllable line. In general, Freneau's patriotic poems differ from Trumbull's in evincing a more persistent and more personal ferocity toward the British than Trumbull was apparently able to muster. Furthermore, although he occasionally indulged in humor of a grim sort, he had small talent for the light comic satire that Trumbull excelled in. Probably almost as well-read as Trumbull, Freneau, in his poems at least, was distinctly the more belligerent of the

---

[29] "Life of Philip Freneau," in *The Poems of Philip Freneau*, edited by F. L. Pattee (3 vols., Princeton, 1902-07), I, xxiv.

[30] It is true that soon after the war began Freneau betook himself to the West Indies, where he spent two languorous years. Furthermore, his *American Independent* (1778) was "a somewhat tardy ratification of the Declaration of Independence."—*Poems of Freneau* (ed. by Harry Hayden Clark. New York, 1929), Introduction, p. xvii. Yet his hatred of British tyranny had only been in abeyance, and he was finally to write some of the fiercest anti-British lines in American poetry (*The British Prison Ship*).

[31] *The Poems of Philip Freneau*, I, 168, 169. Cf. *Poetical Works*, I, [3], 4.

[32] Trumbull had composed the first two cantos of *M'Fingal* by October, 1775; and *The Voyage to Boston* was advertised by the *Constitutional Gazette* on October 21, 1775, as "This day . . . published."

two; and, although a good lyric poet, he was often contented in his patriotic verse with a less finished technique than Trumbull. Although two years younger than Trumbull, Freneau was so prolific in the first six months of the war that he had produced several satires before Trumbull wrote *M'Fingal*. Yet there is no evidence indicating that Trumbull was specifically influenced by any of Freneau's poems. Still loyal to British art at least, Trumbull looked steadily across the water for his poetical inspiration.

Although it was composed rather rapidly when once undertaken,[33] *M'Fingal* did not spring into being suddenly: it was no hasty effort but a substantial work requiring a long period of incubation. The idea for the poem was first suggested to Trumbull in the spring of 1775, but he appears to have done little or nothing with it at that time.[34] In early August, however, he put his pen to practice by producing a burlesque on General Gage's proclamation establishing martial law in Massachusetts on June 19 last.[35] This burlesque, which was printed in successive issues of *The Connecticut Courant* early in August,[36] consisted of more than two hundred lines of strongly satiric verse in Hudibrastic couplets. Bearing the marks of hasty composition, the work is no masterpiece; yet many of the lines are exceedingly effective, and Trumbull later transferred about fifty of them, either *verbatim* or with but slight changes, to *M'Fingal*. This piece was an earnest of what Trumbull could do, and it was doubtless its appearance, as J. H. Trumbull has surmised, which

---

[33] See below, p. 160.

[34] See below, p. 164.

[35] A burlesque of the same proclamation appeared in broadside form in June and was printed in *The Connecticut Courant* on July 17; but although James Hammond Trumbull tentatively ascribed it to Trumbull (*The Origin of M'Fingal* [Morrisania, 1868], p. 9), Victor H. Paltsits has shown it to have been more probably written by Freneau.—*A Bibliography of the Separate and Collected Works of Philip Freneau* (New York, 1903), p. 27.

[36] August 7, 1775, p. [4]; August 14, 1775, p. [4].

M'FINGAL, POEM OF THE REVOLUTION 159

"induced the Author's friends to urge him to the composition of a longer and regularly constructed poem, in the same measure and a similar vein. . . ."[37]

Chief of the friends who must be given credit for bringing matters to a head, as will be seen, was Silas Deane, the prime mover, not only in this project, but in *The Progress of Dulness* as well. For some reason, perhaps because of the odium attached to the name of Deane during the darker days of the Revolution, Trumbull did not choose in later years to specify this indebtedness. After the war, in his oft-quoted letter to the Marquis de Chastellux, he referred to his sponsors merely as "some leading members of the first Congress";[38] and in writing the preface to his collected edition in 1820, he was no more generous than before to his ready counselor, Deane, but distributed the credit merely to "some of his friends in Congress."[39] Who the other members responsible for his going into literary action were he has nowhere specified, but it is reasonable to conjecture that they included John Adams, under whom Trumbull had studied law, and Thomas Cushing, under whose roof he had lived in Boston. The delegates from his own state, besides Silas Deane, were Roger Sherman and Eliphalet Dyer, with both of whom Trumbull was evidently acquainted.[40] A legend cherished by the descendants of Trumbull has it that Washington also added his word by commanding Trumbull to "write something mirthful" on the conflict.[41] The motives

---

[37] *Op. cit.*, p. 11.

[38] *Poetical Works*, II, 231. Trumbull was mistaken in referring in this connection to the "first" Congress: when that body met, the campaign of 1775 had not yet begun. The delegates from Connecticut, however, were the same for the first two congresses.

[39] "Memoir," p. 17.

[40] Trumbull succeeded Roger Sherman as treasurer of Yale College in 1776. See below, p. 208. His acquaintance with Dyer is suggested by a letter he wrote to Deane in October, 1775.—*Collections of the New-York Historical Society for the Year 1886*, Vol. XIX (New York, 1887), "The Deane Papers," I, 86.

[41] Mrs. Charles Horton Metcalf, of Detroit, Michigan, a great-great-grand-

which these gentlemen may have had in mind when they bespoke the services of the poet have been well stated by Samuel Kettell:

In this critical moment [that is, the opening months of the war] the keen sighted politicians of the day did not overlook the influence, which the still lingering respect toward England, and the deep sense of her power, must exert over the colonists. They understood the advantage which would be gained, if this respect and dread of power could be made to give place to scorn and contempt. They foresaw that if the Americans could despise the English, they would more boldly face them in battle; that if they could once laugh at them by their firesides, and in the camp, at night, they would beat them in the field on the morrow.[42]

Actuated by the counsel of his friends, Trumbull wrote the "first part" of *M'Fingal* in the fall of 1775 at New Haven.[43] This part of the poem, soon published as Canto I, consisted of approximately one-half of the entire poem. It was later divided into Cantos I and II. At this time he also "formed the plan of the work, sketched some of the scenes of the third Canto and [wrote] the beginning of the fourth. . . ."[44]

---

daughter of the poet, made this statement in a personal interview. No direct evidence can be adduced in verification of this story, but it is pertinent to note that Washington reviewed the student soldiers on the New Haven green in July, 1775.—H. T. Blake, *Chronicles of New Haven Green*, p. 136. It is at least possible that Trumbull, who was even then a man of some prominence, had an audience with the Commander-in-Chief at that time.

[42] *Specimens of American Poetry*, I, 179.

[43] "Memoir," p. 17. See also Stiles, "Itinerary," IV, [205]. Of the numerous errors that have been made in regard to the place and time of the composition of this part of *M'Fingal*, only a few will be mentioned here. A British notice of the poem referred to it as "Written at Philadelphia."—*The Gentlemen's Magazine*, XLVI (August, 1776), 374; Winnifred King asserts that the first part of the poem was written at Boston.—*The Connecticut Magazine*, X (1906), 407; V. L. Parrington implies that it was written at Hartford.—*Op. cit.*, p. 249; Mrs. Marble erroneously states that "Parts of this satire were written during the latter part of 1774 and at intervals in 1775."—*Heralds of American Literature* (Chicago, 1907), p. 128. John T. Winterich inadvertently gives the name of the author as "Jonathan" Trumbull.—*Early American Books and Printing* (Boston, 1935), p. 143.

[44] "Memoir," p. 17.

The feelings with which Trumbull entered the lists with his pen as an opponent of Great Britain have been slightly misrepresented by certain critics, from whom there have issued a number of loose statements tending to suggest that Trumbull was a fierce and fearless radical. Among these is Theodore Stanton, who writes:

No literary production was ever a more genuine embodiment of the spirit and life of a people, in the midst of a stirring and world-famous conflict, than is *M'Fingal* an embodiment of the spirit and life of the American people, in the midst of that stupendous conflict which formed our great epoch of national deliverance. . . . The author of *M'Fingal* wrote his satire under no personal or petty motive. His poem was a terrific assault on . . . the public enemies of his country . . . *M'Fingal* belongs, indeed, to a type of literature hard, bitter, vengeful. . . .[45]

M. C. Tyler speaks of a "fierce note" which one finds in Trumbull's poetry after 1774 and of Trumbull's "strain of passionate sympathy with the direction and tone of . . . Revolutionary politics."[46] Again, Carl Holliday asserts that Trumbull composed *M'Fingal* "not through an itching for fame, but through genuine love of country."[47] Moreover, Will Howe writes in *The Cambridge History of American Literature* of the "anger" which found expression in the poem.[48] Yet the facts do not bear out the view that Trumbull was a ruthless radical and a fierce propagandist.

Trumbull did not serve his country on the field of battle or in the halls of Congress. His youth did not recommend him for an official position of responsibility. Probably his delicate health and his temperamental aversion to violence prevented him from taking part in the field. It is clear that

---

[45] *A Manual of American Literature* (New York, 1909), p. 56.
[46] *Op. cit.*, I, 429.
[47] *The Wit and Humor of Colonial Days* (Philadelphia, 1912), p. 208.
[48] II, 150.

Trumbull was never a man to welcome physical danger. Twice during the Revolution he retreated to positions of safety. He left Boston in 1774 partly because, as he tells us, "Every thing [was] then verging towards hostility in Massachusetts."[49] He likewise withdrew from New Haven in 1777 when that town was "exposed to invasion."[50] Nor did Trumbull always exhibit fearlessness of a moral sort. His own word attests the apprehension he felt lest *The Progress of Dulness* create for him a "new set of Enemies."[51] His *Elegy on the Times* was anonymous and, the situation considered, somewhat conservative in tone. The anonymity of those poems, as well as of *M'Fingal*, so far from being adequate evidence of Trumbull's modesty or patriotism, may well be construed as a natural measure of caution on Trumbull's part. Certainly the situation which confronted him when he wrote *M'Fingal* was a much more serious one than he faced when he wrote *The Progress of Dulness*. Had the British cause triumphed in the Revolution, it would have done Trumbull no good to be known as the author of such an obnoxious poem as *M'Fingal*; for just as the colonists who chose to remain loyal to the King during the war were either hounded from the country after the war or made exceedingly uncomfortable, it is fair to infer that if the war had gone against the Colonies, the Crown would have made it very uncomfortable for the leaders of the rebellion, including the literary staff.

This is not to question the orthodoxy of Trumbull's politics; he definitely regarded British attempts to control colonial affairs as tyrannical, and he ultimately favored separation. Yet, though a patriot, he was undoubtedly of a different stripe from men like Josiah Quincy, Philip Freneau, Tom Paine, and Samuel Adams. These men held radical views of

---

[49] "Memoir," p. 17.
[50] *Ibid.*, p. 18.
[51] See above, p. 101.

M'FINGAL, POEM OF THE REVOLUTION

a sort that prophesied the political theory of Jeffersonian democrats, whereas Trumbull's political philosophy, like that of Washington and John Adams, pointed toward Federalism. It is by no means certain that Trumbull did not at first disapprove of the Revolution on legal grounds. V. L. Parrington goes so far as to say that had Trumbull's "environment" and "family connections" been different, he might easily have been a Loyalist.[52] This may be an extreme view; but it is safe to say that the leisure-loving, academic poet would have been just as well pleased had the issue never been raised. He was constitutionally a lover of peace. Mobs were not to his taste; and the rude methods of many supporters of the Whig party were repellent to him, for he was no "raving democrat."[53] Despite his talent for satire, he was a gentleman of quiet tastes. His interests were predominantly literary. When he undertook to compose a poem in the interest of American independence, he did so with what warmth his nature possessed: if he was no revolutionist, he was at least a patriot. The poem he produced proved to be a fairly effective Whig weapon.[54] Nevertheless it is clear that when he composed *M'Fingal*, Trumbull was concerned less for its effectiveness as an instrument of liberty than as a literary production which might or might not be a credit to him. A close reading of the poem itself suggests this view. Incontrovertible evidence in its support may be found in a letter which Trumbull wrote to Silas Deane on October 20, 1775, upon the completion of the first part of *M'Fingal*. This letter has remained practically unknown; and no one, so

---

[52] *Op. cit.*, p. 251.

[53] *M'Fingal* (Boston, 1799), Preface, p. v.

[54] It is possible to exaggerate the influence of *M'Fingal* as an agent of liberal propaganda. It had only three editions during the war; its circulation therefore could not be compared with that of Paine's *Common Sense*, which, issued at almost the same instant as *M'Fingal*, ran into a sale of more than one hundred thousand copies in the space of a few months.—*The Cambridge History of American Literature*, I, 141. See also below, pp. 184, 185.

far as can be ascertained, has related it properly to the subject of Trumbull's zeal as a revolutionary writer. It will be observed how casually the poet speaks of his revolutionary purpose. The letter reads in part:

Give me leave, Sir, to introduce to your acquaintance one Squire Mc Fingal, a Gentleman, who has been a Month or six weeks under my care, & who seems desirous of seeing a little of the world. I can say little more in his commendation than that I believe he is perfectly harmless; for indeed I am, upon longer acquaintance, got pretty much out of conceit of him myself, & if you like him no better I shall not wonder if you order him into close Custody. Without a metaphor, you remember, Sir, last spring you recommended to me to attempt a burlesque on General Gage's victories. I wrote you an answer, rather declining it, for reasons I then gave you; & you dropped the matter. It ran, however, in my mind, & I had so much regard for your commands, that I attempted a little sketch or two, but without being able to please myself, & so threw aside the thought for that time. But lately on shewing what I had sketched to one or two friends here, they advised me to throw the whole into some consistent form & go on with it. This (as I had nothing else either of business or amusement) I complied with, & it has produced the thing I here send you[.] I know it is too long, & too tedious & too— in short, too badly written & has too little wit in it. But I am heartily tired of it, & if it has no merit now, I shall never give it any. Many would call it inelegant & incorrect, but as my notions of the degree of elegance & correctness proper for this style are not just like the Ideas of your merely grammatical Critics, I would not wish it altered in that respect. My Plan you will see comprehends yours, & takes in a larger field,—& one main view I had, was to record a few of the most inveterate enemies of our Country, whom I should wish to see otherwise gibbeted up than in my verse. If you approve of the piece on the whole, do what you please with it. If any particular part do not answer, strike it out, & preserve the connection in any way you chuse. I am sensible many couplets may be omitted without affecting the sense. If it should appear broad [sic], more notes would perhaps be wanting. I leave it all to your better judgment. If you shew it to any Gentleman with you, unless M^r. J. Adams, I must beg you not to tell the author's name. Do not let the Copy go out of your hands. If you suppress it, I beg you to return it to me. I have no other, except the first rough draft. I have been doubting this fortnight, for it is so long since it was finished, whether to send it to you, or consign it to oblivion. On the whole I have determined to send it. And so fourthly & lastly, I have to enquire of you, your opinion of the piece, & what you design to do with it: which I beg the favour of you by a line, to inform me,—and beg leave to subscribe myself,

With the greatest Respect,
Your very humble Servant.
[JOHN TRUMBULL][55]

Four unmistakable inferences arise out of this letter. First, Trumbull did not himself originate the idea of his writing the burlesques of General Gage that proved to be a preliminary study for his more general satire on the Tories. Second, far from rushing rashly into print upon the outbreak of the Revolution, he dallied with the idea of writing the poem until he had sufficient leisure. Third, he wished to exercise caution to preserve his anonymity. Fourth, he was not so much excited over the opportunity of serving his country as he was concerned to produce a literary work which would be a credit to him. Moreover, in an age which generally reserved its highest honors for poets who wrote with "elegance and correctness," Trumbull naturally showed a degree of diffidence in staking his reputation on a comic satire abounding in profane wit.[56]

If Silas Deane's political services to his country are unfortunately clouded with ambiguity, it is impossible to im-

---

[55] *Collections of the New-York Historical Society for the Year 1886*, Vol. XIX, "The Deane Papers," I, 86-90.
[56] For an elaboration of this view, see my article, "John Trumbull as Revolutionist," *American Literature*, II (November, 1931), 294, 295.

pugn his services to American literature. He it was who had encouraged Trumbull to put the finishing touches on *The Progress of Dulness*. Far from "suppressing" the manuscript of *M'Fingal* now entrusted to him, he appears to have brought about its prompt publication. The work appeared first at Philadelphia, but the precise date of the publication has remained in doubt. From the welter of conflicting evidence and conjectures on the point, the most plausible inference to be drawn is that although the title-page carries the date 1775, the poem did not actually reach the public until January, 1776, when it was first advertised in a Philadelphia paper as "just published."[57] The first canto bore the title:

M'FINGAL:
A MODERN
EPIC POEM.
CANTO FIRST,
OR
THE TOWN-MEETING

It appeared in a small octavo volume of forty pages for sale by William and Thomas Bradford at the "London Coffee-House."[58] Canto First consists of so much of the poem as was divided in 1782 into Cantos I and II. It was brought out in a second Philadelphia edition in 1776, and a London

---

[57] *The Pennsylvania Journal*, January 31, 1776, p. 3. Trumbull's own testimony on the point is inconsistent. In his "Memoir" (p. [7]) he states that the poem was "printed in the fall of the year 1775." On the other hand, he told President Stiles that it was "printed Jany 1776."—Stiles, "Itinerary," IV, [205]. Doubtless relying on the "Memoir," B. J. Lossing, who brought out three editions of *M'Fingal*, refers the publication of the poem to "the Autumn of 1775."— *M'Fingal* (New York, 1881), Introduction, p. 7. J. H. Trumbull, however, the author of *The Origin of M'Fingal*, asserts (on p. 10 of that work) that the poem appeared in 1776 with a 1775 imprint. This conclusion, in view of the evidence in *The Pennsylvania Journal* cited above, must now be accepted.

[58] A copy of this rare edition may be seen at the Watkinson Library, Hartford, Connecticut.

M'FINGAL, POEM OF THE REVOLUTION 167

reprint also appeared in 1776.[59] These are the only known editions of *M'Fingal* as it originally appeared—in extent, about one-half of the completed poem. Upon the conclusion of the Revolutionary War, Trumbull resumed the composition of *M'Fingal* and cast it into the form in which it is best known today. This involved revising the first canto, dividing it into Cantos I and II, and adding Cantos III and IV. The poem thus altered was slightly more than twice as long as in the original form. It was completed upon the urgent request of Trumbull's friends, who "having obtained his promise, immediately put into circulation a subscription for the work."[60] The composition of the second part was completed between January and April, 1782;[61] and the poem as a whole, Trumbull's principal contribution to American literature, was published for the first time at Hartford between August 20 and September 10, 1782.[62] It was entitled:

> M'FINGAL:
> A MODERN
> EPIC POEM,
> IN FOUR CANTOS.

In conformity with Trumbull's usual practice, the poem appeared anonymously. Since it was promptly pirated in 1782, it is worth noting that the authorized (subscription) edition, a large duodecimo volume of one hundred pages, was printed by Hudson and Goodwin "near the Great Bridge."

So it came about that the scholar-poet commenced his most celebrated poem somewhat mistrustfully at the behest

---

[59] The London edition was published by John Almon, who had previously published Trumbull's *Elegy on the Times*.

[60] "Memoir," p. 18.

[61] Stiles, "Itinerary," IV, [205].

[62] Between July 20 and August 20 it was advertised each week as "in the Press," and on September 10 it was announced as "Just Published."—*The Connecticut Courant*, Nos. 914, 915, 916, 917, 920.

of friends who thought that it might be a useful agent of propaganda during the national crisis in 1775. Whatever the extent of its immediate use, the poem proved to have so much intrinsic value that the author was easily persuaded to expand it after the war as a purely literary work. Ultimately it became one of the most popular poems in the history of American literature. An account of the immediate reception of the poem and its subsequent history, therefore, may be illuminating with respect to the early literary annals of our country. Before this is presented, however, a brief analysis of the contents of *M'Fingal*, a poem now generally read by title and excerpt only, may not be amiss.

M'Fingal is a poem of slightly more than three thousand lines divided into four cantos of nearly equal length. The first two cantos, separated in time merely by a dinner hour, deal with a town meeting held in a church at which the Tory squire, M'Fingal, just returned from Boston to his native town not far distant, engages in a wordy combat with Honorius, proponent of the Whigs. The squire, of Scottish descent, prides himself particularly upon his gift of second-sight through which he gained fame

> . . . . by seeing
> Such things, as never would have being.

Exceedingly powerful of lungs, if inclined to be confused in his thinking, he has enjoyed a fair repute in town meetings, for the town, "torn by feuds of faction," has difficulty in making up its mind:

> As that famed weaver, wife t'Ulysses,
> By night her day's-work pick'd in pieces,
> And though she stoutly did bestir her,
> Its finishing was ne'er the nearer:
> So did this town with ardent zeal
> Weave cobwebs for the public weal,
> Which when completed, or before,

M'FINGAL, POEM OF THE REVOLUTION 169

    A second vote in pieces tore.
    They met, made speeches full long-winded,
    Resolv'd, protested and rescinded;
    Addresses sign'd; then chose committees
    To stop all drinking of Bohea teas;
    With winds of doctrine veer'd about,
    And turn'd all whig committees out.

Now, with the constable waving a staff to keep the peace and the moderator seated in the pulpit above him, and the restless crowd surgimg beneath, Honorius, the Whig leader, arises to address the assembly just as M'Fingal, arriving late, sits down with scowling contenance. Honorius commences by predicting on general principles the approaching dissolution of Great Britain's power. He compares her to an aging woman.

    Thus now while hoary years prevail,
    Good mother Britain seem'd to fail;
    Her back bent, crippled with the weight
    Of age, and debts, and cares of state.
    For debts she owed, and those so large,
    As twice her wealth could ne'er discharge,
    And now 'twas thought, so high they'd grown,
    She'd come upon the parish soon.
    Her arms, of nations once the dread,
    She scarce could lift above her head;
    . . . .
    And Gallic crows, as she grew weaker,
    Began to whet their beaks to pick her.
      And now her powers decaying fast,
    Her grand climact'ric had she pass'd,
    And just like all old women else,
    Fell in the vapors much by spells.
    Strange whimsies on her fancy struck,
    And gave her brain a dismal shock;
    Her memory fails, her judgment ends;
    She quite forgot her nearest friends,

> Lost all her former sense and knowledge,
> And fitted fast for Bedlam-college.

But even in her decline, she

> . . . took a whim to be Almighty;
> Urg'd on to desperate heights of frenzy,
> Affirm'd her own Omnipotency;
> Would rather ruin all her race,
> Than yield supremacy, an ace.

This resolve led her into divers unjust and absurd acts such as annulling our charters and placing in charge of her affairs in America the reprobate General Gage with his bungling "magazine of lies." Proceeding to vituperation of those persons among the colonists who sell themselves for gold, Honorius creates such consternation that the Tories cry him down in order to give tongue to their spokesman, M'Fingal. The Squire's speech, occasionally interrupted by rebuttal from Honorius, is mainly an attempt to frighten the Whigs into submission to the King's will. He argues from the divine right of kings; he cites the dire fate of other nations that have rebelled against authority; and he calls the roll of many prominent Americans, including clergymen, judges, writers, and printers, who have remained loyal to Great Britain. Characteristically, while M'Fingal is glorifying the cause of the Crown and berating the rebel Whigs, he employs such a travesty of reason that he maligns his own cause. Heckled by Honorius when he attempts to defend Governor Hutchinson, he blunders into the admission that in Tory opinion lying is

> The highest privilege of speech
> . . . .
> The only stratagem in war,
> Our generals have occasion for.

And when Gage broke his promise to allow the people of Boston freedom, he says, it was because

M'FINGAL, POEM OF THE REVOLUTION

He'd too much wit, such leagues t'observe,
And shut them in again, to starve.

After further discourse and a brief summary of his denunciation of the Whigs, the Squire gives over, it now being "time t'adjourn for dinner."

Canto II is entitled "The Town-Meeting, P.M." Before plunging into the business of the afternoon, however, Trumbull allows his muse a brief frolic on the green. This digression illustrates one means the poet took to relieve the heaviness of continued political discussion:

> THE Sun, who never stops to dine,
> Two hours had pass'd the mid-way line,
> And driving at his usual rate,
> Lash'd on his downward car of state.
> And now expired the short vacation,
> And dinner o'er in epic fashion,
> While all the crew, beneath the trees,
> Eat pocket-pies, or bread and cheese,
> (Nor shall we, like old Homer, care
> To versify their bill of fare)
> Each active party, feasted well,
> Throng'd in, like sheep, at sound of bell;
> With equal spirit took their places,
> And meeting oped with three *Oh Yesses*.

The Squire takes up the discourse where he had left off, listing the "crimes" of the Whigs; but he frequently injures his own cause by inept allusions, as when, after charging the Whigs with ingratitude, he asks whether the Crown did not send the Colonies governors and judges, as well as

> ... all felons in the nation
> To help you on in population.

He tells Honorius that the Whigs'

> ... boasted patriotism is scarce,
> And country's love is but a farce,

for as Britain knows from experience, there is no such thing as patriotism:

> . . . self is still, in either faction,
> The only principle of action.

Confident that the Whigs are cowards, M'Fingal assures them that they will never be able to withstand the combined onslaught of "Indians, British troops and Negroes." Honorius' reply to these malevolent remarks of M'Fingal is an apt reminder that if the success of the British is to be gauged by her first commander, America need not fear, for that General, with his childlike faith in proclamations,

> Laid nought, but quires of paper, waste.

Blandly taking the cue from Honorius, the Squire naïvely belittles Gage still further by a travesty of praise in which he compares the British general to the goose that saved Rome. Then after offering a farcical defense of Percy, who ran away from the field of conflict, the Squire turns from past events to future and foretells the dreadful days in store for the Whigs upon the arrival of Howe, Clinton, and Burgoyne. After a campaign which will result in the "sack of cities," the hanging of Whig committees, and the confiscation of rebel property—events which are certain to come to pass because of such "signs of the times" as meteors, prophetic stars, apparitions, the prophecies of old women, and the northern lights—the Squire foresees the ultimate ruin of the Whigs. The Crown will then reward the Tories and

> Dispense estates and titles round.
> Behold! the world shall stare at new setts
> Of home-made Earls in Massachusetts. . . .

M'Fingal himself may hope for a reward:

> E'en I perhaps (heaven speed my claim!)
> Shall fix a *Sir* before my name.

> For titles all our foreheads ache,
> For what blest changes can they make!

It would seem hardly necessary to refute the arguments of the befuddled Squire; but Honorius replies to him in a strain of fine dignity, which, considering the childish opposition, seems incongruous. An excerpt from his polemics hints at what an undistinguished work Trumbull might have produced if he had chosen to dispense with humor throughout this poem:

> But, oh my friends, my brethren, hear;
> And turn for once th' attentive ear.
> Ye see how prompt to aid our woes
> The tender mercies of our foes;
> Ye see with what unvaried rancour
> Still for our blood their minions hanker;
> Nor aught can sate their mad ambition,
> From us, but death, or worse, submission.
> Shall these then riot in our spoil,
> Reap the glad harvest of our toil,
> Rise from their country's ruins proud,
> And roll their chariot-wheels in blood?

The words of Honorius, however, are again interrupted: the impatient Tories precipitate an intramural struggle; and outside there arises a still greater uproar. M'Fingal draws his sword; there is a general exodus; and the Squire goes forth to disperse the mob. The moderator, who has nimbly hidden his carcass beneath the desk, now rises and adjourns the meeting *sine die*.

The third canto, entitled "The Liberty Pole," contains the most amusing action of the poem. Sallying forth with "ministerial ire," the Squire sees a portentous thing,

> A pole ascending through the sky,
> Which numerous throngs of whiggish race
> Were raising in the market-place.

> Not higher school-boy's kites aspire,
> Or royal mast, or country spire;
> Like spears at Brobdignagian tilting,
> Or Satan's walking-staff in Milton.
> And on its top, the flag unfurl'd,
> Waved triumph o'er the gazing world,
> Inscribed with inconsistent types
> Of *Liberty* and *thirteen stripes*.

Enraged by this "May-pole of sedition," around which the Whigs are performing rites of dedication by drinking flip, M'Fingal caustically inquires whether they think it will cure "crackt skulls and batter'd noses." He tells them that they are the dupes of rogues and demagogues, under whose tutelage they have come to regard liberty as a patent license for "crimes" and to look upon "public good" as their own. Their clamor for more liberty is ridiculous, says the Squire. The Whig will

> Cry "Liberty," with powerful yearning,
> As he does "Fire!" whose house is burning;
> Though he already has much more
> Than he can find occasion for.

Grown slightly more skilled in dialectic, M'Fingal no longer blunderingly uses arguments that recoil upon himself, but, for a time at least, delivers effective blows. He makes insulting references to the humble station of many of the Whigs, and he ridicules the democratic practice of bringing incompetents into office:

> Each leather-apron'd dunce, grown wise,
> Presents his forward face t'advise,
> And tatter'd legislators meet,
> From every workshop through the street.
> His goose the tailor finds new use in,
> To patch and turn the Constitution;
> The blacksmith comes with sledge and grate

> To iron-bind the wheels of state;
> The quack forbears his patients' souse,
> To purge the Council and the House;
> The tinker quits his moulds and doxies,
> To cast assembly-men and proxies.
> From dunghills deep of blackest hue,
> Your dirt-bred patriots spring to view,
> To wealth and power and honors rise,
> Like new-wing'd maggots changed to flies,
> And fluttering round in high parade,
> Strut in the robe, or gay cockade.
>
> . . . .
>
> For in this ferment of the stream
> The dregs have work'd up to the brim,
> And by the rule of topsy-turvies,
> The scum stands foaming on the surface.
> You've caused your pyramid t'ascend,
> And set it on the little end.
> Like Hudibras, your empire's made,
> Whose crupper had o'ertopp'd his head.

The net result of the efforts of these humble persons is that they have substituted for the British constitution a "Commonwealth" that is

> . . . a common harlot,
> The property of every varlet.

After reviewing sundry misdeeds of the rebels, the Squire concludes they have gone so far that they must now expect not mercy but vengeance.

At this point, the climax of the poem, M'Fingal orders the constable to read the riot act, but that functionary is interrupted in the prosecution of his duties by a shower of stones and clubs. Feigning a wound, he falls to the ground and creeps to a hiding place, but the Whigs fetch him back. M'Fingal now advances, crying "King George" three times, and brandishing his sword. Frightening the Whigs from his path, he strikes "on their Pole a vengeful blow." Despite a volley of stones, the Squire perhaps would have

> . . . fell'd the pole to ground,
> Had not some Pow'r, a whig at heart,
> Descended down and took their part

and urged one of their larger men to use a shovel, which had been instrumental in erecting the liberty-pole, to make war on the Squire. M'Fingal, nothing loath, advances to the combat, but the spade of the burly Whig quickly snaps the Squire's sword. Turning to the Tories for assistance, M'Fingal finds that they have all fled, an action which he would have liked to emulate had not "age unwieldy check'd his pace." Now seeing the "spade-arm'd chief" advancing too near him, the Squire bends over to seize a stone for a missile. But just as he

> . . . tugg'd to raise it from the ground,
> The fatal spade discharged a blow
> Tremendous on his rear below:
> His bent knee fail'd, and void of strength
> Stretch'd on the ground his manly length.
> Like ancient oak o'erturn'd, he lay,
> Or tower to tempests fall'n a prey,
> Or mountain sunk with all his pines,
> Or flow'r the plow to dust consigns,
> And more things else—but all men know 'em,
> If slightly versed in epic poem.

M'Fingal is now a prisoner, but the Whigs choose first to deal with the constable. Fastening a rope to his waist, they swing him up the pole "like a keg of ale" until he reaches the top. There, in the clear air, his thoughts are quickly rectified:

> As Socrates of old at first did
> To aid philosophy get hoisted,
> And found his thoughts flow strangely clear,

M'FINGAL, POEM OF THE REVOLUTION 177

> Swung in a basket in mid air:
> Our culprit thus, in purer sky,
> With like advantage raised his eye,
> And looking forth in prospect wide,
> His Tory errors clearly spied.

He therefore immediately renounces

> . . . the Pope, the Turks,
> The King, the Devil and all their works,

and offers to

> Turn Whig or Christian, what you please.

Then, after voting to accept his confession, the patriots lower him,

> Spread at all points, like falling cat.

Nothing daunted by the constable's experience, the Squire stands his ground, "heroic as a mule." Indeed he defies the Whigs in a vigorous speech during which he points out that punishment only makes a person think less of his oppressor:

> No man e'er felt the halter draw,
> With good opinion of the law.

Prepared to "stand the worst," he takes consolation in the fact that the Whigs will "rue this inauspicious morn." The Whigs prepare to punish the Tory leader, but not without due process of law. They quickly convene a court beside the pole, and presently the clerk reads M'Fingal's sentence, namely, that he should be haltered, tarred and feathered, and drawn through the town in shame. Accordingly the Whigs seize him, tie him to the pole, and pour "o'er his head the smoking tar." The Squire presents a vivid spectacle as

> . . . from the high-raised urn the torrents
> Spread down his sides their various currents;

> His flowing wig, as next the brim,
> First met and drank the sable stream;
> Adown his visage stern and grave
> Roll'd and adhered the viscid wave;
> With arms depending as he stood,
> Each cuff capacious holds the flood;
> From nose and chin's remotest end,
> The tarry icicles descend;
> Till all o'erspread, with colors gay,
> He glitter'd to the western ray,
> Like sleet-bound trees in wintry skies,
> Or Lapland idol carved in ice.

Next the feathering takes place, after which

> . . . all complete appears our 'Squire,
> Like Gorgon or Chimaera dire;
> Nor more could boast on Plato's plan
> To rank among the race of man,
> Or prove his claim to human nature,
> As a two-legg'd, unfeather'd creature.

This ceremony completed, the Whigs, anxious to exhibit their handiwork, place the constable and the Squire in a cart and draw them around the town. Finally tired of this sport, the mob returns the two culprits to the pole and betakes itself to the tavern

> To end in mirth the festal day.

Left alone with the constable, the Squire sits, stuck to the pole,

> Glued by the tar t'his rear applied,
> Like barnacle on vessel's side.

He is no longer defiant or wrathful, but apprehensive. Just as

> . . . all goes wrong in church and state,
> Seen through perspective of the grate:

M'FINGAL, POEM OF THE REVOLUTION

So now M'FINGAL's Second-sight
Beheld all things in gloomier light;
His visual nerve, well purged with tar,
Saw all the coming scenes of war.

His dire forebodings he imparts to the constable, saying that

. . . this feathery omen
Portends what dismal times are coming.
Now future scenes, before my eyes,
And second-sighted forms arise.
I hear a voice, that calls away,
And cries 'The Whigs will win the day.'
My beck'ning Genius gives command,
And bids me fly the fatal land;
Where changing name and constitution,
Rebellion turns to Revolution.

He then instructs his henchmen to call their friends together so that M'Fingal's "prophetic voice" may warn them of what is imminent. But first he bespeaks the assistance of the constable in getting him loose from the liberty-pole.

Canto Fourth is entitled "The Vision." When night comes, the Tories repair to M'Fingal's cellar, there to hear the voice of warning. The chiefs assembled, M'Fingal

Rose solemn from the turnip-bin.

With tears running down his "tar-streak'd visage," he speaks. After briefly reviewing past triumphs, he confesses the error in judgment, persisted in despite his second-sight, which persuaded his "stubborn soul" to have "faith in Hutchinson too long." Now, he frankly states, in order to escape dungeons, horsewhips, and tar "yet in embryo in the pine," he intends to make good his escape while he can. To this decision he has been forced by various omens of which he was advised by one Malcolm, a Scotsman, aide to Governor Tryon, who had been tarred and half hanged in 1774. In a vision M'Fingal has seen Malcolm, he says, on a gallows, whence that individual "unfurl'd" the curtains of future events. The recital of these events constitutes a survey of the course of the Revolution from the capture of Montreal forward. Among the more notable items in the vision are Burgoyne's abortive campaign at Saratoga, Clinton's "moonlight marches" across New Jersey, and Cornwallis's surrender. Finding that his gloomy narrative caused the Squire to grow pale, Malcolm hastened to change the subject to "British valour and humanity"—which included starving, freezing, and shooting prisoners; serving them poisonous food; taunting dying men; introducing the pox (large as well as small); and spreading deliberately the prison fever. Despite these instances of British skill in "th' art and mystery of Murther" exemplified so well by Howe and his hireling, Josiah Loring, the rebel cause triumphed. The lesson was clear to Malcolm; and he passed it on to M'Fingal:

> For know, that fate's auspicious door,
> Once shut to flight, is oped no more;
> Nor wears its hinge, by changing stations,
> Like Mercy's door in Proclamations.

Lest the Squire tarry too long, Malcolm showed him still another vision—that of the rising power of America. This was accompanied by the dwindling of Britain's power. Indeed England, in this view, is so small that

> . . . had it found a station
> In this new world, at first creation,
> Or doom'd by justice, been betimes
> Transported over for its crimes,
> We'd find full room for't in lake Erie, or
> That larger water-pond, Superior,
> Where North at margin taking stand,
> Would scarce be able to spy land.

The inference from these warnings is clear, but another crisis is at hand in the fortunes of M'Fingal. His narrative

M'FINGAL, POEM OF THE REVOLUTION

of the visions revealed to him by Malcolm is interrupted by a shout that betokens discovery by the Whigs of the hiding place of the Tories. Confusion seizes all members of the band:

> The lights put out, each tory calls,
> To cover him on cellar walls,
> Creeps in each box, or bin, or tub,
> To hide him from the rage of mob,
> Or lurks, where cabbage-heads in row,
> Adorn'd the sides with verdant show.

As for M'Fingal, he so far profits by Malcolm's counsel as to deem it

> . . . vain to stay,
> And risk his bones in second fray.

Making use of a window known to him alone, he issues forth and makes all haste to Boston.

> His friends, assembled for his sake,
> He wisely left in pawn, at stake,
> To tarring, feath'ring, kicks and drubs
> Of furious, disappointed mobs,
> Or with their forfeit heads to pay
> For him, their leader, crept away.

Thus the poet takes leave of Squire M'Fingal, the Tory leader—in full flight to Boston regardless of the fate of the comrades he has deserted.

M'Fingal is now so little known to the general public that it is difficult to realize that it was probably the most popular American poem of its length before Longfellow's *Evangeline* and the best political verse-satire of its length before Lowell's *Biglow Papers*. Its fame, though great, has wavered. After a considerable success at the beginning of the war, its popularity diminished somewhat until 1782, when the completion of the poem gave it a new lease of life. The political purpose which brought it into being has been responsible for a tendency in recent years to associate its greatest success with the period of the Revolution. The truth is that its popularity during the Revolution has been exaggerated and that its subsequent vogue was greater than we now remember. During the period of actual warfare, Trumbull's satire was evidently eclipsed by works of less literary merit but greater propaganda value; when the need for the propagandist was past, the poet emerged more clearly. As the Americans, now politically independent, looked about to see upon what basis they might build their literary independence, they seized upon *M'Fingal* as one of their own productions which bid fair to be of enduring value. Consequently a multitude of notices of the poem appeared in the first decade of its existence in its complete form. It was kept to the fore for a number of years thereafter, partly because other good American poetry was scarce and partly because *M'Fingal* possessed real merit. Trumbull's poem bore reëxamination and republication better than most Revolutionary literature—including Freneau's satires. Its high literary flavor, which had perhaps prevented its being enjoyed fully by the rank and file during the war, favored its being accepted by critics as a work of art after its partisan purpose had been served. *M'Fingal* not only survived the Revolutionary period, but it held a respected place in American literature until well toward the middle of the nineteenth century. Thereafter notices of the poem were infrequent, and *M'Fingal* gradually slipped into the class of those poems which are considered to be of "historical importance."

The reputation of *M'Fingal* has not been correspondent to its merit. The extravagant approbation with which the poem was at first regarded was doubtless partly due to the fact that America, not yet blessed with a numerous literary progeny, had to lavish her affection and praise upon what she had. Later, when the muse became more prolific, Trumbull's poem was unduly neglected. *M'Fingal* gradually went out of fashion. The romantic poetry of Poe, the sentimental poetry of Longfellow, and the rough-hewn poetry of Whitman represent three styles of American poetry with which the dusty Hudibrastics and old-fashioned wit of *M'Fingal* could not compete. The Revolution which gave the poem birth also set a limit upon its life. The modern reader resents being called upon to brush up his dubious knowledge of the campaigns of 1776 in order to enjoy a poem. Hence, although it is sometimes sampled (unwillingly) by college students in their anthologies, *M'Fingal* has gradually lost ground, until today it is little more than a problem for research. All things considered, it has deserved a slightly better fate.

The immediate reaction to the publication of Canto I of *M'Fingal* it is impossible to demonstrate fully by direct evidence. This is partly because in 1776 American literature was not thoroughly integrated and self-sustaining. Most American writers before this time, and indeed for some years afterwards, had no other idea than that American letters constituted an outlying branch of English letters, dependent upon the home office for support and direction. American literary opinion was manufactured largely in England and made available to American readers through British reviews. America was slow to perfect the machinery necessary for adequate book reviewing; periodicals were few and uncertain of continued existence.[63] When the first part of *M'Fingal* appeared, there was but one American magazine

---

[63] Although some American magazines dared to appear as early as the fourth decade of the eighteenth century, those that existed before the Revolution were few and short-lived. Only one magazine was started during the Revolution. After 1783, there was more activity, sixteen magazines having been started between 1783 and 1789. But it was not until the last decade of the century that the magazine habit took root firmly: between 1790 and 1800 there were sixty-three "new ventures" in the periodical world.—William Beer, *Checklist of American Periodicals 1741-1800* (Worcester, 1923), pp. 4, 5.

which might have been expected to review it, *The Pennsylvania Magazine*. That magazine failed, however, to notice the poem. No newspaper references to it have been found except a few advertisements which appeared in *The Pennsylvania Journal* early in 1776. Consequently the nature of the reception accorded the first part of *M'Fingal* must be largely inferred from indirect evidence.

It has been generally assumed (on insufficient evidence) that *M'Fingal* was a large secondary factor in the success of the American arms.[64] In partial substantiation of such a view, it must be granted that the poem had two editions within a year, that the British press gave it considerable attention, and that the demand for its completion after the war argues its original popularity. This is not the whole story, however, for the term popularity in this connection needs definition. It is one thing to produce a work of art which wins critical approval and so has a measure of popularity within a restricted circle. But it is quite another to produce a work which is popular in the sense of winning a vast body of general readers. There is a great difference between the popularity, say, of James Branch Cabell and that of Sinclair Lewis. It would seem that the best evidence of the latter type of popularity is the demand for new editions and the appearance of frequent allusions to the work. No editions of *M'Fingal* are known to have appeared during the six long and dreary years between 1776 and 1782, and newspaper advertisements of it or allusions to it during the war were exceedingly rare. Paine's *Common Sense*, which appeared almost simultaneously with *M'Fingal*, was repeatedly advertised and it went through several editions, selling more than one hundred thousand copies within three months. Dickinson's (earlier) *Letters from a Farmer in Pennsylvania* were reprinted in newspapers in each of the thirteen Colonies.

---

[64] See, for example, Annie Marble, *op. cit.*, p. 129; M. C. Tyler, *op. cit.*, I, 441; *The Cambridge History of American Literature*, I, 139.

Such popularity *M'Fingal* could not match. Other competition which *M'Fingal* had in the public mind included Freneau's verse, which was less narrowly literary than Trumbull's, and countless verses that appeared here and there during the Revolution, many of them, like Hopkinson's *Battle of the Kegs*, adapted to be sung as ballads or as marching songs.[65] Moreover, although *M'Fingal* is comic throughout, it should be recalled that its most amusing part, the third canto, did not appear until after the war. In the absence of strong proof to the contrary, it is at least pertinent to suggest the hypothesis that although *M'Fingal* could not fail to appeal to the intelligentsia, it was not so easily appreciated by the man in the street or the man in the trenches as many simpler poems more direct in their attack on the Tory cause. At all events, not much can be said for the roadside popularity of a book which had only two editions in six years.[66]

In England where the critical press was active, *M'Fingal* promptly received a large share of attention for a book emanating from New England. According to whether the journal which reviewed the work was liberal or conservative, *M'Fingal* was alternately praised and condemned. Thus *The Monthly Review*, which compared the poem to *Hudibras*, could not find "the Yankey Poet . . . in any respect, inferior to his predecessor, of merry memory."[67] *The Critical Review*, a conservative organ, summarily damned the poem as "A doggerel rhapsody, extended through forty-four pages, without wit, humour, or any discoverable design."[68] Obviously

---

[65] *The Battle of the Kegs* was "set to music—possibly by Hopkinson himself—and was sung by the soldiers at the front."—George E. Hastings, *The Life and Works of Francis Hopkinson* (Chicago, 1926), p. 295.

[66] Alfred Kreymborg is obviously inaccurate in his statement that "public demand during the war exhausted thirty editions" of *M'Fingal.—Our Singing Strength* (New York, 1929), p. 24. Indeed Mr. Kreymborg's brief discussion of Trumbull (*ibid.*, pp. 23, 24) is wholly unreliable.

[67] First Series, LIV (June, 1776), 504.

[68] First Series, XLI (June, 1776), 481.

the poem called for neither of these extremes of criticism, and at least one of the seven British reviewers who appraised *M'Fingal* shortly after its appearance, found an intelligent middle ground:

Our Yankee is not a Hudibras, nor is the author another Butler; he is not, however, destitute of wit and humour, and the design of his piece is very plain, that of turning into ridicule a town-meeting, in which the late circumstances of the inhabitants of Boston and the American disputes with Great-Britain were canvassed in disputation.[69]

Whatever the precise degree of success attained by *M'Fingal* during the Revolution, it is clear that its greatest vogue was post-Revolutionary. Its reputation was greatest between 1782 and 1830. The period between 1782 and 1820 in American literature is a great abyss into which the average reader does not willingly slip. At the end of that time, Sydney Smith posed the offensive but partially relevant question, "In the four corners of the globe, who reads an American book?"[70] The American novel then boasted no more illustrious names than Hannah Foster, Charles Brockden Brown, and Hugh Brackenridge. Before 1819 Irving had done only the *Salmagundi Papers* and the *Knickerbocker History*. The drama, thus far represented by Thomas Godfrey, Royall Tyler, and William Dunlap, was even then in the doldrums. Our poetry, though prolific, ran largely to cheap, showy varieties or to the pious weeds of elegy. Between 1775 and 1820, excepting Trumbull's *M'Fingal*, Freneau's *British Prison Ship* and a few lyrics, Barlow's *Hasty Pudding*, and Drake's *Culprit Fay*, practically no poetry of permanent interest was published until 1817, when Bryant's *Thanatopsis* made its first astonishing appearance. In this relatively arid period, Trumbull's *M'Fingal*

---

[69] *The London Review of English and Foreign Literature*, III (January-June, 1776), Appendix, p. 536.
[70] *The Edinburgh Review*, XXXIII (January, 1820), 79.

M'FINGAL, POEM OF THE REVOLUTION towered conspicuously for many years. Although Sydney Smith's scornful query was pertinent in that it suggested the dearth of good American books, it could not be applied specifically to *M'Fingal*. There was in this country a large body of readers who were not averse to reading an American production if it revealed ability. Of course no public is homogeneous; there were, from the first, critics who condemned the poem on one or another score. Yet in 1829, almost fifty years after it was first published, Samuel Kettell, a competent observer, remarked that *M'Fingal* had "had a greater celebrity than any other American poem."[71] Signs of this enormous popularity may be read in the annals of the period.

The most obvious sign of the popularity of *M'Fingal* was the extraordinary number of editions it received, most of them unauthorized. In 1820 Trumbull complained of the wholesale pirating to which his poem had been subjected:

As no author, at that period, was entitled by law to the copyright of his productions, the work soon became the prey of every bookseller and printer, who chose to appropriate it to his own benefit. Among more than thirty different impressions, one only; at any subsequent time, was published with the permission, or even the knowledge of the writer; and the poem remained the property of newsmongers, hawkers, pedlars and petty chapmen.[72]

The first of these illicit editions was advertised so shortly after the authorized edition as to interfere seriously with the latter's sale.[73] On the same day that the publication of the pirated edition was announced (January 7, 1783), there appeared in *The Connecticut Courant* an article, evidently from the pen of Trumbull,[74] bitterly attacking literary piracy and

---

[71] *Specimens of American Poetry*, I, 179.
[72] "Memoir," pp. 18, 19.
[73] *The Connecticut Courant*, December 24, 1782, p. [3].
[74] The article was not signed, but strong internal evidence points to Trumbull's authorship.

pleading for a statute to control it.[75] Apparently a bill had already been introduced into the General Assembly of Connecticut by this time, for on the very next day "An Act for the encouragement of Literature and Genius" was passed, which secured to authors the sole right of publication of their works for a period of fourteen years.[76] Yet, since other states did not protect Trumbull, the pirating of *M'Fingal* continued, an exasperating but indubitable sign of his poem's popularity.[77]

In one edition or another, *M'Fingal* was read far and wide. The record of its first decade (1782-1792) is brilliant. During this period the poem had seven editions. It was read by aristocrat and commoner alike. Copies were soon in the hands of John Adams,[78] Thomas Jefferson,[79] David Humphreys,[80] and General Nathanael Greene.[81] Washington was also in possession of a copy, which bears his autograph.[82] In 1784 the Marquis de Chastellux was so favorably impressed with the poem that he asked Trumbull to send him several copies for distribution to persons in France.[83] In 1785 Noah Webster made the poem known to school children by publishing two long excerpts from it in his *Grammatical Institute*.[84] In the

---

[75] *Ibid.*, January 7, 1783, pp. [1], [2].

[76] *Acts and Laws, Made and passed by the General Court or Assembly . . . of the State of Connecticut . . . on the eighth Day of January, Anno. Dom. 1783*, New London, 1783.

[77] A list of the editions of *M'Fingal* is given below in the bibliography.

[78] *The Historical Magazine*, IV (July, 1860), 195.

[79] Letter from Trumbull to Jefferson, June 21, 1784, manuscript in the possession of the Massachusetts Historical Society.

[80] Anson Phelps Stokes, *Memorials of Eminent Yale Men*, II, 315.

[81] "Governor Joseph Trumbull Collection Military and General Correspondence 1760-1867" (5 vols. Manuscript in the possession of the Connecticut State Library), Vol. II, Document 106 d.

[82] *Catalogue of the Famous Library of ... Henry Huth* (9 vols., [London], [1912-20]), VIII, 2077. Exactly when Washington acquired his copy is not known. It was sold in 1919 for the sum of £225.

[83] John Trumbull, *Poetical Works*, Appendix, II, [229], 230.

[84] *A Grammatical Institute of the English Languag* [sic] . . . (3 vols., Hartford, 1785), III, 106-09, 111-13.

M'FINGAL, POEM OF THE REVOLUTION 189

same year the whole poem was printed at Boston. In 1786 *The New Haven Gazette* twice used *M'Fingal* for political propaganda.[85] At Philadelphia during the following year it received a new edition, and it was reprinted in its entirety in Carey's *American Museum*, where it was followed a few months later by a number of shorter poems by the "author of M'Fingall."[86] In 1788 *The Massachusetts Centinel* twice quoted *M'Fingal* for party purposes, and it printed a sentimental eulogy of Trumbull.[87] At Hartford during the same year, *M'Fingal* received flattering attention in two successive issues of *The American Mercury*.[88] Quoted first and last for a variety of purposes, *M'Fingal* was even used (during 1788) to establish a point of historical fact![89] It was appropriate that David Humphreys should dedicate his play, *The Widow of Malabar* (1790), to his friend, the celebrated author of *M'Fingal*, and that he should secure the latter's collaboration in writing its prologue and epilogue.[90] In 1791 Philadelphia, always hospitable to *M'Fingal*, accorded the poem another edition; and in 1792 the liberal party in England was responsible for a London edition. A more flattering record of public appreciation during ten years' time could hardly have been expected for any poem.

The next decade of *M'Fingal's* existence was hardly less glorious. In 1795 a handsome illustrated edition appeared in New York—probably with Trumbull's approval, for its copper plates were prepared from drawings by Elkanah Tisdale, whose illustrations later appeared in Trumbull's *Poet-*

---

[85] See below, p. 193.

[86] *The American Museum*, I (April, 1787), 353-81; II (July, 1787), 95-103, 206-03 [sic].

[87] *The Massachusetts Centinel*, VIII (January 2, 1788), 122; VIII (January 26, 1788), 152; X (September 27, 1788), 16.

[88] August 25, 1788, p. [2]; September 1, 1788, p. [3].

[89] David Humphreys, *An Essay on the Life of the Honorable Major-General Israel Putnam* (Hartford, 1788), pp. 103, 104.

[90] *The Miscellaneous Works of Colonel Humphreys* (New York, 1790), pp. 116, 117.

ical Works. *The Monthly Magazine, and British Register* (London) noted in 1798 that *M'Fingal* was "read with rapture in America" and called attention to Trumbull's position as a pioneer in American literature.[91] This article was copied in the following May by two American periodicals, one in Philadelphia and one in New York.[92] Early in 1799 also, Mathew Carey, the Philadelphia publisher, wrote a controversial poem in Hudibrastic couplets which was furnished with footnotes showing the author's indebtedness to particular passages in *M'Fingal*.[93] Boston also gave its share of attention to *M'Fingal* this year when a new edition was published there. There can be no question, furthermore, that the renewal of interest in *The Progress of Dulness*, toward the end of the century, indicated by the editions of 1794, 1796, and 1801, was in large measure created by the enduring popularity of *M'Fingal*.

With the passage of twenty years, the reputation of *M'Fingal* would seem to have got its growth; yet it increased in weight and heartiness for another score of years. In 1805 a version of the "Epithalamium" was twice printed with the introductory remark that it was the work of "the witty author of Macfingal,"[94] and a request was issued for some of his early unpublished pieces.[95] Other signs of *M'Fingal's* vitality before 1820 included the appearance of an edition at Elizabethtown (1805); the purchase of a copy of the "Elegant London ed^n" by President Madison (1809)[96]; the publication of another New York edition (1810); the use of

---

[91] VI (August, 1798), [81], 82.

[92] *The Dessert to the True American*, I (May 4, 1799), [1]; *The Monthly Magazine, and American Review*, I (May, 1799), 151-53.

[93] *The Porcupiniad, a Hudibrastic Poem . . . Addressed to William Cobbett*, Philadelphia, 1799.

[94] *The Monthly Anthology and Boston Review*, II (May, 1805), 247-50; *The Port Folio* (Philadelphia), V (October, 1805), 319, 320.

[95] *The Monthly Anthology*, II, 247.

[96] Barlow MSS, The Pequot Library, Southport, Connecticut.

passages from the poem for political propaganda in 1811;[97] and the appearance of no less than six editions between 1812 and 1816.[98] It was undoubtedly the abiding popularity of *M'Fingal* which induced S. G. Goodrich to undertake the publication of Trumbull's *Poetical Works* in 1820.

After 1820 the character of *M'Fingal's* reputation underwent a change: popular interest in the poem apparently waned somewhat, but critical approval remained at a high level. In short, *M'Fingal* became a classic. The 1820 edition of the *Poetical Works* was a financial failure,[99] and only one edition of *M'Fingal* appeared between 1820 and 1830.[100] On the other hand, the poem apparently lost no ground in critical quarters. In 1828 Samuel Converse, the publisher of Webster's *Dictionary*, solicited Trumbull's interest in a very ambitious volume of biographies of the most eminent living artists, poets, and novelists, with portraits, the whole to be sold at ten dollars a volume. The work was never completed, but it is significant that its prospectus listed the eight living poets to be included, in the following order: Trumbull, Percival, Hillhouse, Bryant, Halleck, Dana, Pierpont, Sigourney.[101] One year later Samuel Kettell's three-volume anthology, *Specimens of American Poetry*, was published in Boston. If the original plan of publishing the whole of *M'Fingal*[102] had been adhered to, Trumbull would have been accorded space about three times as great as any of the other one hundred and ninety or more poets who graced that anthol-

---

[97] See below, p. 193.

[98] These came out at Baltimore (1812), Albany (1813), Hallowell (1813), Lexington (1814), and (in two editions) Hudson (1816).

[99] S. G. Goodrich, *Recollections of a Lifetime* (2 vols., New York, 1857), II, 111, 112.—Clearly the public was little interested in any of Trumbull's works but *M'Fingal* and, to a less degree, *The Progress of Dulness;* and of these poems there was an abundance of separate editions.

[100] At Boston, 1826.

[101] Burton MSS, CXXVI, 7.

[102] Letter from S. G. Goodrich to Trumbull, April 7, 1827, Burton MSS, CXXV, 50.

ogy. As it was, with only Canto III used for this purpose, Trumbull's space was exceeded appreciably by that of only one poet, his old college-mate, Timothy Dwight; and it exactly equaled the space allotted to Bryant. The anthology was not received favorably on all sides, but it was doubtless a reasonably accurate barometer of contemporary critical opinion. In this work Kettell asserted that *M'Fingal* had "had a greater celebrity than any other American poem."[103]

When Trumbull died in 1831, *M'Fingal* had been before the public about fifty years. Although he had long since ceased to figure as an active writer, the steady fame of his major poem had remained a constant gratification to him. Reasons for *M'Fingal's* astonishing longevity—the paucity of other good American poetry, the aura of patriotism surrounding the work, its adaptability to quotation and declamation, the wealth of sheer fun it contained—have already been suggested. One additional explanation for its vogue needs amplification.

Although *M'Fingal* was originally conceived as an instrument of American independence, Trumbull was detached enough even at the time of the war to perceive absurdities and wrong-headedness in the conduct of the patriots as well as of the Loyalists. After the war he wrote to the Marquis de Chastellux that in *M'Fingal* he had tried to satirize both Whigs and Tories "with as much impartiality as possible."[104] This remark perhaps gives an exaggerated idea of the extent of the poet's ridicule of the Whigs, for the poem was prevailingly patriotic. Yet Squire M'Fingal's speeches in denunciation of the rougher element in the rebel constituency[105] carried heavy invective and keen ridicule which it is highly probable that the patrician Trumbull lawlessly enjoyed writing. At all events, the Squire's harangues on the abuse

---

[103] *Op. cit.*, I, 179.
[104] *Poetical Works*, Appendix, II, 231.
[105] See, for example, above, pp. 174, 175.

M'FINGAL, POEM OF THE REVOLUTION 193

of liberty[106] were later found to afford splendid texts for conservative propaganda in the troubled years after the Revolution, when our government, having won its independence, had much ado to maintain its stability. After the war, many prominent patriots, including Trumbull, became staunch Federalists. If Trumbull's poem could not turn Federalist, it was conveniently found to contain passages which could be removed from their context and made to look very much like Federalist doctrine. The use of *M'Fingal* for the purposes of conservative politics began in 1786, when *The New Haven Gazette* extracted passages from it on two occasions in order to call attention to the weakness of the central government and to the abuse of liberty on the part of incompetent leaders.[107] In 1788, *The Massachusetts Centinel* also twice resorted to *M'Fingal* for the support of Federalist doctrine.[108] In 1811, a disastrous year for the Federalists in Massachusetts, *M'Fingal* was again drawn upon for literary ammunition to be used against the Republicans under Gerry.[109] The peak of irony, however, was reached three months later when *M'Fingal*, originally designed primarily as a revolutionary document, was quoted extensively in condemnation of a revolution in Caracas, Venezuela, where certain insurgents had set up "a noisy, flourishing Demagoguy."[110] The practical use of *M'Fingal* in this way both testified to the popularity of the poem and gave it greater currency. That its lines were acquiring a proverbial character in the minds of the American people is to be inferred from the newspapers' employment of the coined expressions, "M'Fingalick"[111] and

---

[106] See especially *Poetical Works*, I, 87-90.
[107] *The New Haven Gazette*, August 24, 1786, p. 220; September 21, 1786, p. 249.
[108] *The Massachusetts Centinel*, January 2, 1788, p. 122; January 26, 1788, p. 152.
[109] *The Columbian Centinel*, June 15, 1811, p. [4].
[110] *Ibid.*, September 28, 1811, p. [1].
[111] *The Massachusetts Centinel*, January 26, 1788, p. 152.

"A Mac-Fingalism."[112] There is no reason to believe that Trumbull, by nature a somewhat conservative person and by political faith now a Federalist, was disturbed at the tendency to regard his poem as a repository of reactionary or at least conservative opinion. It was but another sign of the power of his pen. *M'Fingal* thus prospered no matter what the direction in which political winds were blowing—for it did not, of course, lose its identity as a patriotic poem.[113]

Not all the attention *M'Fingal* received was complimentary. Although the criticism of the poem during the author's life-time was preponderantly favorable, there were from the beginning discordant notes in the chorus of praise. At first the disapproval was generally based on political or moral grounds, but later the poem was frowned upon by more impartial literary critics. During the war, the first part of the poem was damned by English reviewers of the conservative party.[114] The 1792 (London) edition was also attacked, for although the American Revolution was then over, the liberal bearing of *M'Fingal* was felt to be dangerous in the days when the French Revolution was generating an alarming degree of sympathy in England.[115] Although this sort of politically biased criticism soon disappeared, Trumbull's poem continued to be disparaged because of a certain social rancor that lingered between England and America for many years. Ill feeling was kept alive by the sneering accounts of America brought back by British travelers. Caustic rejoinders from the States provoked a general literary warfare that

---

[112] *The Columbian Centinel*, June 15, 1811, p. [4].

[113] During the War of 1812 *M'Fingal* enjoyed a lively wave of popularity. Four editions appeared between 1812 and 1814.

[114] See above, p. 185.

[115] See, for example, *The Critical Review*, Second Series, VI (December, 1792), 466, 467.—Disapproval of the conservative party was not lessened by the fact that the notes in this edition were written by Barlow, who in the same year published two tracts containing doctrines far more radical than Trumbull would have then sanctioned.

M'FINGAL, POEM OF THE REVOLUTION 195

Washington Irving's *English Writers on America* (1819) was (vainly) designed to mitigate. Books by Captain Hall and Mrs. Trollope did nothing to improve matters, and even Dickens added to the discord between the nations. *M'Fingal*, of course, suffered in the wholesale condemnation of things American. Perhaps the most offensive and unfair bit of criticism of Trumbull's poem emanated from *The Quarterly Review* in 1814.[116] This promptly drew an indignant reply from Timothy Dwight[117] and, a little later, some delicious satire from Trumbull.[118] Many other unfavorable British comments on American poetry directly or indirectly damned *M'Fingal* until for various reasons the poem gradually fell out of sight.

Another type of reproof directed at *M'Fingal* showed that Trumbull was right in believing that many Americans were likely to withhold the highest honors in poetry from a mere satirist or comic poet. In his letter to *The Connecticut Courant* on the subject of copyright he argued that commercial rewards, at least, should be secured to an author, for in a humorous or satirical work a poet always staked his reputation:

If he attempt humour and ridicule, he is at once dreaded and hated as a satirist, and every witty passage in his writings shall be wrested and distorted to found a charge of irreligion and profligacy. Nor can the most unblemished moral character, nor the most well known regard for the doctrines of christianity, be any shield of defence, against wilful slander and malevolent misrepresentation.[119]

Again in his unpublished essay, "On Satirical Productions" (dated January 7, 1783), he attempts to parry the thrusts of his narrower critics who objected to the apparent irreverence of *M'Fingal*. It is significant that in order to confute

---

[116] X (January, 1814), 523, 524.
[117] *Remarks on the Review of Inchiquin's Letters, Published in the Quarterly Review* (Boston, 1815), pp. 107, 108.
[118] "Memoir," p. 8.
[119] *The Connecticut Courant*, January 7, 1783, p. [1].

these critics Trumbull had recourse to quoting Scripture:

> The Graver Part of mankind usually consider humour, & Ridicule as unworthy of a serious character & rank all witty & satirical expressions among those idle words for which we are hereafter to be brought into Judgment. If nevertheless this kind of writing can be vindicated by examples out of the sacred Scriptures, one would imagine the mouth of such censurers would be sufficiently stopped.[120]

Then in order to prove his point, he actually specifies and quotes passages from the Bible, some of which are "sarcastic & contemptuous" and some "highly humorous."[121] The Puritan tendency to distrust satire and to demand unmistakable piety was not of course strong enough to impair *M'Fingal's* reputation seriously, but it persisted for many years. It is probably significant that Elihu Smith's *Columbian Muse*, the first American anthology of poetry (printed 1794), which reproduced many pages of Trumbull's other works, gave no space whatever to *M'Fingal* although the plan of the work did not exclude excerpts. Even as late as 1829, Samuel Kettell, who had great respect for the poem, felt obliged to withhold the ultimate of praise on the grounds that

> Burlesque poetry is but an inferior species of composition . . . We feel it to be in some sense a prostitution of poetry, to busy it with the faults and follies of men. The free and chosen haunts of the muse are in the lofty mountains. . . . Who . . . would wish to see her degraded to the business of a satirist and scourge?[122]

Politics and morality, however, were not responsible for the decline into which *M'Fingal* gradually fell. Ultimately these factors were discounted, and the poem had to stand on

---

[120] Cornell MSS, p. 30.
[121] *Ibid.*
[122] *Specimens of American Poetry*, I, 182, 183.

its own merits before the cool scrutiny of relatively impartial critics. The extremes of both praise and abuse appeared less frequently in notices of the poem. In 1818, Bryant, for example, mentioned *M'Fingal* with little enthusiasm as "a tolerably successful imitation of the great work of Butler."[123] John Neal's *Randolph* (1823) showed scant respect for Trumbull as a poet.[124] Even more significant were the critical comments some years later by Edgar Allan Poe.

No patriotic or ethical considerations dictated the critical decisions of Poe, who, although occasionally prejudiced and blundering in his judgments, often attempted to appraise writing on the basis of its intrinsic merit. Irritated by what he thought to be undue encomia lavished upon an inferior poem, he expressed his dissent from the common opinion in his usual unequivocal fashion. His criticism of *M'Fingal* was at once a reminder of the adulation the poem had received and a prophecy of its future decline. In reviewing a volume of Brainard's poems, in 1842, he remarked that Brainard was

> a man of indisputable genius, who, in any more discriminate system of panegyric, would have been long ago be-puffed into Demi-Deism; for if 'M'Fingal,' for example, is in reality what we have been told,[125] the commentators upon Trumbull, as a matter of the simplest consistency, should have exalted into the seventh heaven of poetical dominion the author of the many graceful and vigorous effusions which are now lying . . . before us.[126]

Seven years later he had not changed his mind (though he often did), but referred to *M'Fingal* as a "clumsy and imitative work . . . scarcely worth mention."[127]

---

[123] *The North American Review*, VII (July, 1818), 201.

[124] *Randolph, a Novel* (2 vols., n. p., 1823), II, 177.

[125] Poe had doubtless seen an extremely enthusiastic review of the 1839 (Philadelphia) edition of *M'Fingal* in *The Southern Literary Messenger*, VII (April, 1841), 321-24.

[126] *The Literati* (New York, 1850), p. 140.—The edition of Brainard's poems to which Poe referred, namely, that issued by Edward Hopkins of Hartford, appeared in 1842. [127] *Op. cit.*, p. 275.

Although Poe's peculiar predilections in poetry forbid taking his critical pronouncements too seriously, it is apparent that toward the middle of the nineteenth century *M'Fingal* had lost its conspicuous position in American poetry. The poem was quietly crowded out of its former place of prominence by the productions of a great many newer poets, especially the Knickerbocker poets and the New England group. Griswold's anthology of American poetry (1842) indicated the large bulk of tolerable poetry by more recent authors with which *M'Fingal* had to vie for prominence.[128] In a British review of the anthology Trumbull was summarily dismissed with the brief observation that he was "flippant and dull."[129] In America Trumbull provoked less hostile criticism: he was not so much attacked as neglected. Nor is this surprising in view of the number of poets who were claiming the national attention about 1850, among them Longfellow, Whittier, Bryant, Lowell, Poe, Holmes, and Emerson, as well as a host of lesser poets such as Halleck, Willis, and William Ellery Channing. Among these newer singers, Trumbull was a voice out of the past. He soon ceased to be heard except by a few. It is significant that in 1854 Benjamin Silliman remarked that Trumbull's "great Epic [is] little known now to our young people."[130] After the middle of the century its descent was even more rapid until it reached such a low state that it was read by few persons except those especially interested in the history of American literature.[131]

---

[128] Rufus W. Griswold, *The Poets and Poetry of America*, Philadelphia, 1842.

[129] *The Foreign and Colonial Quarterly Review*, I (January, 1843), 336.

[130] "Remarks on the late president Dwight" (manuscript in the possession of Yale University), p. [9].

[131] It would not be possible (or profitable) to list in this study all the references to *M'Fingal* that occurred in books and periodicals throughout the nineteenth century. Many of these are brief stereotyped notices such as appeared in encyclopedias and histories of literature. A few editions of the poem have appeared since 1850, but they were evidently not called forth by popular demand.

M'FINGAL, POEM OF THE REVOLUTION 199

The approach to a disinterested criticism of *M'Fingal* is rendered difficult by the twofold purpose which animated the author and the diverse poetical methods he employed. Trumbull's own statement of his purpose contained contradictory elements. In his letter to the Marquis de Chastellux he said that *M'Fingal* was written "merely with a political view," but he added that his design was "to give, in a poetical manner, a general account of the American contest, with a particular description of the characters and manners of the times, interspersed with anecdotes, which no history would probably record or display. . . ."[132] Trumbull admitted, too, that he did not confine himself to one poetical manner. He wrote: "I determined to describe every subject in the manner it struck my own imagination, and without confining myself to a perpetual effort at wit, drollery and humour, indulge every variety of manner, as my subject varied, and insert all the ridicule, satire, sense, sprightliness and elevation, of which I was master."[133] He spoke of the poem as a "burlesque" and as a "parody of the serious Epic"; and in its subtitle he used the term "comic epic." It is clear also that some parts of the poem are mock-heroic in character. But the poem is no one of these things continuously and exclusively. The presence of the serious Honorius precludes the possibility of describing the entire work as burlesque. Inasmuch as the poem does not concern itself with the birth of a new nation so much as it does with the blunders of Great Britain, it is not to be called an epic in the true sense. Nor is *M'Fingal* a truly "comic" poem considered in the light of the definitions of either Fielding or Meredith.[134] Furthermore, the significance of the subject,

---

[132] *Poetical Works*, Appendix, II, 231.

[133] *Ibid.*, p. 232.

[134] It is obvious that Trumbull did not observe Fielding's rule for comic writing, namely, that the author should confine himself "strictly to Nature." —*Joseph Andrews* (London, 1769), Preface. The unnatural stupidity which

especially in Canto IV, forbids classifying *M'Fingal* as a mock-heroic. In short, *M'Fingal* partakes of the nature of so many literary forms that it cannot be justly criticized according to the canons of any one. Therefore certain general standards of literary criticism may best be applied to it.

Broadly speaking, *M'Fingal* contains two conflicting elements, the fictitious and the historical. It derives its good structure principally from the former. Considered as a record of the adventures of the Tory Squire, *M'Fingal* has evident unity of time, place, and action. The poem opens with the Squire's return from Boston to attend the town meeting, and it concludes on the same day with his ignominious flight toward Boston. A small town near the city is the sole scene of the action. The progress of the poem keeps the Squire fairly steadily in the foreground. In Cantos I and II, he is the vociferous protagonist of the Tory party; in Canto III he is the object of the rude attention of the Whigs; and in the last canto, he is the prophet who gloomily foretells the ultimate success of the American cause. It is true that the reader is occasionally inclined to forget the fortunes of M'Fingal when he becomes a mere narrator of events in the Revolution. Moreover, there are a few minor digressions in the poem. Nevertheless, the difficulty of the structural problem considered, Trumbull was justified in priding himself upon having preserved his plan so steadily throughout the poem.[135]

If the action of *M'Fingal* is well unified, it cannot be said that it is highly dramatic throughout. The framework of the whole poem is dramatic: the champions of two opposing causes engage in a public debate; the debate precipitates

Squire M'Fingal shows at times excludes him from the class of comic characters as defined by Fielding. Nor does he meet the requirements of George Meredith for comic characters, namely, that they are actuated by "the fountain of sound sense."—*An Essay on Comedy and the Uses of the Comic Spirit* (New York, 1913), p. 22.

[135] *Poetical Works*, Appendix, II, 232.

violence and a physical catastrophe for the villain; and the action concludes with the flight of the defeated champion. Yet the speeches of the Squire and Honorius are so long that they cause the reader to transfer his interest from the speakers to the substance of their speeches. The fate of Squire M'Fingal is forgotten from time to time. Canto III is by far the most dramatic of the four parts, for in it the exposition is distinctly overbalanced by the directly presented action. Consequently, from the point of view of the general reader, the third canto is clearly the most effective part of the poem, for it suffers least from the conflict between the historical and the fictitious.

The problem of characterization was less difficult, for although some of the characters are real and some fictitious, their paths seldom cross. Nevertheless the characterization probably reveals the weakest aspect of the poem. The principal actor is, in reality, no character at all, but a caricature —an artificial contrivance created to be the butt of Trumbull's ridicule and the object of the mob's contempt. A few of M'Fingal's speeches contain excellent satire of the patriots, but his frequent self-condemnatory speeches cannot be taken seriously as representative of the intelligence of Tory leaders. Furthermore, they tend to subtract interest from the poem, for they render him an unworthy opponent of Honorius, who steadily argues to the best of his ability. Hence there is no real clash of wits. Honorius was also intended to be looked upon as a fictitious character, but public opinion has persistently identified him with John Adams, whom he may be said to resemble in his fondness for controversy, his moral earnestness, and his dignity of bearing.[136] Unfortunately for the action of the poem, Honorius does not appear after Canto II. The British leaders are not fully

---

[136] An attempt has been made to show that Trumbull did not have Adams in mind when he drew Honorius, but the evidence offered is far from adequate. —*The New England Quarterly*, IV (July, 1931), 509-14.

characterized, but are revealed generally in their mean and ridiculous aspects. It is relevant to remark, however, that in a poem containing a large element of burlesque and farce the importance of characterization is diminished.

The description of persons, places, and actions is a far more important element than the characterization in *M'Fingal*. Trumbull excelled in certain types of description. Although he did not have the love of concrete and colorful imagery that betokens a great poet, he had a good eye for outline, and his attention to the laws of good descriptive writing lends vividness to his discourse. The description of the interior of the church in which the town meeting was held shows his skill in selecting effective detail; the British retreat at Concord is vividly sketched; the description of the increasing agitation of the mob just before the meeting is dissolved is an example of Trumbull's ability to create broad effects by the use of a few details.[137] The third canto, however, probably contains the most delightful descriptive writing in the whole poem. Most effective are the pictures of the constable and the Squire in the hour of their extremity. The portrayal of the Squire after he has been tarred and feathered is a masterpiece of descriptive writing.[138] In general, Trumbull's best descriptions are those in which he does not confine himself to picturing a scene, but interpolates humorous comment upon the actors and the situation.

The principal source of the power of *M'Fingal*, however, has not yet been mentioned. Trumbull's temperament was primarily that of an observer, a critic. Hence he was less skilled in reporting action, characterizing persons, creating serious moods, or even describing humorous scenes, than he was in treating of *ideas*, generally in humorous fashion. Consequently those passages in the poem are the best in which the poet comments upon a line of action, dissects a motive,

---

[137] *Poetical Works*, I, 10, 11, 63, 64, 80-83.
[138] *Ibid.*, I, 113-15.

M'FINGAL, POEM OF THE REVOLUTION

or analyzes an argument. Thus the success of the tactical maneuvers of the British against swine and oxen; the rationalizing of General Gage; the Tories' hopes for titles; the Squire's arguments against democracy; the constable's revision of his political views while in midair—these are among the subjects which gave Trumbull the best opportunities for exercise of his genius for satiric interpretation.[139] For Trumbull was essentially not a poet in the sense of *maker*, but a critic or a commentator with an extraordinary genius for the comic interpretation of ideas.

One other source of the effectiveness of *M'Fingal* may be mentioned which has been largely ignored by commentators thus far. It has been too often assumed that *M'Fingal* is a poem embodying a comprehensive view of the Revolution. This, however, is not the case. Such a poem would be intolerable. Comprehensiveness was the death of Barlow and Dwight. Trumbull did not write of the Revolution as a whole, but exercised a rigid selection in the use of materials. In general, he employed only such material as would foster his central purpose of expressing contempt of the British and pouring ridicule upon them (with a lesser amount of ridicule of Whigs), for despite his "impartial" satire of Whigs and Tories, the Tories received the fuller measure of opprobrium. His aim was not to exalt America so much as to abase Britain. The American leaders are not applauded so much as the British leaders are vilified and ridiculed. General Washington is mentioned but twice in the poem, whereas General Gage, that invitation incarnate to satire, is named no less than twenty-three times. Lord North, another object of Whig contempt and hatred, is mentioned ten times, and the jolly but ill-starred Burgoyne receives notice on six occasions. The American leaders are largely neglected. The reason for this is obvious upon a close ex-

---

[139] *Ibid.*, I, 69, 60-62, 76, 88-90, 109.

amination of the poem. The best way to serve the American cause, it appeared, was to belittle the British; and the best way to belittle the British was to emphasize their blunders and retreats. Thus the most conspicuous theme in the poem is suggested by the words "cowardice," "flight," and "retreat." This theme occurs in *M'Fingal* approximately thirty-five times. Among the other threads of ridicule which appear frequently in the pattern of the poem are second-sight, which is alluded to a dozen times; Popery, referred to about a score of times; and astrology and astronomy, which appear as motifs over twenty times. The ideas of fate and superstition saturate the poem. The words "star," "fatal" or "fate," and "vision" dot the text at frequent intervals. The persistent, although perhaps partly unconscious, recourse to these themes was one of the major factors in the success of the poem, for they all lent themselves to the purposes of comic satire.

Although Trumbull never lets the reader forget the satiric aim, his style varies considerably. His rapid and frequent transitions from the playful to the savagely invective, from the "sublime" to the farcical, and from the fanciful to the "elevated" tend to impair the dominant tone of the poem. Trumbull's restless, darting genius was not calculated to produce sustained homogeneous verse. *M'Fingal* has more variety than stability; consequently it tends to be more entertaining and stimulating than satisfying. Nevertheless a certain uniformity is given to the style by the steady employment of the octosyllabic couplet with frequent Hudibrastic rhyme. Hudibrastic rhyme is not, of course, evident upon every page of the poem; it disappears, for example, when the poet wishes to write in a serious heroic strain. Yet it is one of the most prominent elements of the poem and it unquestionably adds greatly to the enjoyment of most readers. Although by nature Trumbull wrote concisely, he occasionally used inconspicuous padding to serve the purposes of rhyme and rhythm. By the judicious use of variation of pauses he escapes the greatest danger attendant upon the use of octosyllabic couplet, namely, monotony. The quality which he appears to have exerted himself most definitely to secure in his verse is rapidity of movement. It is the lightness and rapidity of the verse which enable the reader to bear with equanimity the many classical and modern allusions which adorn the poem. *M'Fingal* reveals its author as learned but not pedantic; for if the scholar in Trumbull was tempted to dally too long in the elaboration of an allusion, the satirist was quick to proffer a sovereign corrective, namely, humor. Thus despite its heavy historical baggage, *M'Fingal* travels lightly, and it is in fact one of the most entertaining poems of its length in American literature.

The entertaining quality of *M'Fingal* will be granted by all who dare to penetrate the barrier of historical allusion which surrounds the poem. Its claim to greatness, however, is another matter. As soon as it was published, it became apparent that it must be compared with Butler's *Hudibras*. Not a few critics have asserted that *M'Fingal* is the greater poem. The truth is that the American poem is quite as readable as *Hudibras* and it is superior in structure. But in other respects it is probably inferior to Butler's poem. Trumbull's genius was genuine but slight. He was just as clever as Butler, but not so wise. If it is true that *M'Fingal* is one of the best political verse-satires in modern English literature, it achieves its position by virtue of the relative scarcity of great poems in that category. With the greatest of these, *Absalom and Achitophel*, it cannot bear comparison; Dryden's massive genius was of a higher order than Trumbull's. Nor does Trumbull's skill in mock-heroic entitle him to be ranked with Pope. In American poetry, as Poe observed, good satire has been exceedingly rare. Among the extended political satires which American poets have produced, probably only Lowell's *Biglow Papers* can be held to surpass

M'Fingal. Yet *M'Fingal* cannot be accounted a truly great poem. Probably the single quality it most lacks is a quality often absent from poetry written under the aegis of the neoclassical school, namely, a sufficient emotional basis. *M'Fingal* has too much head and too little heart. Conceived in a situation that should have bred in the author a high degree of moral fervor, it reveals more care for literary finish than for the accomplishment of a large purpose. *M'Fingal* exhibits brilliant craftsmanship, but it possesses too little humanity. Trumbull's intellect was a marvelously delicate and harmonious mechanism which enabled him to design and adorn a work of art, but his imaginative gift was not of the first order. And yet, all things considered, fate has not dealt unkindly with the author of *M'Fingal*. Covetous of the name of a great epic or elegiac poet, he would have prospered for a time but would soon have perished had not circumstance and friendship caused him to write the poem for which his slender but authentic genius was best adapted, *M'Fingal*.

CHAPTER VIII

APOSTATE POET

AFTER THE publication of *M'Fingal* in 1782, the active career of John Trumbull as a poet became less and less significant. To be sure, his fame remained bright for many years; but his actual production was meagre and, from the point of view of belles-lettres, inconsequential. For the last thirty years of his life he almost abandoned the muse. Reasons for his apostasy are obvious. The time not yet being ripe for a professional literary career, Trumbull practised law for a livelihood. Although literary history records countless cases of men who have forsaken law for letters, it provides few instances in which law and letters have gone hand in hand. At all events, Trumbull's legal and judicial activities absorbed more and more of his energies as time went on. Moreover, they gave him not only a financial income but also an independent reputation which must have been a source of satisfaction. Perhaps the principal reason for his failing production, however, is that he was not essentially a creative artist. A book-lover, a scholar, and a critic, he was also a facile writer; but he does not appear to have had that overpowering passion for self-expression that often accompanies literary genius. His temperament was judicial and self-contained rather than ebullient. He was more naturally the spectator or the critic than the creator. As he grew older, his talent for witty commentary did not desert him, but he lacked a suitable occasion to employ it. The exhortations of his friends were not sufficient to persuade him to undertake another literary project worthy of the author of *M'Fingal*. Hence, like Fitz-Greene Halleck, he allowed his poetry to lapse while he gave himself to business and professional interests. Trumbull the jurist survived Trumbull the poet.

It would profit little for the student of literary history to follow in detail the career of Trumbull during the years after he largely relinquished the pen. His outward life was devoid of spectacular events. Having left Boston in 1774, when the Revolution seemed imminent,[1] he returned to New Haven in order to practise law. In 1776 he was married to Sarah Hubbard, the daughter of a prominent New Haven attorney.[2] His connection with Yale College was renewed in 1776, when he was appointed college treasurer.[3] In 1777, when New Haven seemed likely to be invaded, he betook himself to Westbury, his birthplace—doubtless believing with the poet in *Joseph Andrews* that it was "his business to record great actions, and not do them." Here he remained, practising such civil law as was needed in those martial days, until 1780, when he removed to Hartford, then "a small commercial town . . . dealing in lumber, and smelling of molasses and old Jamaica."[3a] At Hartford he stayed for forty-five years, engaged in law, politics, judiciary duties, social life, and literary avocations. His active concern with politics began in 1789, when he became attorney for the county of Hartford. He was a member of the state legislature in 1792 and in 1800. As a strong Federalist he incurred much political enmity, and it was even asserted that he gave up satirical writing in order to better his chances of securing a judgeship.[4] After 1801 he forswore politics upon being appointed a judge of the superior court of the state of

---

[1] See above, p. 143.

[2] The marriage took place on November 21.—*Parish Register*, First Church of Christ, New Haven, Connecticut.

[3] "Yale College Register," I, 212.

[3a] S. G. Goodrich, *op. cit.*, I, 436.

[4] As "M'Fingal, a Poet,—late Student with J. Adams" he was satirized in a play that had considerable success in 1801, *Federalism Triumphant in the Steady Habits of Connecticut Alone, or, the Turnpike Road to a Fortune* (printed 1802).

Connecticut. Further recognition came to him in 1808 when he was appointed judge of the supreme court of errors in Connecticut. Both these posts he held until 1819. Now nearly seventy years old, he returned to private life. In 1825 he left Hartford for Detroit, Michigan, there to live with his daughter Julia Woodbridge, the wife of the governor of Michigan. He died at Detroit on May 12, 1831, at the age of eighty-one. Although a somewhat frail person, he had lived a long and for the most part healthy life, despite one almost fatal illness in 1798.

Excepting a few unimportant occasional pieces, the writing that Trumbull actually produced after 1782 was mainly political in its bearing. He collaborated in the composition of *The Anarchiad* and *The Echo*, two somewhat inchoate poetical works with prose introductions and commentary, which had considerable currency between 1786 and 1805. The more famous of these, *The Anarchiad*, was written by Trumbull, Humphreys, Barlow, and Hopkins to combat the forces of decentralization and insurrection after the Revolution. In particular, it attacked paper money and the Shays Rebellion. It took the form of a series of "American Antiquities" and was published serially in *The New Haven Gazette* between October 26, 1786, and September 13, 1787. Various numbers were reprinted in other newspapers throughout New England.[5] The work was exceedingly popular among conservative readers on account of its shrewd analysis of contemporary affairs, but its literary merit was insufficient to give it permanent interest. Now it is an antiquity in fact.[6] The part Trumbull played in its composition probably will never be known exactly, but such is the nature of the work

---

[5] The whole was not published in book form until 1861, when Luther G. Riggs edited it at New Haven.

[6] A more detailed discussion of *The Anarchiad* may be found in T. A. Zunder's *The Early Days of Joel Barlow* (New Haven, 1934), pp. 196-200. See also V. L. Parrington, *op. cit.*, pp. 363-67.

that it can make little difference to his reputation how much he did on it. He had already proved himself capable of better things.

The authorship of *The Echo* is a matter of still greater doubt. It was produced in collaboration by certain members of the Hartford Wits, probably including (besides Trumbull) Theodore Dwight, Richard Alsop, Elihu Smith, and Mason Cogswell. It consisted of approximately twenty numbers, which were published in various newspapers (principally *The American Mercury* and *The Connecticut Courant*) between 1791 and 1805. Some numbers also appeared as broadsides. The papers were collected and published in book form in 1807. Like *The Anarchiad*, *The Echo* was primarily an agent of Federalist propaganda. It originated in a desire to ridicule the "pedantry, affectation and bombast" of literary pieces in the newspapers of the time and in general to "check the progress of false taste in American literature."[7] But the menace of French political philosophy soon gave the authors of *The Echo* something more serious to satirize, and they made it their business to assist in "stemming the torrent of jacobinism in America."[8] Their productions were widely copied throughout New England and the middle states, especially Pennsylvania, and thus had a considerable political influence. Notwithstanding their indubitable force and generous wit, however, their political character so far overshadows all other interest in them that they belong essentially to history rather than to literature.

Trumbull's defection was not perceived immediately: a poet may rest. *M'Fingal* earned a sufficient reputation to sustain its author for a number of years in relative idleness. Meanwhile he was generally regarded as the leader of the Hartford Wits, an illustrious group of writers who for the last two decades of the eighteenth century enjoyed a reputa-

---

[7] *The Echo* (n. p., 1807), Preface, p. [iii].
[8] *Ibid.*, p. iv.

tion disproportionate to their real achievements in letters. Their obsession with the idea that the corner stone of American letters must be an epic ultimately proved the undoing of Dwight and Barlow, and the political bearing of much of their writing marked it for oblivion. During the declining days of Federalism in Connecticut they were sorely beset politically, but their productions in belles-lettres were praised on all sides. For the most part they were a homogeneous group—educated at Yale College, trained in the learned professions, possessed of ample financial means, and inclined toward "steady" political habits. They did not look upon themselves as merely littérateurs, for among them were men of unusual eminence in law, industry, medicine, surgery, politics, and diplomacy. Moreover it was a sign of social distinction to be a member of the "Friendly Club" in which these gentlemen were convivially united.[9] Trumbull was a man of attainments in more than one field of activity, but it was doubtless his literary prowess and his wit (for, unlike many comic writers, he was a sparkling conversationalist) that entitled him to move in this brilliant constellation as a principal luminary.

It was of course expected that sooner or later the literary leader of the Hartford Wits would again prove his right to the position of eminence he held. Trumbull's friends importuned him to resume the pen. Some of them wished him to demonstrate his capacity for serious poetry by producing an heroic poem on a large scale. Among these was John Adams, who wrote (in 1784) that, although in his opinion *M'Fingal* would "live as long as '*Hudibras*,' " Trumbull was capable of better things than burlesque poetry:

Give me leave, however, to repeat, what I believe I have formerly said to you, in some Letter or Conversation—at least I

---

[9] An account of this club may be found in Francis Parsons, *The Friendly Club and Other Portraits* (Hartford, 1922), pp. 15-45.

have long thought of it, and said it to others—that altho' your Talent in this way is equal to that of any one, you have veins of Poetry of superior kinds. I wish you to think of a subject which may employ you for many years, and afford full scope for the pathetic and sublime, of which several specimens have shown you master in the highest degree. Upon this plan I should hope to live to see our young America in Possession of an Heroick Poem, equal to those the most esteemed in any Country. . .[10]

Trumbull did not follow the flattering but pernicious advice of Adams. Perhaps the polite but relatively unenthusiastic reception of the heroic poems of Dwight and Barlow (*The Conquest of Canaan* and *The Vision of Columbus* were published after long delay in 1785 and 1787, respectively) convinced him that the Yankees did not really want a serious epic. At all events he refrained from any such undertaking. Nor did he do anything else to justify the reputation of a man who was "supposed by many to possess a genius equal to Swift."[11] His silence was so prolonged that it became impossible to ignore it. When *The Monthly Anthology and Boston Review* published a version of Trumbull's "Epithalamium" in 1805, the editors issued a request for other unpublished pieces that might be in the hands of those "who knew Trumbull in his better days."[12] This comment was significant, and the passing of the years confirmed the belief that Trumbull had survived himself as a poet. Nor did the romantic poetry of Wordsworth, Byron, Keats, and Shelley awaken his poetic faculties. He remained to the last an eighteenth-century wit. When his collected poems were published in 1820, they contained, besides *M'Fingal* and *The Progress of Dulness*, a great many shorter poems all but one of which were written before 1780. In short, Trumbull had written

---

[10] *The Historical Magazine*, IV (July, 1860), 195.
[11] *The Anarchiad* (New Haven, 1861), p. 76 n.
[12] *The Monthly Anthology*, II (May, 1805), 247.

practically nothing that he deemed worthy of preservation for nearly forty years.

Although Trumbull ceased to figure as a productive poet, the author of *M'Fingal* was not forgotten. Personal honors came to him until the very end of his life. In 1818 Yale College bestowed on him the honorary degree of Doctor of Laws. In 1824 he was elected to Phi Beta Kappa.[13] In the same year he was guest of honor at a literary dinner in New York City at which the most prominent writers of the day, including Cooper and Halleck, gathered in compliment to the patriarch of American letters. The toasts offered on that occasion testified to the amazing popularity of *M'Fingal*.[14] On the eve of his departure for Detroit in the following year, a similar dinner was tendered him at Hartford.[15] Nor was Detroit indifferent to the arrival of the "venerable Judge Trumbull, the author of that witty and patriotic poem, M'Fingal."[16] These marks of recognition which came to him late in life seem to indicate that contrary to V. L. Parrington's opinion Trumbull was not "pretty much forgotten before he died,"[17] but that he was very much remembered—as the author of one of the nation's classics.

As Trumbull grew older, he also grew, according to a well-known law, increasingly conservative. This manifested itself not only in his politics, but also in his attitude toward his poetical productions. He had made his first success by writing a satirical poem, *The Progress of Dulness*. He had

---

[13] Cornell MSS, p. 53.

[14] *The New York American*, July 16, 1824, p. 2. Most of the toasts were conventional allusions to Trumbull or *M'Fingal*, but James Fenimore Cooper managed in characteristic fashion to satirize his contemporaries while turning a neat compliment to the "patriarch" Trumbull: "The present generation—They think themselves wiser than the last—may they prove it."—*Ibid*.

[15] *Ibid.*, September 29, 1825, p. 2.

[16] *The Detroit Gazette*, October 11, 1825, p. 430.

[17] *Op. cit.*, p. 250.

reached the pinnacle of fame in American poetry in an unorthodox manner by writing a comic epic. Furthermore, he had on one occasion expressed regret that in some of his early "more laboured productions" he had indulged to excess in "Swelling Epithets" and "pompous versification";[18] and he had become an apologist for comic writers and satirists.[19] Yet as old age crept upon him a delusion of his earliest days seems to have returned, which caused him once more to place part of his hope for future fame on his odes and elegies. The 1820 edition of his *Poetical Works* naturally contained *M'Fingal* and *The Progress of Dulness*; but it also contained a great many shorter poems, more than half of which were serious poems, either "elegant" or "sublime" in character, written under the influence of the neoclassical school. The first of these in order was a dreadful ode entitled *The Genius of America*, and the last was the author's chef-d'œuvre in this genre, *An Elegy on the Times*. Trumbull wished to be more than a humorist. Yet posterity, which has scant regard for the secret hopes of authors, quickly stripped him of all tinsel and fustian, and bade him face the years simply as the author of *The Progress of Dulness* and *M'Fingal*. Doubtless his ghost is still troubled by the fate of his odes and elegies, but the modest fame of Trumbull rests secure in *M'Fingal*.

---

[18] Cornell MSS, p. 30.
[19] See above, pp. 195, 196.

BIBLIOGRAPHY

Part I

A Selected List of Works Relating To John Trumbull

Trumbull has been the subject of innumerable brief biographical and critical articles, but most of these are either cursory or stereotyped. Many of them, especially those which undertake to characterize the Connecticut Wits as a group, are inaccurate as well as superficial. It has seemed wise to omit them from consideration here and to confine this bibliography to the more useful and accessible materials. In most instances the bibliographical data given adequately suggest the nature of the article, but critical comment has occasionally been added. Detailed reference to original manuscripts and other rare materials upon which this book has been largely based may be found in the footnotes.

American Annual Register for the Year 1831-32, The, VII, 381-85 (Appendix).
American Antiquarian Society, "John Trumbull Checklist," *Proceedings* for October 17, 1934, pp. 26-28. (Contains useful data from title-pages of editions of *M'Fingal, The Progress of Dulness,* and certain of Trumbull's other publications. There are minor inaccuracies, and no entry is made for the second [Philadelphia] edition of *M'Fingal.*)
Anderson, Joseph (ed.). *The Town and City of Waterbury, Connecticut, From the Aboriginal Period to the Year Eighteen Hundred and Ninety-Five.* 3 vols., New Haven, 1896. III, 923-27.
Beers, Henry A. *The Connecticut Wits and Other Essays.* New Haven, 1920. Pp. 7-29.
Bronson, Henry. *The History of Waterbury, Connecticut.* Waterbury, 1858. Pp. 441-43.
Cogan, Clare I. "John Trumbull, Satirist," *The Colonnade,* XIV, [79]-99. (This volume of *The Colonnade* contains a reprint of

the 1820 collected edition of Trumbull's poetical works. It was edited by Arthur H. Nason for the Andiron Club at New York in 1922.)

Cowie, Alexander. "John Trumbull as Revolutionist," *American Literature*, III (November, 1931), 287-95. See also the same author's forthcoming article on John Trumbull in *The Dictionary of American Biography*.

Dexter, Franklin B. *Biographical Sketches of the Graduates of Yale College with Annals of the College History*. 6 vols. New York and New Haven, 1885-1912. III, 251-57.

Duyckinck, Evert A., and George L. *Cyclopaedia of American Literature*. 2 vols. New York, 1856. I, 308-12.

Dwight, Timothy. *Travels in New England and New York*. 4 vols. New Haven, 1821, 1822. IV, 330.

Everest, Charles W. *The Poets of Connecticut*. Hartford, 1843. Pp. 35-40.

Farmer, James E. *Brinton Eliot From Yale to Yorktown*. New York, 1902. Pt. I, Chap. VII. (Fiction.)

Goodrich, S. G. *Recollections of a Lifetime*. 2 vols. New York, 1857. II, 111, 112, 114, 115. (Goodrich published Trumbull's *Poetical Works* in 1820.)

Griswold, Rufus Wilmot. *The Poets and Poetry of America*. New York, 1842. Pp. 41, 42.

Holliday, Carl. *The Wit and Humor of Colonial Days*. Philadelphia, 1912. Pp. 199-226.

Kettell, Samuel. *Specimens of American Poetry, with Critical and Biographical Notices*. 3 vols. Boston, 1829. I, 175-83.

King, Winnifred B. "First American Satirists," *The Connecticut Magazine*, X (July-September, 1906), 403-11. (Useful for outline but not always accurate in detail.)

Marble, Annie. *Heralds of American Literature*. Chicago, 1907. Pp. 107-45. (More readable than reliable.)

Mitchell, Donald G. *American Lands and Letters*. 2 vols. New York, 1897, 1899. I, 152-62. (Genial.)

Monthly Magazine, and British Register, The, VI (August, 1798), [81], 82.

New York Commercial Advertiser, May 30, 1831, p. [2].

Otis, William Bradley. *American Verse 1625-1807*. New York, 1909. Pp. 92, 102-4, 106, 130-31.

Parrington, Vernon Louis. *The Colonial Mind*. New York, 1927. Pp. 248-52. (Notwithstanding a few factual errors, the best statement of Trumbull's political views. Approximately the same material is available in *The Connecticut Wits* [ed. by V. L. Parrington, New York, 1926], Introduction, pp. xxxvi-xxxix.)

Parsons, Francis. *The Friendly Club and Other Portraits*. Hartford, 1922. Pp. 27-29.

Patterson, Samuel White. *The Spirit of the American Revolution as Revealed in the Poetry of the Period*. Boston, 1915. Pp. 83-99.

Sheldon, F. "The Pleiades of Connecticut," *The Atlantic Monthly*, XV (February, 1865), 187-201.

Stokes, Anson P. *Memorials of Eminent Yale Men*. 2 vols. New Haven, 1914. I, 114-25.

Trumbull, James Hammond. *The Origin of M'Fingal*. Morrisania [New York], 1868.

[Trumbull, John]. "Memoir of the Author," *The Poetical Works of John Trumbull, LL.D.* 2 vols. Hartford, 1820. I, [7]-22. (Trumbull's memory betrayed him on a few points, but in general this sketch must be accepted as a trustworthy though not a detailed guide to his life as far as 1819.)

Tyler, Moses Coit. *The Literary History of the American Revolution*. 2 vols. New York, 1897. I, 187-221, 426-50. (The best brief treatment of Trumbull as a man of letters.)

Wright, R. W. "The Poets and Poetry of the Revolution," *Papers of the New Haven Colony Historical Society*, II (1877), [93]-115.

PART II

WORKS OF JOHN TRUMBULL, WRITTEN 1755-1775

This part contains those works of Trumbull, published and unpublished, which were written before or during 1775. After that date Trumbull's contributions to belles-lettres were few and, except for the last two cantos of *M'Fingal*, relatively unimportant. A number of unpublished (and largely unfinished) prose essays

218 BIBLIOGRAPHY

written after 1775 as well as a few poems, may be found among the Tyler Papers at the Cornell University Library. The "Critical Reflections" referred to in the text *passim* were written between 1778 and 1783. For the unpublished works here listed, the date of composition and the location of the manuscript are given. In cases in which no title appears on the manuscript, the first few words, placed within brackets, are used in lieu of a title. For the works published prior to 1775 the date and the place of publication are given. For the works not published until after 1775 the date of composition (in parentheses) is given together with the place and date of publication. The titles are arranged chronologically according to the date of composition. Only the first publication of each work has been noted except in the cases of Trumbull's two principal poems, *The Progress of Dulness* and *M'Fingal*, for which subsequent printings have also been noted.

[Come, Blessed Saviour, quickly come], 1755, Cornell MSS, p. 6.
First lines of a Translation of the Beginning of the Poem of Silius Italicus on the Punic War, 1765, Cornell MSS, p. 7.
[So some fair tower], 1765, Cornell MSS, p. 11.
From a Pastoral, 1766, Cornell MSS, p. 8.
Introduction to a satirical poem, 1766, Cornell MSS, p. 7.
Poetical Inspiration, 1767, Cornell MSS, p. 9.
[While You, my Friend, to flow'ry meads resort], 1767, Cornell MSS, p. 9.
[And as when Adam met his Eve], 1768, Cornell MSS, p. 10.
Funeral Oration, 1768, Cornell MSS, p. 11.
[Mount "Fancy's horse"], 1768, Cornell MSS, p. 12.
On t[he] Philanthropy of the Author of Tristram Shandy, 1769, Cornell MSS, p. 34.
An Epitaph on Phinehas [*sic*] White, Student of Yale Col. Septr 1769, 1769, Burton MSS, CIII, 4.
Epithalamium, 1769, manuscript in the possession of Yale University. *The Monthly Anthology, and Boston Review*, II$\frac{1}{2}$(May, 1805), 247-50. (Expurgated version.)
"The Meddler," *The Boston Chronicle*, September 4, 1769, to January 15, 1770, *passim*.
"The Speech of Proteus to Aristaeus, Containing the Story of

Orpheus and Eurydice" (1770), *The American Museum* (July, 1787), II, 95-97.

"The Correspondent," *The Connecticut Journal*, February 23 to July 6, 1770, *passim*.

An Essay on the Use and Advantages of the Fine Arts. Delivered at the Public Commencement, in New-Haven. September 12th. (1770). New Haven, [1770].

[Join too the hooting Owl], 1770, Cornell MSS, p. 10.

Epistle to Mr H......, 1771, Burton MSS, CIII, 5.

"Ambition—An Elegy" (1771), *The American Museum*, II (August, 1787), 206-03 [sic]. (This poem is more commonly known by the title *On the Vanity of Youthful Expectations. An Elegy.*— See *Poetical Works*, II, [165]-168.)

Elegy on B. St. John, 1771, Cornell MSS, p. 13. (This is part of a preliminary study for the *Elegy* cited immediately below.)

An Elegy, On the Death of Mr. Buckingham St. John, Tutor of Yale College, (1771). Broadside, n.p., [1771].

"Advice to Ladies of a Certain Age" (1771), *Poetical Works*, II, [171]-178.

Epistle [Addres]s[ed] to Mr. I. J., 1771, Cornell MSS, p. 36.

Speculative Essays on Various Subjects, 1771, 1772, Cornell MSS, p. 24.

"The Owl and the Sparrow, A Fable" (1772), *Poetical Works*, II, [149]-154.

The Progress of Dulness, Part First Or the Rare Adventures of Tom Brainless. [New Haven], 1772.

The same, second edition. [New Haven], 1773.

The Progress of Dulness, Part Second: Or an Essay on the Life and Character of Dick Hairbrain of Finical Memory. [New Haven], 1773.

The Progress of Dulness, Part Third, and Last: Sometimes Called, The Progress of Coquetry, or the Adventures of Miss Harriet Simper. New Haven, 1773.

The Progress of Dulness [Parts First, Second, and Third]. Exeter, 1794.[1]

---

[1] Some of the more vituperative parts of the original prefaces were omitted from this and subsequent editions. In 1785 Trumbull even contemplated sup-

The same. Carlisle, 1797.
The same. Wrentham, 1801.
The same. Hartford, 1820. (*Poetical Works*, II, [8]-90.)
The same. New York, 1922. (*The Colonnade*, XIV, [413]-462.)
"To My Good Catechist, the Lover of Virtue and Good Manners," *The Connecticut Journal*, February 5, 1773, p. [1].
"The Correspondent," *The Connecticut Journal*, February 12 to September 3, 1773, *passim*.
"The Prophecy of Balaam," (1773), *The American Museum*, II (July, 1787), 99-101.
"Ode to Sleep" (1773), *Poetical Works*, II, [113]-120.
Epitaph to be inscribed on the Marriage Bed of Miss S........ W........, 1773, Burton MSS, CIII, 21.
To a Lady on returning her thimble, 1773, Cornell MSS, p. 27.
Epistle [Dear Friend, this verse], 1773, Cornell MSS, p. 14.
On the Marriage of Two special Friends of the Author, Mr. D. L. and Miss S. C., 1773, Cornell MSS, p. 13. (The manuscript bears the incorrect date "1769.")
"An Elegy on the Times," *The Massachusetts Spy*, September 22, 1774, p. [4]; September 29, 1774, p. [4].
"The Downfall of Babylon" (1774), *The American Museum*, II (July, 1787), 97-99. (This poem is more commonly known under the title "The Destruction of Babylon."—See *Poetical Works*, II, [195]-201.)
On some Ladies joining to hiss Mr. Q.......s oration at the Commencemt. at Harvard College, 1774, Cornell MSS, p. 34.
"Advertisement" for "Poems on Several Occasions; Part first— designed as a specimen of about three thousand Volumes of the same species of poetry, composed by the Author & others," 1774, Cornell MSS, p. 27.
"To a Young Lady, Who Requested the Writer to Draw Her Character. Sept. 1774. A Fable" (1774), *Poetical Works*, II, [123]-128.
["By Thomas Gage . . . A Proclamation"], *The Connecticut Courant*, August 7, 1775, p. [4]; August 14, 1775, p. [4].

---

pressing the whole poem.—See *Passages From the Correspondence and Other Papers of Rufus W. Griswold* (Cambridge, 1898), p. 8.

BIBLIOGRAPHY

M'Fingal: a Modern Epic Poem. Canto First, or The Town-Meeting. Philadelphia, 1775.[2]

The same. Philadelphia, 1776.

The same. London, 1776.

M'Fingal: a Modern Epic Poem, in Four Cantos. Hartford, 1782. (Hudson and Goodwin.)

The same. Hartford, 1782. (Nathaniel Patten.)

The same. Hartford, 1782. (Bavil Webster.)

The same. Boston, 1785.

The same. Philadelphia, 1787.

The same. Philadelphia, 1787. (*The American Museum*, I, 353-81.)

The same. Philadelphia, 1789. (*The American Museum*, Vol. I, second edition, pp. 311-39.)

The same. Philadelphia, 1791.

The same. London, 1792.

The same. London, 1793.

The same. New York, 1795.

The same. Boston, 1799.

The same. Elizabethtown, 1805.

The same. New York, 1810.

The same. Baltimore, 1812.

The same. Albany, 1813.

The same. Hallowell, 1813.[3]

The same. Lexington, 1814.

The same. Hudson, 1816. (146 pp.)

The same. Hudson, 1816. (145 pp.)

The same. Hartford, 1820. (*Poetical Works*, I, [1]-177.)

The same. Boston, 1826.

---

[2] This edition bears a 1775 imprint, but it probably did not appear until 1776. See above, pp. 160, 166. Although Trumbull asserted in his "Memoir" (p. 19) that *M'Fingal* had "more than thirty different impressions," this bibliography lists only twenty-three editions which appeared before 1820. If Trumbull did not err in his facts the discrepancy may perhaps be accounted for by the number of pirated editions that appeared, some of them printed on cheap paper.

[3] The publication of this edition is sometimes referred to Augusta (Maine), where it was printed. This edition apparently reappeared in 1824 with the cover imprint "Boston: F. Bedlington."—See *Proceedings of the American Antiquarian Society*, October 17, 1934, p. 27.

The same. Philadelphia, 1839.
The same. Hartford, 1856.
The same. New York, 1860.
The same. New York, 1864.
The same. New York, 1881.
The same. New York, 1922. (*The Colonnade*, XIV, [309]-407.)

PART III

CALENDAR OF LETTERS WRITTEN BY JOHN TRUMBULL

This list includes letters or fragments of letters written by Trumbull. Seven of these, designated by asterisks, remain unpublished. The order of arrangement is chronological. Indication is made of the name of the addressee, the place and date of composition, and the location of the letter or the place where it has been printed.

* 1. To Silas Deane. New Haven, January 8, 1772. In the possession of the Reverend Anson Phelps Stokes.
  2. To John Adams. Boston, August 20, 1774. Printed in part in H[ezekiah] Niles, *Principles and Acts of the Revolution in America*. Baltimore, 1822. P. 323. The manuscript is not available.
  3. To Silas Deane. New Haven, October 20, 1775. "The Deane Papers," I, 86-90, *Collections of the New York Historical Society for the Year 1886*. Vol. XIX (New York, 1887).
* 4. To Andrew Adams. March 30, 1776. In the possession of W. Benjamin, New York City. No place of composition appears on the manuscript.
  5. To General Nathanael Greene. Waterbury, January 28, 1780. Anson Phelps Stokes, *Memorials of Eminent Yale Men*, 2 vols. New Haven, 1914. I, 123, 124.
* 6. To Thomas Jefferson. Hartford, June 21, 1784. In the possession of the Massachusetts Historical Society.
  7. To Francois-Jean, Marquis de Chastellux. Hartford, May 20, 1785. *Poetical Works*, Appendix, II, 230-33. The entire letter is not available.

8. To Mathew Carey. Hartford, June 4, 1785. *Passages From the Correspondence and Other Papers of Rufus W. Griswold.* Cambridge, 1898. Pp. 8, 9.
9. To Oliver Wolcott. Hartford, December 9, 1789. In the possession of the Connecticut Historical Society, "Wolcott Papers," Vol. XI, Document 44. This letter has been printed, with many errors, in George Gibbs, *Memoirs of the Administrations of Washington and John Adams*, 2 vols. New York, 1846. I, 25, 26.
*10. To Oliver Wolcott. Hartford, July 8, 1794. In the possession of the Connecticut Historical Society, "Wolcott Papers," Vol. XI, Document 45.
*11. To David McClure. Hartford, October 12, 1799. In the possession of the Historical Society of Pennsylvania.
*12. To Oliver Wolcott. Hartford, May 12, 1800. In the possession of the Connecticut Historical Society, "Wolcott Papers," Vol. XI, Document 46.
*13. To James Hillhouse. Hartford, April 4, 1820. In the possession of Thomas Madigan, New York City.
14. To S. Converse. Detroit, March 28, 1826. *The New-York Evening Post*, May 17, 1826, p. [2].

INDEX

Adams, John, 125, 129, 131, 132, 140, 141, 143, 159, 163, 165, 188, 201, 208 n, 211, 212
Adams, Samuel, 58, 139, 162
Adams family, 8
Addison, Joseph, 4, 54, 55, 56, 83, 86, 87, 92, 147; *The Spectator*, 17, 22, 54, 55, 92; *The Tatler*, 54, 92
Allen, James, 156
Almon, John, 139 n, 167 n
Alsop, Richard, 210
American Annual Register, The, 122
American Mercury, The, 189, 210
American Museum, The, 77, 189
American Revolution. *See* Revolutionary War
Amesius, Gulielmus, 26, 29
Anarchiad, The, 209, 210
Arbuthnot, John, 147
Aristophanes, 147

Bacon, Asa, 53 n
Bacon, Francis, 15, 85
Barlow, Joel, 31 n, 63, 186, 194 n, 203, 209, 211, 212
Bay Psalm Book, The, 38
Beattie, James, 147
Beaux' Stratagem, The, 75
Bellamy, Joseph, 80 n
Berkeley, George, 37 n, 81, 84 n
Berkeley Scholarship, 36, 37
Blackmore, Sir Richard, 147 n
Bolingbroke, Henry, 22, 80, 111, 113
Boston Chronicle, The, 54
Boston Massacre, 138, 156
Boston Port Bill, 125, 131, 133, 138
Boston Tea Party, 131

Brackenridge, Hugh Henry, 186
Bradford, William and Thomas, 166
Bradstreet, Anne, 38
Brainard, John G. C., 197
Breval, J. D., 98
Brinton Eliot From Yale to Yorktown, 73 n
Brooke, Henry, 147
Brothers in Unity, 31 n
Brown, Charles Brockden, 186
Browne, Isaac Hawkins, 147
Browne, Sir Thomas (quoted), 81
Bruce, King Robert, 9
Bryant, William Cullen, vii, 122, 186, 191, 192, 197, 198
Bunyan, John, 45, 119, 147 n
Burgoyne, General John, 172, 180, 203
Bute, Lord, 152
Butler, Samuel, vii, 52, 70, 98, 115, 147, 148, 149, 150, 151, 152, 155, 186, 197, 205; *Hudibras*, vii, viii, 52, 148, 149, 150, 151, 175, 185, 186, 205, 211
Byles, Mather, 54
Byron, Lord, 212

Cabell, James Branch, 184
Calvinism, 2, 22, 81
Camp, Statira, 128
Carey, Mathew, 77, 189, 190
Cervantes, 147
Channing, William Ellery, 198
Chastellux, François Jean, Marquis de, 151, 159, 188, 192, 199
Chaucer, 147
Chivers, Thomas Holley, 3 n
Church, Benjamin, 156

INDEX

Churchill, Charles, vii, 4, 98, 147, 148, 151, 152, 153, 155
Cibber, Colley, 147
Cicero, 21, 26, 100, 147
Clap, Thomas, 26, 27, 30, 32, 34, 35, 36, 43, 71, 75
Clarissa Harlowe, 55
Claudian, 49, 147 n
Clinton, Sir Henry, 172, 180
Cogswell, Mason, 210
Coke, Sir Edward, 130
Collins, William, 148
Columbian Muse, The, 3, 69, 77, 140, 196
Congress, Continental, 140, 143, 156, 159
Connecticut Courant, The, 158, 187, 195, 210
Connecticut Gazette, The, 20
Connecticut Journal, The, ix, 62, 65, 79, 82, 83, 91, 114
Connecticut Wits. *See* Hartford Wits
Converse, Samuel, 191
Cooper, James Fenimore, 213
Cornwallis, General Charles, 180
Correspondent, The, 79, 81, 82-92, 93, 101 n, 127 n, 142
Cowley, Abraham, 4, 147
"Critical Reflections," 96, 97, 98, 147, 151
Critical Review, The, 185
Critonian Society, 31 n
Cushing, Thomas, 131, 140, 159

Daggett, Naphtali, 36
Dana, Richard Henry, the elder, 191
Deane, Silas, 72, 82, 101, 102, 144, 159, 163, 165
Declaration of Independence, 8, 157
Deism, 23, 80, 81, 82, 84, 105, 113
Dennie, Joseph, 54
Dickens, Charles, 195
Dickinson, John, 5, 58, 138, 184
Drake, Joseph Rodman, 186
Dryden, John, vii, 22, 97, 147, 205

Dunlap, William, 186
Dwight, Timothy, 43, 63, 71, 73, 74, 83, 96 n, 192, 195, 198 n, 203, 210, 211, 212
Dyer, Eliphalet, 159

East India Company, The, 133
Echo, The, 209, 210
Edwards, Jonathan, 14, 26, 80 n
Elegy on the Death of Mr. Buckingham St. John, 67-69
Elegy on the Times, An, 124, 125, 131, 132, 133-140, 144, 156, 162, 167 n, 214
Emerson, Ralph Waldo, 198
Emmons, Nathanael, 31, 80 n
"Epithalamium," 48-53, 54, 63, 190, 212
Erasmus, 147
Essay on the Fine Arts, An, 59-62, 68 n, 79

Farmer, J. E., 73 n
Federalism, 5, 163, 193, 194, 208, 210, 211
Fielding, Henry, 199
Fingal, 152
First Book of the American Chronicles of the Times, 156
Foster, Hannah, 74 n, 186
Franklin, Benjamin, 5, 38, 54, 88, 134, 138
Franklin, James, 54
French and Indian War, 21, 32
French Revolution, 194
Freneau, Philip, vii, 63, 126, 139, 156, 157, 158, 162, 182, 185; *British Prison Ship*, 145, 157 n, 186

Gage, General Thomas, 157, 158, 164, 165, 170, 172, 203
Gay, John, 38, 70, 78, 147, 148

General Assembly (of Connecticut), 34, 86, 188
George III, 133, 138, 175
Gerry, Elbridge, 193
Gil Blas, 148 n
Godfrey, Thomas, 186
Goldsmith, Oliver, 4, 77, 147, 148
Goodrich, S. G., 191
Gray, Thomas, 4, 69, 147, 148
Green, Thomas and Samuel, 116, 139
Greene, General Nathanael, 188
Griswold, R. W., 198

Hall, Captain Basil, 195
Halleck, Fitz-Greene, 191, 198, 207, 213
Hancock, John, 5, 138
Hart, William, 80 n
Hartford Wits, vii, viii, 210, 211
Harvard College, 76, 123, 141, 142 n
Helvetius, Claude, 84 n
Hillhouse, James, 16 n, 191
Hobbes, Thomas, 84 n
Hogarth, William, 97
Holbach, Baron d', 84 n
Holmes, Oliver Wendell, 198
Homer, 21, 40, 147, 154, 155, 171
Hopkins, Edward, 197 n
Hopkins, Lemuel, 209
Hopkins, Samuel, 80 n
Hopkinson, Francis, 156, 185
Horace, 21, 147
Howe, Joseph, 71, 73, 74, 115
Howe, General William, 172, 180
Hubbard, Sarah. *See* Trumbull, Sarah Hubbard
Hudibras. *See* Butler
Hudibrastic verse, 41, 46, 52, 62, 66, 70, 78, 96, 98, 120, 148, 149, 151, 153, 154, 158, 183, 190, 204
Hudson and Goodwin, printers, 167
Hume, David, 23, 80, 82, 111, 113
Humphreys, David, 31 n, 65 n, 77 n, 83, 89, 188, 189, 209

Hutchinson, Governor Thomas, 153 n, 170, 179

Irving, Washington, 55, 186, 195
Isocrates, 147

Jefferson, Thomas, 188
Johnson, Samuel, 4, 77, 147, 148 n
Joseph Andrews, 199 n, 208
Juvenal, 147

Keats, John, 212
Kettell, Samuel, 122, 160, 187, 191, 192, 196
Knickerbocker poets, 198
Kreymborg, Alfred, 185 n

La Bruyère, Jean, 147
Leonard, Daniel, 153 n
Lewis, Sinclair, 184
Lewisohn, Ludwig, 2
Lexington, battle of, 156
Liberty Song, The, 156
Linonian Society, 31 n, 75
Livy, 147 n
Locke, John, 26, 81, 84 n
Longfellow, Henry W., vii, 145, 181, 183, 198
Loring, Josiah, 180
Lowell, James Russell, 147, 148, 181, 198, 205
Loyalists, 128, 153, 163, 192
Lucan, 39
Lucian, 147
Lyman, Daniel, 34 n, 128

M'*Fingal*, sources, 147-158; composition, 158-165; publication, 166-168; analysis, 168-181; reception and reputation, 182-198; criticism, 199-206; mentioned, vii, viii, x, 5,

7, 8, 14, 41, 52, 56, 58, 70, 78, 98, 101, 121, 122, 124, 125, 126, 127 n, 131, 140, 141, 143, 144, 145, 146, 207, 208 n, 210, 211, 212, 213, 214
Macpherson, James, 148
Madison, James, 190
Malcolm, John, 179, 180, 181
Mansfield, Lord, 152
Mark Twain, 63
Marmontel, Jean François, 147
Mason, William, 147
Massachusetts Centinel, The, 189, 193
Massachusetts Spy, The, 133, 134 n
Mather family, 8
Meddler, The, 54-57, 79, 142
Meredith, George, 199
Metcalf, Mrs. Charles H., x, 159 n
Milton, John, 4, 22, 23, 44, 55, 67, 77, 99 n, 126, 147, 148 n, 174
Mitchell, Stephen Mix, 48, 49, 53 n, 101 n
Monthly Anthology and Boston Review, The, 49 n, 212
Monthly Magazine, The, 190
Monthly Review, The, 148, 149, 185

Neal, John, 197
Neoclassicism, viii, 1, 3, 4, 5, 6, 7, 63
New England Courant, The, 54
New Haven Gazette, The, 189, 193, 209
North, Lord, 135, 136, 152, 180, 203

Ode to Sleep, 126, 127, 144
Oliver, Thomas, 153 n
Otis, James, 139
Ovid, 147

Paine, Tom, 58, 139, 145, 162, 163 n, 184
Parrington, V. L., 122, 160 n, 163
Pennsylvania Journal, The, 184
Pennsylvania Magazine, The, 184

Percival, James Gates, 191
Percy, Lord, 157, 172
Phillips, John, 147
Pierpont, John, 191
Plato, 147 n, 178
Pliny, the Younger, 147
Poe, Edgar Allan, 183, 197, 198, 205
Poetical Works (Trumbull), 1, 15 n, 16 n, 47, 102, 104 n, 109, 127, 130, 139, 144, 189, 190, 191, 212, 214
Pope, Alexander, vii, 4, 22, 62, 65, 70, 78, 99, 111, 115, 147, 148, 205; *The Dunciad*, 99, 100; *The Rape of the Lock*, 127
Popery, 88, 127, 177, 204
Port Folio, The, 49 n
Prince, Thomas, 54
Prior, Matthew, 4, 38, 78, 97, 147, 148, 153, 154, 155
Progress of Dulness, The, 4, 6, 22, 27, 28, 41, 56, 70, 74 n, 76, 77, 78, 81, 82, 85 n, 89, 93, 94-124, 125, 129, 144, 153, 159, 162, 166, 190, 191 n, 212, 213, 214
Psalms, The, 23, 38
Puritanism, 1, 2, 3, 4, 5, 6, 7, 22, 38, 39, 64, 137, 196

Quarterly Review, The, 195
Quebec Act, 127 n
Quincy, Josiah, 58, 133, 162

Rabelais, 147 n
Revolutionary War, The, 1, 4, 5, 6, 7, 8, 21, 36, 41, 47, 57, 58, 59, 121, 122, 124, 125, 140, 144, 145, 146, 156, 157, 159, 161, 162, 163, 165, 167, 179, 180, 182, 183, 185, 186, 193, 194, 200, 203, 208, 209
Richardson, Samuel, 119, 147
Riggs, Luther G., 209 n
Rochester, Earl of, 110
Rousseau, Jean Jacques, 80, 82

INDEX

St. John, Buckingham, 65, 66, 67, 68, 71
Saratoga, battle of, 180
Shaftesbury, Anthony Ashley Cooper, Earl of, 23, 80
Shakespeare, William, 61, 147
Shays Rebellion, The, 209
Shelley, Percy B., 212
Shenstone, William, 147
Sherman, Roger, 159
Sigourney, Lydia H., 191
Silliman, Benjamin, 198
Smith, Elihu, 3, 69, 77, 78, 139, 196, 210
Smith, Sydney, 186, 187
Smollett, Tobias, 148 n
Socrates, 176
Sons of Liberty, 58
Southmayd, William, 19, 20
Spectator, The. See Addison
"Speculative Essays," 79-82, 84 n, 93
Spenser, Edmund, 49, 147
Stamp Act, 58, 155
Steele, Richard, 54, 75, 92, 147
Sterne, Laurence, 47, 48, 147, 148 n
Stiles, Ezra, 13 n, 15 n, 16, 19 n, 21, 22, 23, 26, 27 n, 36 n, 75, 166 n
Stoddard, Solomon, 14
Strong, Nehemiah, 72, 75
Swift, Jonathan, vii, 4, 38, 82, 92, 97, 115, 147, 148, 151, 153, 154, 155, 174, 212

Tacitus, 147
Tasso, 147
Tatler, The. See Addison
Thomson, James, 4, 22, 147, 148
Tickell, Thomas, 147
Tisdale, Elkanah, 189
Tories, 5, 7, 132, 145, 149, 165, 168, 170, 172, 173, 176, 177, 179, 181, 185, 192, 200, 201, 203
Toy Shop, The, 75

Treadwell, Governor John, 29 n, 31
Tristram Shandy, 47, 110
Trollope, Mrs. Anthony, 195
Trumble, Benoni, 11
Trumble, Elinor Chandler, 10
Trumble, Elizabeth, sister of the poet, 15 n
Trumble, Elizabeth, named for Elizabeth mentioned above, sister of the poet, 15 n
Trumble, John of Newcastle-on-Tyne, 10, 11
Trumble, John of Suffield, 11, 15 n
Trumble, John of Watertown, father of the poet, 11-15, 16, 19, 20, 21, 22, 25
Trumble, Joseph of Rowley, 11
Trumble, Joseph, father of the first Governor Jonathan Trumbull, 11
Trumble, Lucy, sister of the poet, 15 n
Trumble, Samuel, brother of the poet, 15 n
Trumble, Sarah, sister of the poet, 15 n
Trumble, Sarah Whitman, mother of the poet, 14, 15 n, 16, 17, 19
Trumbull, Benjamin, 11
Trumbull, James Hammond, 158, 166 n
Trumbull, John, the artist (second cousin of the poet), 8
Trumbull, John, the poet, ancestry, 9-14; birth, 14, 15; childhood marked by precocity, 15-17, 20, 21; earliest poem, 17; mistaken conception of his poetical endowment, 18; anecdotes of boyhood, 19, 20; examination for admission into Yale at seven years of age, 20; astonishing memory, 23; undergraduate at Yale, 25-37; early verse, 37-41; graduate student, 41-44; miscellaneous verse, 44-54; first venture as a newspaper essayist, 54-57; Master's essay, 59-62; resi-

dence in Wethersfield, 65-71; tutor at Yale, 71-79; writer of philosophical essays, 79-82; new series of newspapers essays, 82-92; composition and publication of *The Progress of Dulness*, 94-124; removal to Boston, 125, 126, 130, 131; experiments in belles-lettres, 126-30; first extended poem on a national theme, 131-40; expression of conservative political views, 141; poetical trivia, 141-43; return to New Haven, 143; composition and publication of *M'Fingal*, 145-206; declining production in letters, 207; career as jurist, 208; works written in collaboration, 209, 210; a leader of the Connecticut Wits, 209-11; failure to respond to the romantic movement, 212; publication of collected poems, 214; death, 209

Trumbull, Governor Jonathan (cousin of the poet's father), 8, 11
Trumbull, Julia (Woodbridge), daughter of the poet, 209
Trumbull, Sarah Hubbard, wife of the poet, 127 n, 208
Trumbull, Sir William, 10
Tryon, Governor William, 179
Tyler, Moses Coit, 112, 126, 161, 184 n
Tyler, Royall, 186

Vergil, 21, 26, 116, 147
Virginia Banishing Tea, 156
Voltaire, 80, 82, 111, 113

Wadsworth, Joseph Bissell, 35 n
Wales, Samuel, 31
War of 1812, 194 n

Warton, Thomas, 98, 99
Washington, George, 159, 160 n, 163, 188, 203
Watts, Isaac, 16, 17, 61
Webster, Noah, 44, 188, 191
Wells, Jonathan, 75
West, Stephen, 80 n
Wheatley, Phyllis, 88
Whigs, 6, 149, 150, 153, 163, 168, 169, 170, 171, 172, 173, 174, 175, 176, 177, 178, 179, 181, 192, 200, 203
Whitefield, George, 32 n, 129
Whitehead, William, 147
Whitman, Elizabeth, 74 n
Whitman, Samuel, 14, 15 n
Whitman, Walt, 183
Whittelsey, Chauncey, 36 n
Whittier, John Greenleaf, 198
Wilkes, John, 58, 89
Willis, Nathaniel Parker, 198
Wolcott, Oliver, 73
Wollebius, Johannus, 26, 29
Woodhull, Richard, 27
Wordsworth, William, 60, 212
Writs of Assistance, 88

Yale College, curriculum of in Trumbull's day, 21, 26-29, 42-43, 71-72; discipline at, 29-30, 35-37, 92; "poison plot" at, 32; and the Revolution, 58; Trumbull's attitude toward curriculum of, 43-44, 73-76, 92-93, 103; Trumbull's criticism of in his writings, particularly *The Progress of Dulness*, 85-86, 95-96, 103, 107, 109, 123; mentioned, 11, 12, 13, 14, 16, 20, 23, 25, 61, 62, 65, 159, 208, 211, 213.
Young, Edward, 4, 77, 147, 148

www.ingramcontent.com/pod-product-compliance
Lightning Source LLC
Chambersburg PA
CBHW021401290426
44108CB00010B/330